1711.

The Passion Narratives of the Synoptic Gospels

STUDIES IN THE SYNOPTIC GOSPELS

by Herman Hendrickx, CICM

The Infancy Narratives
The Passion Narratives of the Synoptic Gospels
The Resurrection Narratives of the Synoptic Gospels
The Sermon on the Mount

The Passion Narratives of the Synoptic Gospels

Herman Hendrickx

Geoffrey Chapman
London

A Geoffrey Chapman book published by
Cassell Ltd
1 Vincent Square, London SW1P 2PN

First edition copyright 1977 by East Asian Pastoral Institute, PO Box 1815,
Manila, Philippines
Revised edition © Geoffrey Chapman, a division of Cassell Ltd, 1984

Cum permissu superiorum

This edition first published 1984

ISBN 0 225 66400 3

Scripture quotations, unless otherwise indicated, are from the Revised Standard
Version Bible (RSV), Catholic Edition, copyrighted © 1965 and 1966 by the
Division of Christian Education of the National Council of the Churches of
Christ in the USA, and used by permission. The abbreviations JB, NAB and NEB
denote, respectively, the Jerusalem Bible, the New American Bible and the New English
Bible.

British Library Cataloguing in Publication Data

Hendrickx, Herman
    The passion narratives of the synoptic gospels.
    —Rev. ed.
    1. Jesus Christ—Passion   2. Bible.N.T. Gospels—Commentaries
    I. Title
    232.9′6   BT431

Printed and bound in Great Britain by Biddles Ltd, Guildford

Contents

Preface

This book had its beginning in a series of lectures on the synoptic passion narratives given to several groups of theology students and catechists. The positive reactions to my earlier book on the infancy narratives encouraged me to revise my notes thoroughly and to write this book.

My teaching experience has indicated that people generally do not expect 'surprises' in the study of the passion narratives, unlike the infancy and resurrection narratives. While not intending to startle readers, I hope to convince them that a serious study of the passion narratives can be very rewarding for one's personal life as well as for better appreciation of the Holy Week celebrations.

The introductory chapter discusses some questions concerning the passion narratives in general. This is followed by five chapters, each discussing a stage of the story. Each chapter is divided into three sections, commenting consecutively on Mark, Matthew and Luke. In the last chapter I try to state the chief characteristics of each of the passion narratives and to show that these characteristics are in keeping with the overall theological tendencies of each of the evangelists. Although throughout the book I have attempted to summarize the more interesting results at the end of each section, it may prove helpful to read the last chapter first to avoid failing to see the wood for the trees.

It is impossible to account in detail for every idea or formulation for which I am indebted to New Testament scholarship and such an apparatus would be beyond the scope and format of this book. Notes have therefore been kept to a minimum but a full bibliography is included, together with suggestions for further reading. I am deeply indebted to the work of many biblical scholars and I wish to record here my appreciation and thanks.

I should like to thank all those who had a share in the publication of this book. I am especially indebted to Rev. John Linskens, CICM, Rev. Daniel Clifford, SJ, and Rev. John O'Regan, OMI, for reading the manuscript and giving a number of very valuable suggestions; to Rev. Martin Ramsauer, SJ, for accepting the manuscript for publication, and to Sister Victoria de la Paz, SCMM, and Rev. Robert McKee, CSC, Publications Managers in the East Asian Pastoral Institute, whose kind concern was so obvious at all times.

Note on the revised edition

The first edition of this book was published at the beginning of 1977 and could take into account the literature on the passion narratives only up to 1975.

Therefore the author and the publisher, Geoffrey Chapman, decided to complete and update the bibliography and make some, mostly minor, revisions of the text. We trust that these changes will make the book more readable and useful for the reading public we have in mind.

I should like to express here my gratitude to Miss Anne Boyd, Chief Editor, without whose interest this second edition would not have been possible, and Miss Fiona McKenzie, Senior House Editor, for her excellent editing.

1 Introduction to the Passion Narratives

A continuous narrative?

It is clear that the passion narrative, i.e., the story of how Jesus suffered (Latin *passio* = 'suffering') and died, occupies an extremely important place in all four gospels. In Mark especially this is so striking that since the beginning of this century it has become common to refer to the gospel of Mark as a passion narrative with a long introduction.

Under the influence of Martin Kaehler and Martin Dibelius, it has been widely accepted that, while the pre-passion traditions (Mk 1 – 13) reached Mark in the form of isolated short passages (pericopes), or sometimes in small collections (partial compilations), he received the passion narrative in the form of a continuous narrative. It has been said that while Mark was free to arrange the traditional materials concerning Jesus' public ministry according to his own theological concerns and those of his Church, the passion narrative had practically reached its final form when Mark wrote his gospel. At a very early stage of the Christian tradition it was a continuous narrative for the most part in the real chronological sequence in which the events happened, following the more or less fixed order of events in the arrest, trial and condemnation of any person. It has also been noted that the details of the passion would be meaningless unless from the start they were fitted in a sequence leading from arrest to crucifixion. And it has been emphasized that the chronological continuity and the homogeneity of the passion narrative among the four evangelists are unique in the gospel literature.

This was believed to apply especially to what is called the *shorter* passion narrative, beginning with the arrest of Jesus (Mk 14:43; Mt 26:47; Lk 22:47; compare Jn 18:1ff.). Nowhere else do the gospels coincide as closely as in the passion narratives, particularly in the story of the crucifixion. Contrary to their presentation of Jesus' pre-passion public ministry, from the arrest onwards all four evangelists recount the events in the same order: appearance before the high priest and the Roman governor, the choice of Barabbas, the crucifixion, death and burial. Coupled with this remarkable agreement in sequence is a continuity in each narrative unparalleled elsewhere in the gospels. All these points were believed to confirm what was considered probable on other grounds, that the passion narrative was narrated in a connected form at a very early stage of the Christian tradition.

The *shorter passion narrative* was then later developed into what is called the *longer passion narrative*. Gradually an introduction to the passion proper was added consisting of the plot (Mk 14:1–2; Mt 26:1–5; Lk 22:1–2), the anointing at Bethany (Mk 14:3–9; Mt 26:6–13; compare Lk 7:36–50), the betrayal by Judas (Mk 14:10–11; Mt 26:14–16; Lk 22:3–6), the preparation for the Passover (Mk 14:12–16; Mt 26:17–19; Lk 22:7–13), the Last Supper (Mk 14:17–25; Mt 26:20–29; Lk 22:14–38), and the agony at Gethsemane (Mk 14:26–42; Mt 26:30–46; Lk 22:39–46).

However, some scholars have recently insisted that the consensus about the status of the passion narrative should be re-examined, and studies conducted in that line suggest that all the sections composing the passion narrative went through some development and that the evangelists, including Mark, were quite active in the final form of the narrative. Analysis of the passion narratives leads to conclusions similar to those reached by previous analysis of the pre-passion materials, namely that they show as many signs of editorial work as the other parts of the gospels. There is no evidence that any of the evangelists knew of a generally accepted, pre-Marcan formulation of the passion narrative. Apparently much of the material found in these chapters existed independently, and was combined for the first time by Mark. Matthew and Luke then recast that passion narrative in conformity with their own theological perspectives.

This development in the study of the passion narrative is not altogether new. Martin Dibelius attempted to distinguish primary and secondary elements in the passion narrative. Rudolf Bultmann held that there was a connected narrative, prior to Mark, but that the pre-Marcan passion narrative cannot as a whole be considered an organic unity. Vincent Taylor attempted to distinguish two separate narratives at the basis of the Marcan passion narrative, an older passion account, referred to as narrative B, and another account of Jesus' sufferings, narrative A, written by Mark himself, and into which he integrated narrative B.

Recently, Eta Linnemann succeeded quite well in proving that the previously almost generally accepted existence of a pre-Marcan passion narrative is untenable and that the features which make the passion narrative appear as a connected narrative are to be attributed to Mark.

Finally, Ludger Schenke concluded that while Mk 14:43 – 16:8 may reflect to some extent a pre-Marcan passion tradition, Mk 14:1–42 definitely consists of separate, individual units of tradition. As the present study hopes to show, the same may have to be said of Mk 14:43 – 16:8.

In any case, even the most critical scholars accept that there was some kind of (disconnected) account of the passion before the composition of the gospel of Mark. It is to this not so clearly defined primitive narrative that we turn in the next section.

The situation in life of the earliest passion narrative

The sayings and deeds of Jesus were handed on and adapted for practical purposes, in order to answer particular problems and questions in the early Christian communities. These particular situations were to a large extent responsible for the handing on of a particular saying of Jesus or a story about him. They are called the *situation in life* (in German, *Sitz im Leben*) of a text, meaning the practical situation in the life of the early Christian communities in which this particular saying or story was used and which influenced the form in which this saying or story has been handed on.

If we look for the *situation in life* of the earliest passion narrative, there cannot be much doubt that this passion narrative was from the beginning part of the eucharistic celebration. This seems clear from St Paul's eucharistic text in I Cor 11:23–24, especially from the command, 'Do this in remembrance of me', which is literally repeated in Lk 22:19.

The eucharistic celebration is a memorial, a representation, a reactualization, just as the Jewish Passover was a reactualization of the liberation from Egypt and the conclusion of the covenant. What exactly was remembered and reactualized in the Christian eucharistic celebration? St Paul is quite clear about this: 'For as often as you eat this bread and drink the cup, you proclaim the Lord's death until he comes' (I Cor 11:26). New Testament scholars, therefore, have little doubt that the earliest passion narrative took shape in the early Christian eucharistic celebration. It came into being as an anamnesis, that is, as a recalling of the night of the betrayal, the events of the crucifixion, and the happenings at the tomb. The remembrance of Jesus' death and resurrection characterized the liturgy of the early Church, and it is probable that in the early Christian celebration of the Eucharist Jesus' passion and death were recounted, and that consequently anamnesis was more extensive than is the case today. The recital of the passion narrative was associated with the sacramental reactualization of the death of the Lord, just as among the Jews the recital of the Exodus stories was built into the Passover meal. No wonder that in our gospels the account of the Last Supper became part of the introduction to the passion narrative proper.

Other elements that shaped the earliest passion narrative

The shape of the primitive account of the passion was further determined by *constant reference to the Old Testament*, since the early Christians were intent upon showing that God's will, as expressed in the scriptures, was fulfilled in Christ. Other factors, as *paraenesis* or exhortation, e.g., presenting Simon of Cyrene as a man who takes up his cross and follows Jesus, inviting Christians to do the same, and *apologetics*, intent upon proving the innocence of Jesus, were also at work.

But most of all it was the *confession of faith* of the Christian Church that influenced the growth and character of the passion narrative. The suffering Jesus was proclaimed as the Son of man to whom is given all power in heaven and on earth (cf. Mt 28:18); by his death and resurrection he redeemed mankind and gained a new people; and one day he will come to judge the living and the dead.

The clearest expression of this is found in the gospel of Mark. At the hearing before the Sanhedrin, Jesus is proclaimed as the 'Son of the Blessed', the Messiah, and 'the Son of man' (Mk 14:61–62). At his death, the Jews remained insensible, but a Gentile soldier acclaimed the humiliated one as the Son of God (Mk 15:39). The cosmic signs (darkness, earthquake, etc.) show that the Christ event has universal implications. Everybody must face up to this question: 'Is this not the Messiah, the Son of the Blessed One?' And we who are reading the passion narrative nowadays? Are we scandalized at what we read, or do we confess with the centurion, 'Truly this man was the Son of God' (Mk 15:39)? Thus we should read the gospels, and in particular the passion narratives, in the spirit in which they were written – as *confessional documents* which are meant to elicit the response of faith rather than to inform us about the minute details of the passion and death of Jesus.

The passion narrative is 'historical'

In the past, many biblical scholars, including Martin Dibelius, have repeatedly insisted on the general historicity of the passion narrative, and rightly so. It does not admit of any doubt that Jesus appeared before Pilate and died by crucifixion, and several other elements of the narrative are historically probable.

But recent studies, though most of the time they do not directly deal with questions of historicity, show how difficult it is to go beyond that affirmation of basic historicity. Here, as elsewhere in the gospel narratives, we are given, combined in a single picture, the historical Jesus and the Church's understanding and proclamation of Jesus as they developed for several decades before the composition of the gospels. Rarely, if ever, can we make a confident distinction between what is history and what is interpretation. In fact, there is no such thing as 'pure history'.

The theological interpretation and proclamation of the passion do not have absolute priority over the history of the passion; it has been rightly said that the two stand in dialectical relationship. The passion narrative is indeed an interpreted and 'kerygmatized' history of the passion.

We should go beyond questions of mere historicity in order to arrive at a deeper appreciation of the gospels. However, historical truth can be discovered through the proclamation of the Church, as basis of what is proclaimed. In the light of the impact of the resurrection experience, the early Church interpreted Jesus' suffering and death as the coming of the endtime, indicated by apocalyptic signs (the earthquake, the eclipse, the cry from the cross, the resurrection of the saints, etc.). The impelling basis for this interpretation was the Old Testament. Indeed, the use of Old Testament citations and allusions colours the factual account, giving it a theological character and showing that the evangelists were not writing mere history. But it is also clear that what was interpreted was basically historical fact.

The synoptic passion narratives have their own perspective

Although the synoptic gospels are in substantial agreement as to the course of the events and the nature of the passion, fidelity towards the message does not prevent the evangelists from writing personal works. We note some freedom in the choice of materials. Luke in particular introduces into the narrative many touches of his own. Mark and Matthew resemble each other very much, but both have nevertheless elements which are not found in the other. However, the most striking difference is that of perspective. We should understand this correctly: none of the passion narratives is systematic and none of them gives exclusive attention to one sole perspective to the exclusion of others. But each passion narrative has its own emphasis.

All three evangelists interpret the passion positively: in fulfilling the scriptures it reveals the person of Jesus and constitutes the consummation of his work. Messianic expectations (Ps 110[109]), apocalyptic manifestation (Dan 7), the suffering of the Just (Pss 22[21] and 69[68]) – all find their realization or purpose. By assuming the role of the suffering servant (Isa 53), Jesus enters into his glory, not as earthly Messiah, but as Son of God, transforming at the same time the spiritual condition of man.

While Jesus is never called 'the suffering righteous one' in the passion narratives, there are enough allusions to this theme there to allow the conclusion that Jesus' passion and death were understood by the early Church as prefigured by the suffering righteous one of the Old Testament. In the Old Testament as well as in later Jewish writings this theme is related to that of exaltation as a reward for suffering and that of the expiatory value of suffering.

Illumined by their post-resurrection faith, the evangelists saw that it was in his very death that Jesus inaugurated the new era. Mark recognized this in the two signs which immediately followed Jesus' death: the rending of the Temple curtain and the confession of the centurion. Matthew evokes it by describing impressive cosmic repercussions: the earthquake and the raising of the saints. Luke pays special attention to the internal repercussions: the conversions brought about by Jesus' death.

2 The Arrest of Jesus

I. Mark 14:43–52

Verse 43: And immediately, while he was still speaking, Judas came, one of the twelve, and with him a crowd with swords and clubs, from the chief priests and the scribes and the elders.

The introductory words, 'And immediately, while he was still speaking, Judas came . . .', are to be attributed to the evangelist and form an editorial connection with the preceding. If we pay attention to what Jesus said in Mk 14:42, 'Rise, let us be going; see, my betrayer is at hand', it is seen that this connection stresses a Christological point: Jesus knew what was going to happen and his prophecy was fulfilled immediately. He was not caught by surprise. Mark emphasizes that God is at work and that Jesus submits to this experience in conscious obedience.

Judas is introduced as 'one of the twelve', although this had already been stated in Mk 14:10 (compare also Mk 14:18, 20). Both passages are copied by Matthew (Mt 26:14, 47) and Luke (Lk 22:3, 'who was of the number of the twelve', and Lk 22:47). The reference to the fact that Judas was one of the Twelve emphasizes the tragic aspect of the scene. The traitor is not a hostile Jew but one of those whom the Lord had chosen to be his companions.

It is not some misguided outsiders, but the official Jewish leaders, 'the chief priests and the scribes and the elders', who carry out the arrest. The rejection of Jesus is no accident but a conscious, deliberate refusal, foretold in Mk 8:31, the first prediction of the passion.

Verse 44: Now the betrayer had given them a sign, saying, 'The one I shall kiss is the man; seize him and lead him away safely.'

Judas' betrayal will mainly have consisted in making known to the Jewish leaders the time and place where Jesus could be arrested without too much commotion. That Judas should give a sign with a kiss is strange. It would seem to confirm that the people who came to arrest Jesus were not acquainted with him. But Jesus had taught publicly in the Temple. Therefore, it is improbable that nobody among the arresting party would have known him. It may be that the visible action of Judas' kiss is used figuratively to express Judas' inner attitude and the hideous character of his action ('it is as if you would betray a close friend with a kiss'), in much the same way as painters have represented Judas' inner attitude during the Last Supper by his outward appearance.

Verse 45: And when he came, he went up to him at once, and said, 'Master!' And he kissed him.

Mark seems to emphasize the approach of the betrayer: 'see, my betrayer is at hand' (verse 42), 'and immediately . . . Judas came' (verse 43), 'and when he came, he went up at him at once' (verse 45). Judas addressed Jesus as 'Rabbi' and kissed him. In this verse, the Greek verb for 'to kiss' is somewhat different from that in the previous verse, and has most probably a stronger meaning. Some suggest here a reference to Prov 27:6, '. . . profuse are the kisses of an enemy'.

Verses 46–47: And they laid hands on him and seized him. (47) But one of those who stood by drew his sword, and struck the slave of the high priest and cut off his ear.

The arrest itself is reported very soberly. There is not the slightest suggestion of any form of resistance or protest on Jesus' part.

It is not clear whether the phrase 'one of those who stood by' intends to refer to a disciple. The verb 'to stand by' is used five times in Mark's passion narrative (Mk 14:47, 69, 70; 15:35, 39; compare 15:40) without any clear pattern. It could very well be that Mark is thinking of someone from a larger circle of onlookers who wanted to defend Jesus. At any rate, the verse does not change the impression we were given in verse 46, that Jesus was arrested almost without any resistance.

There is very little if any connection between the scenes which follow verse 46. Verse 47 is loosely attached to the narrative. It has been suggested that verses 48–49a are an addition which is apologetic in nature and supersede an older motivation of verse 50. It is difficult to see how Jesus could utter verses 48–49a in this particular situation, since they imply the presence of the priests. Their presence at the arrest is very unlikely, but Jesus' words would be very relevant during the following hearing. Verses 48–49a seem, therefore, to be an isolated piece of tradition which Mark has attached to the account of the arrest. Verses 51–52, too, are obviously appended.

Verses 48–49: And Jesus said to them, 'Have you come out as against a robber, with swords and clubs to capture me?

> (49) Day after day I was with you in the temple teaching, and
> you did not seize me. But let the scriptures be fulfilled.'

It should be noted that Jesus objects not so much to the humiliation of being treated as a common criminal, but rather against the manner of the arrest, which misrepresented his true nature and that of his activities.

Throughout the gospel of Mark we are given the impression that Jesus' main activity was teaching. Mark presents Jesus as a teacher and his teaching is certainly connected with the understanding of his death and resurrection. It has been noted that the reference to the scriptures is very general: 'But let the scriptures be fulfilled' (Mk 14:49b). Though some have thought here of a vague reference to texts like Ps 41(40):9, 'Even my bosom friend in whom I trusted, who ate of my bread, has lifted his heel against me' (applied to Judas in Mk 14:18), Isa 53:12, 'he was numbered with the transgressors', and Zech 13:7, 'Strike the shepherd, that the sheep may be scattered', the evangelist has more probably no specific text in mind. The reference to the scriptures expresses the belief of the early Christian community that the whole of Jesus' passion happened 'according to the scriptures'. It may be used even where there is no particularly suitable passage of scripture available.

Verse 50:   And they all forsook him, and fled.

If in the previous verse Mark had Zech 13:7 in mind, the desertion of the disciples marks the fulfilment of that prophecy. We should, however, notice that Mark, who has not used the word 'disciple' (*mathētēs*) since Mk 14:32, will not use it again before Mk 16:7. According to Mark, Jesus' followers do not behave as disciples during the passion.

The present verse emphasizes the isolation of the Son of man. He is insulted by his enemies and abandoned by his friends. This process is continued by the flight of the young man, the rejection by the Sanhedrin, the denial of Peter, and reaches its climax in Jesus' final words on the cross: 'My God, my God, why have you forsaken me?' (Mk 15:34). Mark suggests strongly that Jesus' real suffering does not so much consist in the physical suffering (note, e.g., that the crucifixion is just mentioned, not described), but in the loneliness of the Son of man at the time that, more than any time before, he wants to identify himself with sinful men.

Verses 51–52:   And a young man followed him, with nothing
but a linen cloth around his body; and they seized him, (52)
but he left the linen cloth and ran away naked.

Though it is an attractive guess that the unidentified young man was

Mark, the evangelist, himself, these verses should rather be understood as an appendix to the statement of verse 50 that 'all fled'. After the flight of the disciples, this incident serves to emphasize that this 'follower' of Jesus also fled.

In their attempts to find an Old Testament parallel for this incident, some have referred to Gen 39:12LXX, where we are told that Potiphar's wife caught Joseph by his garment, but he left his garment in her hands, and fled. However, we do not seem to have here more than a merely formal parallelism. Others have referred to Amos 2:16, 'and he who is stout of heart among the mighty shall flee naked in that day'. But most commentators have hesitated to accept either of these solutions.

It has also been pointed out that several verbal links with the rest of Mark's passion narratives suggest that the episode constitutes, in the Marcan redaction, a kind of enigmatic prefiguration of Jesus' lot. Closely associated with Jesus at his arrest, the young man is also arrested (*kratousin;* cf. Mk 14:46), but escapes leaving the linen cloth (*sindōn*) to his adversaries. Jesus, whose clothes have been divided by lot (Mk 15:24), is wrapped in a linen cloth (*sindōn*) at the moment of his burial (Mk 15:46). Mark seems to emphasize the term *sindōn*, for he repeats it in each case (cf. Mk 14:51, 52 and Mk 15:46). This prefiguration remains at present intentionally ambiguous. It will become clear at the resurrection, where we hear again of a young man (Mk 16:5; *neaniskos*, in Mark only here and at Mk 14:51).

But it is possible that Mark mentioned the young man in the record simply because he wanted to draw our attention to an actual eyewitness, upon whose testimony the narrative of the arrest may have been based.

In summary, we can say that on the level of the Marcan redaction and in the context of the passion narrative, the account of the arrest of Jesus serves the following purposes:

(1) It describes the person and action of Judas who betrayed a friend with a kiss (verses 44–45) and shows that, notwithstanding the swords and the clubs, Jesus was a teacher-Messiah who performed his task quite openly (verses 48–49). Both elements play a part in the early Church's concern to emphasize the innocence of Jesus.

(2) It shows that what happened was 'in accordance with the scriptures', i.e., according to the will of God as expressed in the scriptures (verse 49b), and records the fulfilment of the prophecy pronounced by Jesus in Mk 14:27, 'You will all fall away; for it is written, "I will strike the shepherd, and the sheep will be scattered" ', thus confirming Jesus' foreknowledge of the events (verse 50).

(3) It may also have been intended to refer to the existence of eyewitnesses on which the narrative was based (verses 51–52).

(4)   Strong emphasis is laid on the solitude in which Jesus goes to his death (verses 50, 51–52).

No or little explanation is given. The entire passage is narrated in a direct and concise manner and is entirely intended to indicate how in his obedient response to the will of the Father Jesus has to go his way alone, separated from his enemies as well as his disciples. Painted in a few bold strokes, the scene is disconcerting.

II. Matthew 26:47–56

> **Verse 47:** While he was still speaking, Judas came, one of the twelve, and with him a great crowd with swords and clubs, from the chief priests and the elders of the people.

This verse sets the stage for the scene that follows. Matthew avoids Mark's redundant expression, 'immediately, while', by omitting 'immediately' and retaining 'while'. The addition of *idou* ('see', usually not rendered in English translations) before the name of Judas emphatically announces the arrival of the betrayer. Matthew's framework is basically the same as Mark's but a more continuous chronological sequence underlies the approach of Judas:

	Matthew		*Mark*
26:46	see, my betrayer is at hand	14:42	see, my betrayer is at hand
26:47	see, Judas came (*ēlthen*)	14:43	Judas came (*paraginetai*)
26:48	Judas gave (*edōken*) a sign	14:44	Judas had given (*dedōkei*) a sign
		14:45a	and when he came (*elthōn*)
26:49a	And he came up (*proselthōn*) to Jesus.	14:45b	he went up (*proselthōn*) to him.

As at several other points of the gospel, Matthew enlarges the size of the crowds in comparison with Mark by the addition of the adjective 'great' (*polus*). And his typical grouping 'the chief priests and the elders of the people' replaces Mark's 'the chief priests and the scribes and the elders'.

> **Verse 48:** Now the betrayer had given them a sign, saying, 'The one I shall kiss is the man; seize him.'

The aorist *edōken* should be translated 'gave' instead of 'had given'. The instructions given by Judas to his accomplices are reported with only minor changes, the cumulative effect of which is to underline the importance of Judas in the arrest scene. The omission of Mark's concluding phrase, 'and lead him away safely', is a typically Matthean simplification. The evangelist may also intend to clarify Mark's report by mentioning the 'leading away' in Mt 26:57 where it makes more sense.

Verse 49: And he came up to Jesus at once and said, 'Hail, Master!' And he kissed him.

Judas' coming and the giving of the kiss which signals the arrest is formulated as in Mark with only minor changes. The only notable change is the addition of the greeting 'Hail' (*chaire*). We find a parallel in the mocking greeting of the soldiers (Mt 27:29), but since there is definitely no pejorative connotation in the third and final use of the word in Mt 28:9, it is difficult to know whether Matthew intends an allusion to mocking in Mt 26:49.

Verse 50a: Jesus said to him, 'Friend, why are you here?'

These words of Jesus, found in Matthew only, reflect the peculiar Matthean interest in Judas which is found several times in the course of the passion narrative (cf. especially Mt 26:25, 'Judas, who betrayed him, said "Is it I, Master?" He said to him, "You have said so" ' – found in Matthew only).

The word 'friend' (*hetaire*) is found only in Matthew's gospel. It has usually a somewhat formal and even ironical tone (cf. Mt 20:13, the greeting of the owner of the vineyard to the complaining worker; Mt 22:12, the king to the man found without a wedding garment).

The words which follow have been translated 'why are you here?' (RSV) or 'do what you are here for' (JB and NAB; compare NEB). The latter translation stresses Jesus' knowledge of Judas' intention and of the fact that the time for the betrayal has come.

Verse 50b: Then they came up and laid hands on Jesus and seized him.

The second half of the verse returns to the text of the Marcan source (Mk 14:46), but there are a number of differences. We get the impression that the words of Jesus rather than the kiss of Judas (as in Mark) trigger off the arrest. This subtle change of accent which could easily be overlooked is indicative of the evangelist's subordination of Judas to the dominant figure of Jesus.

The addition of the phrase 'Then they came up' (cf. verse 49, 'and he came up') suggests that both Judas and his accomplices had each in turn to come forward to confront Jesus.

Verse 51: And behold, one of those who were with Jesus stretched out his hand and drew his sword, and struck the slave of the high priest and cut off his ear.

The changes introduced in this verse do not basically alter Mark's version of the incident of the sword. Instead of 'one of those who stood by' Matthew has 'one of those who were with Jesus', thus clearly identifying the sword-bearer as a disciple. It has been suggested that the use of the phrase 'with Jesus' might indicate that the saying which follows has an ecclesial application. It is one of Jesus' disciples who strikes with the sword, and Jesus' words in Mt 26:52–54 are addressed to this disciple (see Mt 26:52, 'Jesus said to him . . .'). Thus these words are addressed to the Christian reader, or the Christian community, those 'with Jesus'.

The added expression 'stretched out his hand' is often used in the Old Testament and indicates a gesture of strength or threat.

Matthew gives greater prominence to the incident by using it as an opportunity to insert some special material of his (Mt 26:52–54). This insertion, however, is not arbitrary, and a close study of these verses shows that the sayings on violence, on the authority of Jesus and on the fulfilment of scripture betray some kinship with the surrounding Marcan context (Mk 14:47–49).

Verse 52: (a) Then Jesus said to him, 'Put your sword back into its place;
(b) for all who take the sword will perish by the sword.'

Verse 52a seems to be an introductory phrase composed by Matthew in order to link the saying of verse 52b to the incident of the sword in verse 51. Jesus says solemnly: 'Put your sword back into its place'. Luke's brief and banal version, 'No more of this!' (Lk 22:51), helps us to grasp better the solemn style of Matthew.

In verse 52b, Jesus continues in the same solemn style to reject the use of violence. Many authors are of the opinion that this clause represents a proverb or saying which circulated in the early Christian tradition and was inserted by the editor into the arrest scene, perhaps adapted somewhat to its present context. For the existence of some such proverb some authors refer to Rev 13:10b, expressing the same idea: 'if any one slays with the sword, with the sword must he be slain'.

Others remark that reference to such a pre-formed saying, the existence of which is not even proven, does not really elucidate the meaning of Jesus' words. They refer to the similarity of Jesus' words to a Jewish Aramaic paraphrase of Isa 50:11, 'Behold, all you (that) kindle a fire, (that) take the sword: go, fall into the fire that you have kindled, and fall into (or: by) the sword you have taken. From my word (*Memra*) you have this: you shall return to your destruction.'

The source of the saying can also be traced in Matthew's own tradition as found especially in the Sermon on the Mount, more specifically in Mt 5:39, the saying on physical violence, and Mt 5:44, the exhortation to love, which reflect the same spirit as Jesus' warning to the disciples in Mt 26:52b. Both here and there, trust in God is strongly emphasized.

Jesus' words, then, would not simply be a proverbial saying, but a free scriptural quotation, in line with Matthew's theology, affirming that God's will is being fulfilled and that nothing can hinder it. Jesus rejects any intervention which would interfere with his obedience to the divine plan.

Verse 53: 'Do you think that I cannot appeal to my Father, and he will at once send me more than twelve legions of angels?'

Our interpretation of verse 52 is confirmed by this verse. Jesus' rejection of any intervention that would interfere with his obedience to the divine plan is extended to the superhuman level.

Jesus' words are first of all an affirmation of power. He claims the authenticity of his mission: even in this moment his Father goes on acknowledging him as the Messiah. The core of the saying concerns Jesus' ability to call upon the Father for aid. The form of aid which the Father might send is described by Jesus as the sending of 'more than twelve legions of angels'. Similar expressions have been found in rabbinic writings and in the Dead Sea Scrolls, which speak of God's 'legions' in reference to angels. The angels play an important part in the doctrine of the Qumran community. The prince of light and the prince of darkness command not only men but also angels. The *Rule of War*, describing the decisive battle between the prince of light and the prince of darkness, says that the engagement between the terrestrial armies is paralleled by a similar confrontation in heaven. In this context, Jesus' words could be understood as referring to the possibility of calling on heavenly reinforcements.

But, notwithstanding these parallels, the immediate source of the phrase can best be sought within Matthew's own gospel. The temptation scene with its quotation from Ps 91(90):11, 'For he will give his angels charge of you to guard you in all your ways', provides an interesting background for the reference to angels in Mt 26:53. In Mt 4:6 the devil refers to angels as a means of extraordinary rescue. The number 'twelve' may also fit into this general context, as a reference to the disciple(s) to whom Matthew has directed the saying. In Mt 26:51 we are told that it was one of those who were 'with Jesus' (against Mark's 'one of those who stood by') who drew his sword. In Mt 26:52 Jesus rebukes him and rejects any form of armed intervention by the disciples. He now rejects any similar action on a supernatural level.

twelve sword-wielding disciples or twelve legions of angels are equally unacceptable if they hinder Jesus' obedience to the command of the Father and the fulfilment of Scripture.[1]

Interpreted in this way, the present verse fits very well in Matthew's overall purpose. In fact, it accomplishes a double objective. Firstly, it rejects any intervention which is not in conformity with God's will as expressed in the scriptures. Secondly, it reaffirms Christological statements found throughout the gospel (cf. Mt 4:11; 13:41; 16:27; 24:31; 25:31), and reveals an intimate relationship with the Father already mentioned in Mt 11:25–27. The verse also contains an implicit reference to Jesus' prayer at Gethsemane.

Verse 54: 'But how then should the scriptures be fulfilled, that it must be so?'

This verse constitutes both the end and the climax of the Matthean insertion. The idea of fulfilment gives meaning to the whole passage. The central importance of verse 54 is confirmed by the fact that the evangelist has another reference to the fulfilment of scripture in verse 56.

Mt 26:54 is very similar to Mk 14:49b (the parallel to Mt 26:56). This similarity suggests that Matthew has composed verse 54 on the basis of Mk 14:49b. Starting from Mark's reference to the fulfilment of scripture, Matthew has developed this thought and has given it a central place in the pericope.

The fulfilment of scripture plays an important role in Matthean theology. Matthew's particular way of using the Old Testament quotations is part of his attempt to express and emphasize the traditional Christian message that Jesus is the Messiah who fulfils God's plan of salvation.

That both verses 54 and 56 lack any explicit Old Testament quotation may be due to the fact that Matthew is inspired by a direct Marcan parallel (Mk 14:49b). He repeats the reference to fulfilment (Mt 26:54 and 56, against Mk 14:49b alone), but respects the absence of any explicit quotation in Mark. Throughout the gospel Matthew shows a striking faithfulness to his source, even in the midst of profound changes.

The phrase 'it must be so' means that the events of the passion must take place because they have been foretold in the scriptures, i.e., because they are the will of God as expressed in the scriptures. The rejection of the use of violence (verse 52) or the possibility of the intervention of angels (verse 53), and the emphasis on the fulfilment of scripture (verses 54, 56), all work together to emphasize Jesus' obedience to the divine will.

Verse 55: At that hour Jesus said to the crowds, 'Have you come out as against a robber, with swords and clubs to capture me? Day after day I sat in the temple teaching, and you did not seize me.'

The phrase 'at that hour' indicates the return to the narrative sequence of the Marcan source interrupted by the insertion of Mt 26:52–54. The use of 'the crowds' instead of Mark's indefinite pronoun ('them') illustrates again Matthew's concern to clarify the account by identifying the subjects of his source.

The other minor changes introduced in the verse are in line with the dignified portrait of Jesus we find earlier in this pericope and elsewhere in the gospel of Matthew. The reference to Jesus' 'sitting' in the Temple (instead of Mark's 'with you') evokes the authority of the rabbi who was seated while instructing his disciples (cf. Mt 5:1; 13:2; 15:29).

Jesus' words challenge the ambiguous attitude of the Jewish leaders. They did not arrest him while he taught openly in the Temple. But now they do so under the cover of darkness. The secretive attitude of his opponents is contrasted with the dignified attitude of Jesus.

Verse 56: 'But all this has taken place, that the scriptures of the prophets might be fulfilled.' Then all the disciples forsook him and fled.

Since Matthew drops Mark's obscure incident about the young man (Mk 14:51–52), he concludes the scene with verse 56. Again he emphasizes that the arrest, as well as the other incidents of the passion, fulfils the prophecy of scripture.

Instead of Mark's 'but', Matthew has the phrase 'but all this has taken place' (cf. Mt 1:22 and 21:4). This may suggest that the words which follow should not be taken as Jesus' own but as representing the evangelist's editorial comment. If this is so, then verses 54 and 56 constitute less of a repetition, since in verse 54 we get Jesus' own comment on the necessity of his arrest and passion, while verse 56 would be the evangelist's conclusion about the meaning of the initial incident of the passion proper.

By using the word 'all' (*holon;* cf. Mt 1:22) the redactor applies the concept of fulfilment to the arrest scene as a whole. The betrayal by one of the Twelve (Mt 26:47–50), Jesus' rejection of any attempt to rescue him (Mt 26:51–54), and the possibility of the arrest at *this* moment (Mt 26:55), 'all' happen to fulfil the plan or will of God expressed in the scriptures.

In a way characteristic of Matthew, Mark's 'the scriptures' is qualified with 'of the prophets'. For Matthew all of scripture is 'prophetic' in so far as it refers to the promised Messiah.

By the phrase 'then' (instead of Mark's 'and'), Matthew links the desertion of the disciples with the idea of fulfilment. It can take place because it belongs to God's plan (Mt 26:56a) and because it was predicted by Jesus (Mt 26:31). Again Matthew identifies Mark's 'all' as 'all the disciples', which may be a reference to Mt 26:31–35, where Jesus emphasizes that 'you will all fall away . . .'. To this Peter replies that he will not deny Jesus, even if he must die with him. And Matthew concludes the pericope with the words, 'And so said all the disciples' (Mt 26:35; compare Mk 14:31, 'And they all said the same').

Summing up, we should say that the cumulative result of Matthew's editorial changes and additions is a confession of faith that Jesus' suffering and death are possible because they are the will of God and because Jesus obediently accepts them.

In contrast with Mark's rather disconcerting scene, Matthew tries to explain things well. He drops certain details (e.g., he omits 'and lead him away safely'), avoids negligences of style and ambiguities (e.g., 'one of those who stood by' is changed into 'one of those who were with Jesus', Mt 26:51). But especially he clarifies the situation by attributing to Jesus a series of sayings which are not found in Mark.

Matthew shows how Jesus dominates the scene: he decides. It is after he has said, 'do what you are here for' (alternative translation for 'why are you here?'; see JB and NAB; compare NEB), that 'they came up and laid hands on Jesus and seized him' (Mt 26:50). The hour has come in which the scriptures will be fulfilled (Mt 26:54, 56; two references to the fulfilment of scripture, against one in Mark). In these ways Matthew informs us from the beginning about the perspective of the narrative. We are not dealing here with a mere report of the facts. The primitive Christian community contemplates the passion through the lens of the scriptures in the awareness that God's design is realized in these disconcerting events. And Matthew invites us to do the same.

III. Luke 22:47–53

Verse 47a: While he was still speaking, there came a crowd, and the man called Judas, one of the twelve, was leading them.

As in Matthew, Mark's initial words, 'and immediately', are omitted. Contrary to Mark (and Matthew), the crowd is mentioned before Judas. This may be an example of Luke's artistry: we see the crowd first, and only afterwards do we notice the man who 'was leading them'. Since there is no trace of 'swords and clubs', nothing in the verse suggests an armed group hostile to Jesus. Luke does not say that the crowd was sent 'from the chief priests and the scribes and the elders' (Mk 14:43), because he makes them present in person to be addressed by Jesus (cf. Lk 22:52). Neither does he mention a sign arranged by Judas to identify Jesus.

Verses 47b–48: He drew near to Jesus to kiss him; (48) but Jesus said to him, 'Judas, would you betray the Son of Man with a kiss?'

Luke does not say that Judas actually kissed Jesus (Mark and Matthew both say that he did), but formulates things indirectly: 'he drew near to Jesus to kiss him'. Similarly Luke will avoid other repulsive or shocking details throughout the passion narrative; for instance, he avoids all insistence on Jesus' arrest, and will nowhere say that Jesus was bound (compare Mk 15:1; Mt 27:2; Jn 18:12).

Judas remains silent (contrary to Mark's 'Hail' and Matthew's 'Hail, Master'), but Jesus addresses him: 'Judas, would you betray the Son of man with a kiss?' It is possible that by the time the gospel was written the kiss had become an important symbol of Christian love (cf. e.g., Rom 16:16; I Cor 16:20; II Cor 13:12; I Thess 5:26), and that Luke found it distasteful to think of Judas using it.

More important is that Jesus is made to refer to himself as the Son of man. Thus it is clearly stated that Judas delivers the Son of man (*paradidōs;* cf. Lk 9:44, 'the Son of man is to be delivered – *paradidosthai* – into the hands of men').

Verses 49–51: And when those who were about him saw what would follow, they said, 'Lord, shall we strike with the sword?' (50) And one of them struck the slave of the high priest and cut off his right ear. (51) But Jesus said, 'No more of this!' And he touched his ear and healed him.

While Mark avoids the term 'disciple' throughout this scene as well as throughout the whole passion narrative, Luke refers to Jesus' followers not simply as 'those who stood by' (Mk 14:47), but as 'those who were about him', a phrase which expresses solidarity (cf. Acts 13:13). Before taking over Mark's abrupt reference to the blow with the sword, Luke tells us that the disciples asked Jesus whether they were to make use of their swords. The dialogue reported in Lk 22:35–38, where the disciples say that they have two swords, may explain this addition. The address 'Lord' suggests that the disciples are aware of Jesus' authority. No answer on Jesus' part is reported and we are told at once that one of the disciples 'struck the slave of the high priest and cut off his *right* ear', thus aggravating the injury mentioned in Mk 14:47.

As in Matthew, but much less solemnly, Jesus rejects all use of force: 'No more of this!' Luke then adds that Jesus touched the servant's ear and healed him. This healing, found in Luke only, is discordant with the gospel tradition as a whole; there is no other example of the healing of a limb severed from the body. But it is a detail which is very much in keeping with Luke's portrait of Jesus as the compassionate Lord, whose moral nobility he repeatedly stresses (cf. Jesus' address to Judas, his refusal to use violence, and finally the healing of the servant). Jesus used the power at his disposal, not to save himself (cf. Lk 23:35), but to do good to his enemies (cf. Lk 6:35–36).

In Mark the blow with the sword *follows* the arrest (Mk 14:47) and is therefore naturally interpreted as an attempt to rescue the prisoner. In Lk 22:50 (and Jn 18:10) it *precedes* the arrest and appears rather as an attempt to resist. Luke mentions the actual arrest only in Lk 22:54.

> **Verses 52–53:** Then Jesus said to the chief priests and the captains of the temple and elders, who had come out against him, 'Have you come out as against a robber with swords and clubs? (53) When I was with you day after day in the temple, you did not lay hands on me. But this is your hour, and the power of darkness.'

It is clear that verses 52c and 53a ('Have you come out as against a robber, with swords and clubs? When I was with you day after day in the temple, you did not lay hands on me') derive from Mark. This passage seems to have been inserted into another Lucan source, 'Then Jesus said to the captains of the temple, "This is your hour, and the power of darkness" '. Luke himself then added to verse 52a 'the chief priests' and the whole of verse 52b, 'who had come out against him'. Thus the members of the Sanhedrin are now present at the arrest. This would also explain why in Lk 22:47 it is not said that the crowd came 'from the chief priests and the scribes and the elders' (compare Mk 14:43 and Lk 22:47). The whole of this editorial intervention gives the present passage a marked tone of hostility to the Jewish authorities which is typically Lucan.

It is rather improbable that 'the chief priests . . . and elders' should have been present in person at the arrest. On the other hand, it is also most unlikely that the arrest would be effected by a hired mob, guided by Judas, though this is the impression left by the account of Mark. The arrest was almost certainly the work of the Temple police. This would explain the presence of the 'captains of the temple' (not mentioned by Mark and Matthew). But the presence of the chief priests and elders remains hard to explain. It is possible that Luke has deduced from the words of Jesus, 'When I was with you day after day in the temple', that some of the Jewish leaders must have been present. At any rate, it gives Luke a more effective setting for the words of Jesus. It should also be noted that Luke, who up to that point quotes Jesus' address in exactly the same words as Mark, omits the final phrase, 'to capture me'.

The resemblance has been noted of the words 'When I was with you day after day in the temple . . .' to Jesus' answer made before Annas, 'I have always taught in synagogues and in the temple' (Jn 18:20; a saying found in John only, but many scholars accept some degree of contact between the Lucan and Johannine passion narratives). The latter saying could obviously have been addressed only to the Jewish authorities.

The words 'But this is your hour, and the power of darkness' are found in Luke only. Together with 'Then Satan entered into Judas' (Lk 22:3; also in Luke only), it refers to the end of Luke's version of the temptation narrative (Lk 4:1–13): 'And when the devil had ended every temptation, he departed from him until an opportune time' (Lk 4:13; again in Luke only). Lk 4:13 should not be understood as a suspension of all diabolical activity. It means rather that the devil kept out of Jesus' way. The struggle goes on, but after the temptation story the devil is on the defensive; he avoids as far as he can any further confrontation with Jesus – 'until an opportune time'. Those who arrest Jesus are instruments of Satan (cf. Lk 22:3). The 'hour' in which they carry out their plans is the hour in which 'the power of darkness' is permitted to exercise its influence.

Luke omits the reference to the fulfilment of scripture. Neither Judas' free act, nor Jesus' arrest, the immediate result of Judas' betrayal, are considered the fulfilment of a scriptural prophecy. This approach had already led Luke to omit the prophecy of Judas' betrayal found in Mk 14:18 which refers to Ps 41(40):9. He makes a clear distinction between the roles of human freedom and the realization of the predetermined divine plan. A similar distinction is found in Acts 2:23, where Jesus is 'delivered up according to the definite plan and foreknowledge of God', but the Jews 'crucified and killed (him) by the hands of lawless men', i.e., the Romans.

The disciples' forsaking of Jesus (cf. Mk 14:50; Mt 26:56) is also omitted. Similarly Luke has previously omitted Jesus' prophecy that all the disciples would fall away (cf. Mk 14:27; Mt 26:31). Instead Luke spoke there of Satan's 'shaking' the disciples 'like wheat' (Lk 22:31; RSV: 'sift'). This saying contains a clear reference to the passion: the action of Satan's instruments against Jesus will subject the disciples to a major spiritual crisis intended to shake them loose from Jesus. But Jesus prayed for them and so, according to Luke (unlike Mark and Matthew), they never really fall away from Jesus. Finally, Luke (like Matthew) omits the reference to the flight of the young man.

In summary, then, we can see that Luke greatly abbreviated the Marcan story. The action is reduced to a minimum and subordinated to Jesus' teaching. He softens or omits everything that affronts the dignity of Jesus, whose moral nobility is emphasized, especially his generosity. Even more than in Matthew, Jesus decides for himself and dominates the scene.

3 Jesus before the Sanhedrin and Peter's denial[2]

I. Mark 14:53–72; 15:1

In Mark, this loosely constructed narrative contains the following:
(1) Three introductory verses which provide the setting for the trial scene and the denial of Peter (Mk 14:53–55);
(2) The accusation of the false witnesses about Jesus' saying concerning the destruction of the Temple (Mk 14:56–59);
(3) The interrogation of Jesus by the high priest about the former's identity and the reaction of the Sanhedrin to Jesus' answer (Mk 14:60–64);
(4) The mocking scene (Mk 14:65);
(5) The denial of Peter (Mk 14:66–72);
(6) Jesus is delivered to Pilate (Mk 15:1).

Introduction (Mk 14:53–55)

Verse 53: And they led Jesus to the high priest; and all the chief priests and the elders and the scribes were assembled.

We learn from this verse that Jesus is led to the high priest (verse 53a) and that the chief priests and the elders and the scribes, i.e., the Sanhedrin, gather (verse 53b). The reference to 'the high priest' stands in tension with the reference to the three groups, 'the chief priests and the elders and the scribes' who compose the Sanhedrin, in the second half of the verse. In all other references to Jesus' passion or being handed over, Mark speaks of the 'chief priests', who, together with 'the priests and scribes', become, from Mk 8:31 onward, the agents of Jesus' death (cf. Mk 8:31; 10:33; 11:18, 27; 14:1, 10, 43, 55; 15:3, 11, 31; but compare also Mk 3:6).

In describing the assembling of the Sanhedrin, only Mark mentions that *all* the chief priests, elders and scribes assemble. This use of *all (pantes)* is quite typical of Mark, and indicates an inclination for 'universalizing' scenes – a tendency which both Matthew and Luke repeatedly alter in their rewriting of their Marcan source. Here in the trial scene it is only Mark who implies that the *whole* Sanhedrin gathers

(Mk 14:53b). The whole body is involved in the plan to call on witnesses (Mk 14:55, 'the chief priests and the whole council', and takes part in the condemnation (Mk 14:64, 'and they all condemned him'). By introducing all the members of the Sanhedrin, whose presence was required for a formal trial, Mark turns a simple hearing into a trial scene. In fact, the Sanhedrin's action was a preliminary process of investigation which resulted in accusing Jesus before Pilate of pretending to be the Messiah, and this charge was the cause of the crucifixion.

> **Verse 54:** And Peter had followed him at a distance, right into the courtyard of the high priest; and he was sitting with the guards, and warming himself at the fire.

This verse may be considered as a traditional introduction to the narrative of Peter's denial. In Mark's composition it is separated from its original context (cf. Mk 14:66–72) in order to intercalate the trial scene within the story of the denial. In its present situation the verse stands in tension with the surrounding verses. In Mk 14:50 it is said that 'all forsook him, and fled', yet the reappearance of Peter in our present verse is not explained.

> **Verse 55:** Now the chief priests and the whole council sought testimony against Jesus to put him to death; but they found none.

The verse serves a double purpose. Firstly, it is a secondary introduction to the trial scene after the reference to Peter's following in Mk 14:54. Secondly, it summarizes the following four verses in stating that no testimony was found against Jesus. Attention is called to the first important issue in the trial scene, the matter of the false witnesses against Jesus.

In the evangelist's eyes, 'the chief priests' are a sort of executive board enforcing the decisions of the Sanhedrin. He seems to take the phrase to mean 'ruling priests'. Presenting them as the implacable enemies of Jesus, he may be conveying to us his hostility towards the police powers exercised by these chief priests. As such we may be listening to the voice of a church which suffered from these powers.

It is said that the 'chief priests and the whole council *sought* testimony against Jesus *to put him to death*'. The same combination of ideas is found at four other important stages of Mark's gospel (Mk 3:6; 11:18; 12:12; 14:1) and has been explained as 'a definite Marcan pattern whereby the whole gospel is written from the viewpoint of the death of Jesus'.[3]

By mentioning the plan to kill Jesus here for the fifth and final time, Mark tells us that the opposition to Jesus which began in Mk 3:6 has reached its climax. Our present verse is in fact reminiscent of

Mk 3:6, 'The Pharisees went out, and immediately held council with the Herodians against him, how to destroy him'. The result of the trial has been decided more or less from the very beginning. Moreover, by adding the phrase 'and the whole council', Mark gives the plan to kill Jesus the approval of the Sanhedrin and thus makes it possible to call the narrative a trial before the Sanhedrin.

The false witnesses and the Temple-saying (Mk 14:56–59)

Verses 56–59: For many bore false witness against him, and their witness did not agree. (57) And some stood up and bore false witness against him saying, (58) 'We heard him say, "I will destroy this temple that is made with hands, and in three days I will build another, not made with hands." ' (59) Yet not even so did their testimony agree.

The most important difficulties in this passage are caused by the reference to false witnesses and the saying about the destruction of the Temple. In such a short passage as Mk 14:53, 55–59, four verses deal with an issue which is apparently of no importance for the rest of the narrative, since the question of the Temple saying is not taken up in Mk 14:60–64.

We note an unusual reiteration of references to the falseness or inadequacy of witnesses (Mk 14:55, 56a, 56b, 57, 59). Moreover, Mark quotes *false* witnesses as referring to a threat of Jesus against the Temple which, in other passages, he does not qualify as false (cf. Mk 13:2; 15:29) and which, in other gospels, is recorded as a genuine saying of Jesus (cf. Jn 2:19–22; Mt 26:60–61 edits the Marcan source in such a way that the saying is not directly attributed to false witnesses).

Most previous explanations have tried to harmonize the content of the pericope and have given little attention to the fact that Mark allows the problems mentioned above to exist in his final redaction. The latter should be given more attention.

The paragraph begins with the words, 'for many bore false witness', in which the phrase 'for many' *(polloi gar)* is recognized as Marcan. Two activities are attributed to the witnesses in verses 57–58: first, they stood up (*anastantes*, 'rose', Mk 14:57; cf. *anastas*, Mk 14:60); second, they bore false witness (*epseudomarturoun*, Mk 14:56, 57). A reference to the Psalms has been discovered here.

Ps 27(26):12 . . . for false *(adikoi)* witnesses have risen against me, and they breathe out violence.

Ps 35(34):11 Malicious *(adikoi)* witnesses rise up *(anastantes)*; they ask me of things that I know not.

Both psalms belong to the category of the lament of the just or innocent sufferer which can easily be applied to Jesus in the present context. The apparent difficulty that the psalms speak of witnesses who are *adikoi* ('injust') instead of *pseudeis* ('false') is solved when we go back to the Hebrew text, where the same word underlies both Greek terms (in addition to the texts already quoted, see Ex 20:16; Prov 6:19; 19:5, 9).

The earliest affirmation of Jesus' innocence before his accusers seems to have used Pss 27(26):12 and 35(34):11. The presence of the false witnesses in the trial scene is due to Mark's adaptation of this tradition. By saying that 'their witness did not agree', he softens the earlier tradition of *false* witnesses.

The presence of very similar expressions in verse 56 ('their witness did not agree') and verse 59 ('yet not even so did their testimony agree') suggests the presence of a literary device which has been called 'Marcan insertion'. Careful study of the text of Mark as a whole shows that there are approximately forty-five instances where a phrase or sentence is repeated soon after its first mention (cf. Mk 2:6 and 8b; 3:7 and 8; 10:23b and 24b, etc.). Further investigation shows that Mark has a precise purpose by including material within the insertion (here by including verses 57–58 about the Temple saying within verses 56 and 59). It has been shown that Mark uses the insertions, firstly to draw attention to the material, which does not necessarily belong to the context in which it now occurs (in our case, the Temple saying would not originally have belonged to the context of the trial), and secondly to introduce into the pericope a dimension which illumines the context in which it is finally placed.

The saying about the Temple in Mk 14:58 was brought to its present place by Mark, who is also responsible for the final form of the saying as we find it here. It is found in the following forms and contexts:

> 'I will destroy this temple that is made with hands, and in three days I will build another, not made with hands' (Mk 14:58).

> This fellow said: 'I am able to destroy the temple of God, and to build it in three days' (Mt 26:61).

> 'Aha! You who would destroy the temple and build it in three days' (Mk 15:29).

> 'You who would destroy the temple and build it in three days, save yourself!' (Mt 27:39).

> . . . (they) set up false witnesses who said, 'This man never ceases to speak against this holy place and the law; for we have heard him say that this Jesus of Nazareth will destroy this place, and will change the customs which Moses delivered to us' (Acts 6:13–16).

Jesus answered them, 'Destroy this temple, and in three days I will raise it up' (Jn 2:19).

The presence of the saying in different contexts (trial of Jesus, trial of Stephen, cleansing of the Temple) and in different traditions (Mark/Matthew; Acts; John) confirms the widespread observation that it represents a pre-Marcan tradition.

The saying consists of two parts: the first represents a threat of destruction against the Temple, the second (not found in Acts 6:14) refers to the building of a new temple. All previous attempts to recover the original (or previous) form of the saying have presupposed that we deal here with a unified saying. This is suggested by the strong chiastic (A-B-B-A) structure of Mk 14:58 in the Greek; but it is generally admitted now that the contrast 'made with hands' / 'not made with hands' is to be attributed to the final redactor.

There are, however, some indications that we are faced here with two sayings at the basis of the present statement, and that the respective authors quoted above use the second to interpret the first in line with their personal theological purposes. The first part of the present saying is in the form of a threat against the Temple which, in content, is similar to Mk 13:2, 'There will not be left here one stone upon another, that will not be thrown down' (compare Mt 24:2; Lk 21:6; both Mk 14:58 and 13:2 use the verb *kataluein*, 'destroy', 'throw down'). The second part of the saying (except in Acts 6:14) contains the picture of Jesus as building another temple (*naos*). In the New Testament *naos* has different nuances and usages, one of which is the communal and eschatological one. If we understand the term 'temple' in this sense in our present verse, we may say that Mark made a single saying out of two originally independent sayings, one affirming opposition to the Temple, the other pointing to the (Christian) community as the substitute for the destroyed Temple.

From Mk 11:1 on, Mark presents Jesus as increasingly opposing the Jerusalem Temple, but simultaneously preparing the eschatological community which will be the substitute for the Temple. We should note more specifically that already in Mk 11:27–33, where Jesus' authority is questioned by 'the chief priests and the scribes and the elders' (Mk 11:27), we have a kind of 'trial before the Sanhedrin'! But at that stage we are in the middle of a section in which the *messianic secret* is predominant, namely Mk 11:1 – 12:44 (note that there is not one Christological title in the section; Jesus is always addressed as teacher or rabbi). Jesus' opponents fail to recognize the authority (*exousia*) of Jesus displayed in the Temple cleansing (Mk 11:15–19). In the second 'trial before the Sanhedrin' (Mk 14:53–65), however, the veil of the *messianic secret* is lifted in the Christological affirmation of Mk 14:61–62, which may be understood as vindicating the statement against the Temple in Mk 14:58.

The anti-Temple motif found all through Mk 11 – 12 is continued in Mk 13, at the beginning of which we are told that Jesus leaves the Temple (Mk 13:1) never to return there again, and in which we find a discourse pronounced by Jesus 'on the Mount of Olives opposite the temple' (Mk 13:3). The reference to the plan of the chief priests and the scribes to arrest and kill Jesus seems to be in reaction to both Mk 13 and Mk 11 – 12.

Beside the anti-Temple motif there is the motif of the eschatological community which will replace this Temple. It is not as obvious as the anti-Temple motif, but can nevertheless clearly be noticed in Mk 12:10–11, Jesus quoting the text about the cornerstone, and Mk 13:27, speaking of the gathering of the elect. This motif of the eschatological community is expressed in the second part of Mk 14:58. Jesus will build a new 'temple' in place of the rejected Temple. His earthly ministry is the beginning (*archē*, cf. Mk 1:1) of the foundation of this new community, but its realization is still in the future, and its present members are still to live in a state of watching (cf. Mk 13:33–37).

Mark did not intend to write a 'life of Jesus', but to explain the significance of Jesus' person and mission for readers of his own time. If, as is increasingly suggested, the gospel of Mark was prompted by the questions raised by the troubles of A.D. 65–70 (and specifically by the destruction of the Temple?), then the anti-Temple motif may express the growing alienation of Mark's Church from Judaism. At the same time it may have provided them with an explanation of the destruction of the Temple, namely that it had to give way to the new 'temple', the eschatological community.

But all this leaves the Christological question unanswered. Mark has not yet said *who* Jesus really is. This he does in Mk 14:61–62, a Christological affirmation, culminating in the reference to the coming of the Son of man, which serves to vindicate the anti-Temple statement of Mk 14:58.

Jesus' self-affirmation and the reaction of the Sanhedrin (Mk 14:60–64)

Verses 60–61a: And the high priest stood up in the midst, and asked Jesus, 'Have you no answer to make? What is it that these men testify against you?' (61a) But he was silent and made no answer.

Verses 60–61a affirm Jesus' silence three times: twice by the use of the verb 'to make no answer' with a double negative (*ouk apokrinēi ouden, ouk apekrinato ouden*), and once by the use of the verb 'to be silent' (*esiōpa*). They also introduce the high priest as the principal person who will ask the decisive question in verse 61b.

The high priest asks Jesus, 'Have you no answer to make?' In Mk 15:4, we find the same question on the lips of Pilate. A similar reference to the silence of Jesus making use of the same words (the middle voice of *apokrinein*) is found in Luke's account of Jesus' appearance before Herod (Lk 23:9). These references to Jesus' silence, found in different traditions, but using similar language, indicate that the motif of the silence of Jesus was part of the early Christian tradition before its incorporation into any particular pericope. Some see here a direct reference to Isa 53:7, '. . . yet he opened not his mouth', while others are more reserved in their judgment because there is no verbal contact between Mark and the Greek text of Isaiah.

Whatever should be said of the exact Old Testament reference, Mark seems to use this tradition with a double purpose; first, to provide a contrast between Jesus and his accusers and, second, to create a link between the accusation about the Temple and the Christological question in verses 61b–62.

Verses 60–61b also isolate Jesus and the high priest. In verses 53 and 55 we were told that the whole council assembled, and in verse 56 that many bore false witness. Now the chief protagonist stands up and confronts Jesus. By isolating Jesus and the high priest Mark succeeds in making the Christological confession the dramatic climax of the trial narrative.

Verses 61b–62: Again the high priest asked him, 'Are you the Christ, the Son of the Blessed?' (62) And Jesus said, 'I am; and you will see the Son of man sitting at the right hand of Power, and coming with the clouds of heaven.'

These verses constitute a 'compendium' of Christological titles found nowhere else in the gospel of Mark.[4] The title *Christ* appears as a designation of Jesus six times in the gospel of Mark (Mk 1:1; 8:29; 9:41; 12:35; 14:61; 15:32), but prior to Mk 14:62, it is applied directly to Jesus as a title only in Mk 8:29. In both Mk 8:29 and 14:62 Jesus accepts the title, but in each case it is qualified – in Mk 8:31 by Jesus' statement on the suffering of the Son of man and in Mk 14:62 by Jesus' reference to the coming of the Son of man.

The title *Son of the Blessed* is usually interpreted as a surrogate for *Son of God*. This or a very similar title appears seven times in the gospel of Mark ('Son of God', Mk 1:1; 3:11; 5:7; 15:39; 'beloved Son', Mk 1:11; 9:7; 'Son of the Blessed', Mk 14:61; to these some add the 'beloved son' of the parable of the wicked tenants, Mk 12:6). There is no agreement on the meaning of the title in the passages mentioned, but it seems that here in Mk 14:62 Mark intends to give it definite content. We find here also the third of three statements concerning the future Son of man (see Mk 8:38; 13:26).

Nowhere else in Mark are all the titles so closely related. The convergence of titles, which should be attributed to Marcan composition, strongly suggests that in Mk 14:62 the *messianic secret* is about to be revealed so that we may expect a clear Christological statement.

Jesus' answer begins with the words, 'I am; and you will see . . .' The use of the phrase *egō eimi* ('I am') as a formula of revelation or identification in Mk 6:50 and 13:6 prevents our considering it here in Mk 14:62 as a simple affirmation. Mark uses it as a revelation formula and its meaning will be determined by the continuation of verse 62.

'And you will see.' Mark uses the verb 'to see' repeatedly in relation to the parousia (cf. Mk 13:26; 14:62; 16:7; see also 9:1; 13:14). In all these passages Mark uses the verb 'to see' in connection with some future event associated with the parousia, the coming either of the kingdom, or of the Son of man, or of the events in the final crisis which precipitates this coming. Thus the parousia is characterized as a manifestation or epiphany, and the revelational quality of the coming of the Son of man is emphasized by the 'seeing'.

There is a growing consensus that Mk 14:61–62 does not represent an authentic saying of Jesus but is rather the product of early Christian theology and more specifically the end-product of early Christian use of the Old Testament. It has been debated whether Jesus' answer contains a parousia Christology, referring to the final vindication of Jesus and his access to full authority at the second coming, or an exaltation Christology, referring to his sitting at the right hand of the Father in virtue of his resurrection. But the question should not be answered in an either-or way. There is no conflict between exaltation at the resurrection and return at the parousia. If we tend to emphasize the parousia expectation, it is not in an exclusive sense, since, for Mark, Jesus is the one who is exalted at the resurrection as well as the one who will return at the parousia. The same combination of exaltation and parousia has been found in the Marcan version of the transfiguration (Mk 9:2–9).

It has already been noted that the most important Christological titles of Mark's gospel ('Christ', 'Son of the Blessed' or 'Son of God', and 'Son of man') are brought together in the trial scene. Several scholars have also observed that in the trial scene 'Son of man' is used to interpret and give content to 'Son of God'. Finally, there is an almost general consensus that the trial scene reaches its culminating point in Jesus' answer 'I am' and that Mk 14:62 explains that affirmation. All this leads to the conclusion that the future Son of man saying in Mk 14:62 is a key to the interpretation of the whole trial scene.

A detailed study of the other Son of man sayings in Mark and their relation to our present saying in Mk 14:62 leads to the conclusion that Mark did not simply receive the future Son of man sayings from the tradition, but that he was active in composing the final form of these sayings. In contrast to the sayings found in the Q tradition[5] which lack almost all imagery (e.g., Lk 11:30/Mt 12:40; Lk 12:8/Mt 10:32;

Lk 12:40/Mt 22:44, etc.), the Marcan sayings are characterized by their imagery of coming, power, glory, clouds of heaven, seeing, which give them their apocalyptic colour. This apocalyptic imagery is also found in I Thessalonians (1:9–10, etc.) and the Book of Revelation (three references to Dan 7:13 in Rev 1:7, 13; 14:14).

It seems, then, that two lines of tradition converge in Mark's future Son of man sayings, one emphasizing the return of the Son of man for judgment, the other filling out this return with the use of apocalyptic imagery.

The first of Mark's future Son of man sayings (Mk 8:38) is found in the context of Mk 8:27 – 9:1, a section which can be considered the real beginning of Mark's Christology, while at the same time emphasizing the meaning of the death of Jesus for the disciples. We have already noted the relation of Mk 8:27 – 9:1 to the trial scene. In this passage the suffering Son of Man (Mk 8:31) clarifies the title 'Christ' (Mk 8:29), and the future Son of man saying (Mk 8:38) brings together the expected one and the suffering Jesus.

The second future Son of man saying is found in Mark's eschatological discourse (Mk 13:26). Here, too, as in Mk 8:38, Mark uses a future Son of man saying with a definite theological purpose. By using the whole apocalyptic imagery he succeeds in making clear that the Jesus who will suffer is the same as the one who will return as the Son of man. At the same time he orients the community to the return of Jesus and says that his return will constitute the inauguration of the new community. Thus it can rightly be said that in Mk 8:38 as well as in Mk 13:26, Mark makes a Christological, as well as an eschatological and an ecclesiological statement. In both Mk 8:38 and 13:26 and their respective contexts, we find a pattern of suffering, vindication and judgment through the parousia, and a reference to a new community.

In the third and final future Son of man saying, Mk 14:62, the motif of the *suffering* of the Son of man has to be gathered mainly from the context. The motif of *vindication* is found in what commentators have usually referred to as the 'dramatic irony' in the answer of Jesus to the high priest: he who is at present being judged will sit in judgment against his enemies. In the midst of his humiliation Jesus is proclaimed to the world as the coming Son of man.

The motif of *judgment* is strongly emphasized in Jesus' answer which is a combination of Ps 110(109):1, 'The Lord says to my lord, "Sit at my right hand . . ." ' and Dan 7:13, 'and behold, with the clouds of heaven, there came one like a son of man . . .'. Commentators have often noted the tension between these two parts of Jesus' answer. They note that the early Christian communities used Ps 110(109) in a context of exaltation/resurrection. But they do not pay enough attention to the use of the whole psalm in the New Testament. This royal psalm speaks of the victorious enthronement of a king (verse 1), who rules in the midst of his foes (verse 2), and who is vindicated by judgment when his victory is complete (verses 5–7). Looked at in this way the psalm bears a striking resemblance to the trial scene: Jesus is referred to as sitting at the right hand of God, while he is actually in the midst of his enemies; by the exaltation/resurrection God vindicates him and subjects his enemies to him. Support for the influence of the total meaning of the psalm on the trial narrative comes from its use in I Cor 15:24–25 and Rom 8:33–34. From these two Pauline passages we can gather that there is no tension between exaltation, judgment and parousia.

The arrival of the Son of man inaugurates also a new stage of God's activity in history, the establishment of the kingdom (Mk 9:1), and the gathering of the elect (Mk 13:27). This aspect is found in the second half of the Temple saying (Mk 14:58b), but whereas the former two statements are addressed to the disciples and put directly on the lips of Jesus, the Temple saying of Mk 14:58 is not put directly on his lips, and the Christological affirmation of Mk 14:62 is addressed to opponents, not to disciples! It seems that the community is not immediately involved.

This is most probably to be related to the fact that the trial narrative is found after the flight of the disciples (Mk 14:50) and intercalated within the story of Peter's denial (Mk 14:54, 66–72). Several studies have shown that in Mark the disciples represent attitudes of faith present in Mark's community. Their dealings with Jesus reflect the situation of the Christian community at the time of the writing of the gospel. From Mk 14:62 it appears that Jesus' enemies will experience the return of the Son of man as judgment. But what will it mean for the disciples? They could not follow Jesus on the way to the cross (cf. e.g., Mk 8:31–33; 14:50). Therefore, they cannot fully understand the meaning of the coming of the Son of man either. This explains why Mark's reference to the expectation of the return of the Son of man and the establishment of a new community is less explicit here than in previous sections of the gospel.

Since neither of the titles mentioned in the high priest's question ('Christ' and 'Son of the Blessed') appears in Jesus' answer (the affirmation 'I am', and the quotations from Ps 110[109]:1 and Dan 7:13), this answer should be understood as not simply an answer, but a reinterpretation of the question. Only here and at Mk 8:29 does Jesus respond when the title 'Christ' is addressed to him. But in both instances he qualifies it. In Mk 8:29 he imposes silence and then refers to the necessity of the suffering of the Son of man. In Mk 14:62 Jesus openly accepts the title ('I am'), but only in relation to the coming of the Son of man. This indicates a definite progression and shows that Mark does not want to give the definitive meaning of the title 'Christ' before Mk 14:62. It cannot be defined without reference to the necessity of suffering. But at the same time it refers also to the parousia, when Jesus receives the fullness of his messianic prerogatives.

A close study of the title 'Son of God' or 'Son of the Blessed' shows that Mark gives a definite structure to his Son of God Christology. In Jesus' public life, the title is used only by demons and expresses a Christology which Jesus rejects; when the title is apparently considered accurate, it is not used publicly. Thus Mark temporizes and keeps the real meaning of the title in store for the trial scene.

Recent study has brought to light that Mark uses the title 'Son of man' to react against a false Christology which represents Jesus as a divine man who did not have to suffer. It has also been suggested that 'Son of God' was a title attributed to Jesus by advocates of a false Christology. It seems, therefore, that the title 'Son of God' too is given its definitive meaning in the trial scene. Jesus publicly accepts the title 'Son of the Blessed', but not without reference to the future Son of man. Thus Mark states that the true meaning of Jesus as Son of God will be seen only when he comes in glory as the victorious Son of man. Therefore, the title 'Son of man' provides the correct perspective not only for Jesus' earthly ministry and suffering, but also for his position as Son of God.

> **Verses 63–64:** And the high priest tore his mantle, and said, 'Why do we still need witnesses? (64) You have heard his blasphemy. What is your decision?' And they all condemned him as deserving death.

'The high priest tore his mantle' as a sign that he had heard a blasphemy, and expressed the same in words. But, strictly speaking, Jesus was not guilty of blasphemy, since he did not expressly pronounce the Name of God. It has also been noted that neither Luke nor John records the charge in the trial (but see Jn 10:33, 36 and 19:7 for charges of blasphemy outside the trial before the Sanhedrin). Only Mk 14:64, and Mt 26:65 in close dependence on Mark, mention the charge of blasphemy. All this is true, but it is more important to ask *why* Mark presents things this way. Mark makes the high priest accuse Jesus of blasphemy and thus creates a striking inclusion or framing repetition with Mk 2:7, where the scribes also say: 'Why does this man speak thus? It is blasphemy!' This is hardly accidental: the first and last accusation against Jesus is that of blasphemy. This blasphemy did not consist of the abuse of God's Name, but of the fact that Jesus claimed divine prerogatives. This may reflect the fact that the Jewish authorities accused Christians of blasphemy because they confessed Jesus as the Son of God. It seems, therefore, that the accusation of blasphemy in the trial narrative sheds light on the Christological impact of Mk 14:62. It is addressed to Christians who are bound to undergo the same sufferings as Jesus when they confess him as the Christ.

Again, according to Mark, the gathering of the Sanhedrin ends with a real condemnation. Notwithstanding historical and other difficulties, this is clearly the meaning intended by Mark: *katakrinein* is to be understood as 'to condemn' and the expression *enochos thanatou* means undoubtedly 'deserving death'; or, as NAB translates: 'They all concurred in the verdict "guilty", with its sentence of death.'

The mocking scene (Mk 14:65)

> **Verse 65:** And some began to spit on him, and to cover his face, and to strike him, saying to him, 'Prophesy!' And the guards received him with blows.

According to the first half of the verse, 'some' members of the Sanhedrin 'began to spit on him, and to cover his face, and to strike him'; for the 'some' can hardly refer to any other persons than some of the 'all' mentioned at the end of the previous verse; moreover, the 'guards' are not mentioned until the second half of the present verse. But it is most improbable that members of the supreme court would engage in undignified action of this kind at the end of a session.

The wording of the scene has undoubtedly been influenced by Isa 50:6,

> I gave my back to the smiters,
> and my cheeks to those who pulled out the beard;
> I hid not my face from shame and spitting.

There may also be an allusion to Isa 53:3–5 and Mic 5:1 (4:14 in Hebrew) 'with a rod they strike upon the cheek the ruler of Israel'. Although some suggest that this mocking scene is altogether derived from Isa 50:6, most scholars allow some measure of historicity to Mk 14:65, attributing the similarities between the two passages to the evangelist's reference to the suffering servant.

The denial of Peter (Mk 14:66–72)

> **Verses 66–67:** And as Peter was below in the courtyard, one of the maids of the high priest came; (67) and seeing Peter warming himself, she looked at him. and said, 'You also were with the Nazarene, Jesus.'

These verses take up again the situation of Mk 14:54. This can clearly be seen in the repetition of the phrases 'in the courtyard' and 'warming himself'. Originally Mk 14:54 belonged to the denial account, but the intercalation of the trial scene led to the repetition of the situation in Mk 14:66. The result is a juxtaposition of Mk 14:65 and

Mk 14:66–72. At the very moment that Jesus is rejected by the Sanhedrin because of his messianic claim, he is denied by Peter. Indeed, more than Judas' betrayal, the denial of Peter underscores the total rejection of Jesus and his Messiahship by the disciples.

It has been said repeatedly that the servant girl's designation of Jesus as 'the Nazarene' followed by his proper name is contemptuous, but it seems that in general Mark's use of 'Nazarene' is positive (cf. Mk 1:9, 24; 10:47; 16:6). It may simply be a popular way of referring to Jesus and his followers. 'To be with Jesus' is practically a technical term for discipleship in Mark (cf. Mk 3:14, 'And he appointed twelve, to be with him, and to be sent out to preach').

> **Verse 68:** But he denied it, saying, 'I neither know nor understand what you mean.' And he went out into the gateway.

Peter's first reply, meant to be a denial, is quite involved in its wording. Some have recognized in it the form common in rabbinical law for a formal denial. In its New Testament use, 'to deny' *(arneisthai)* implies a previous relationship of obedience and fidelity. Some manuscripts have here a first mention of a cockcrow which sounds as a warning.

> **Verses 69–70:** And the maid saw him, and began again to say to the bystanders, 'This man is one of them.' (70) But again he denied it. And after a little while again the bystanders said to Peter, 'Certainly you are one of them; for you are a Galilean.'

Presumably the maid followed Peter and now repeats her statement in the presence of some bystanders. Though not directly addressed, Peter repeats his denial. The first two denials can be interpreted as a mere disputing of acquaintance with Jesus ('But he denied it' – 'But again he denied it'). The bystanders now take over the role of the maid and confidently challenge Peter: 'Certainly you are one of them; for you are a Galilean'. The words are apparently uttered by people who thought of those attached to Jesus as Galileans.

> **Verse 71:** But he began to invoke a curse on himself and to swear, 'I do not know this man of whom you speak.'

Mark's account of Peter's denial rises here to a climax. This denial goes considerably beyond the previous two in intensity. Peter began to swear, i.e., to deny the allegation under solemn oath; this is the third of the predicted denials. This is accompanied by the invocation of a curse (on himself). Peter swears that he does not know Jesus, and on top of that invokes the divine ban (on himself and on what he says).

It has been noted that in the Greek text the verb 'to curse' is intentionally left without object to denote that he curses both himself if he lies and also the people present if they go on insisting that he is a disciple. But it has also been suggested that Peter, under attack in spite of the first two denials, resorts to the strongest possible way of dissociating himself, namely, cursing Jesus! This theory is supported by several considerations. First, the words, 'I do not know this man', understood as the content of the oath, recall the form of words used in the rabbinic ban formula: 'I have never known you'. Secondly, instead of *anathematizein* the *Gospel of the Nazarenes* uses the verb *katarasthai* which is always transitive and therefore cannot be understood as self-cursing. Thirdly, the younger Pliny mentions in the early second century that to curse Jesus could serve as proof of innocence in the case of a person accused of being a Christian. This theory therefore has a certain probability.

Peter's way of speaking of Jesus as 'this man of whom you speak' is deliberate and seems to refer to Mk 8:38, '. . . ashamed of me and my word'. Peter's initial rebuke of Jesus' understanding of his mission (Mk 8:32) is now restated in even more hardened and final terms.

> **Verse 72:**   And immediately the cock crowed a second time. And Peter remembered how Jesus had said to him, 'Before the cock crows twice, you will deny me three times.' And he broke down and wept.

Right after Peter's third denial, 'the cock crowed a second time. And Peter remembered . . . .' With these words Mark stresses that this was the denial predicted by Jesus (Mk 14:30). This is clearly indicated by the presence of 'a second time' in Mk 14:72a, corresponding to 'twice' in Mk 14:30 and 14:72b, and by the formally quoted saying of Jesus found in Mk 14:72b, recalling Mk 14:30 almost literally. In a real sense, then, the denial account is subordinate to the prediction of Mk 14:30, and is intended to expound it. The account as we have it now is written up to show that what Jesus had said is fulfilled. That is, the denial account treats the saying of Jesus in a way similar to that in which scripture is treated in certain other places in the New Testament; in other words, it is given an almost canonical standing. Just as Old Testament texts are said to have been fulfilled, so Jesus' words are presented here as fulfilled.

'And Peter remembered *how* Jesus had said to him' suggests that Peter recalled not only the words of Jesus but also the situation in which they were addressed to him. Remembering all this, Peter was overwhelmed with grief, 'and he broke down and wept'. The phrase 'he broke down' causes difficulty. It should most probably be understood as 'and he began to weep' (cf. NAB: 'He broke down and began to cry'; JB and NEB: 'And he burst into tears'). Others suggest: 'And he dashed out and wept'.

Marcan activity in the trial narrative can be summarized as follows. He has taken over a number of early Christian traditions and has combined them into what now appears as a trial before the Sanhedrin. A pre-Marcan saying about the Temple, itself of composite nature, is inserted by Mark into a framework of false witness, or testimony that did not agree, and then related to the Christological issue, focusing on the final question of the high priest and Jesus' answer (Mk 14:61–62) which is a Marcan compendium of Christology, giving Mark's final word on Jesus as Son of man and Son of God, the latter being qualified by the former.

Mark has intercalated this whole trial account in the narrative of Peter's denial (Mk 14:54, 66–72). This creates the impression that Peter was present throughout the hearing before the Sanhedrin. The ultimate reason for this intertwining of the two originally independent accounts of the hearing and the denial lies most probably in Mk 14:62, the first and the only passage in Mark where Jesus publicly affirms that he is 'the Christ, the Son of the Blessed'. As we pointed out, the present combination of texts results in the juxtaposition of the rejection by the Sanhedrin (Mk 14:63–65) and the denial of Peter (Mk 14:66–72). Thus Jesus pronounces his self-affirmation, not only at the moment when he is rejected by the Jewish leaders, but also at the moment when he is denied and deserted by the last of his followers (see Mk 14:29, 'Even though they all fall away, I will not', and Mk 14:54, 'Peter had followed him at a distance'). Thus this section again lays strong emphasis on the solitude in which Jesus goes to his death.

All this editorial activity leads to a strongly contrasted composition. A first paradox is that the hearing seems to lead to the opposite of the result expected: instead of establishing the guilt of the accused, it ends with the revelation of his supreme dignity. Once this dignity is established one would expect it to be acknowledged. But here comes the second paradox: the revelation of who Jesus really is does not raise any positive answer. It arouses only opposition. He is accused of blasphemy; he is said to deserve death; he is ill-treated and Peter denies him. Through the order adopted, Mark brings to the fore the paradoxical contrast between Jesus' affirmation of his dignity and his treatment thereafter.

Jesus is delivered to Pilate (Mk 15:1)

Verse 1: And as soon as it was morning the chief priests, with the elders and scribes, and the whole council held a consultation; and they bound Jesus and led him away and delivered him to Pilate.

The phrase 'the chief priests, with the elders and scribes' clearly takes up again the reference of Mk 14:53, where the same people are mentioned in the same order. It is somewhat strange that we are told here for the first time that 'they bound Jesus'. We would have expected this at the arrest (cf. Jn 18:12, 14). It is possible that Mark thought of Isa 8:9–10LXX, which contains a reference to a 'consultation' (*bebouleuntai boulēn*) as well as to 'binding' (*dēsōmen*). The phrase 'and delivered him to Pilate' firmly relates this verse to the continuation of the narrative. The third prediction of the passion stating that '... they will ... deliver him to the Gentiles' (Mk 10:33) is now fulfilled. Moreover, the remark of Mk 15:10, 'For he perceived that it was out of envy that the chief priests had delivered him up' clearly refers back to Mk 15:1.

On account of considerations of style, which indicate that the verse was formulated by Mark, and its close connection with the context, which indicates that Mark is taking up again the course of the Jewish trial interrupted by the denial of Peter (Mk 14:66–72), recent studies have led to the conclusion that we have here an entirely redactional verse, and that there is no tension between Mk 15:1 and Mk 14:53–65. The latter passage has recorded the decision to condemn Jesus (Mk 14:64); now we are told that they 'held a consultation' as to how and when to bring Jesus to Pilate. This verse, therefore, directs the action to the Roman trial. It forms a bridge between the Jewish and the Roman trial.

II. Matthew 26:57–75; 27:1–10

Matthew follows Mark very closely, and so we get the following outline:

(1) Introductory verses (Mt 26:57–60a);
(2) The accusation by the false witnesses (Mt 26:60b–61);
(3) The interrogation by the high priest, Jesus' answer, and the reaction of the Sanhedrin (Mt 26:62–66);
(4) The mocking scene (Mt 26:67–68);
(5) The denial of Peter (Mt 26:69–75);
(6) The conclusion of the Jewish trial (Mt 27:1–2);
(7) The fate of Judas (Mt 27:3–10).

Introduction (Mt 26:57–60a)

Verse 57: Then those who had seized Jesus led him to Caiaphas the high priest, where the scribes and the elders had gathered.

The text is in substantial agreement with Mark's beginning of the trial narrative, but several minor changes should not be overlooked. Matthew adds the phrase 'those who had seized (Jesus)' *(kratēsantes)*, thus identifying Mark's vague 'they' but also relating the following scene more closely to the arrest, where the same verbal expression is repeatedly used (cf. Mt 26:48, 50, 55; compare also Mk 14:51, omitted by Matthew).

As a whole, the verse is quite similar to Mt 26:3, 'then the chief priests and the elders of the people gathered in the palace of the high priest, who was called Caiaphas' (compare Mk 14:1b, 'And the chief priests and the scribes were seeking . . .'). There we were told that the Jewish leaders were gathered in the palace of the high priest to plan how they might seize him *(kratēsōsin)*. Now that they have seized Jesus *(kratēsantes)*, they gather again in the same place for the trial. In both Mt 26:3 and Mt 26:57, Matthew identifies the high priest by name and thus gives him more prominence than Mark.

> **Verse 58:** But Peter followed him at a distance, as far as the courtyard of the high priest, and going inside he sat with the guards to see the end.

Matthew again basically follows Mark but with a few interesting changes. Matthew clearly distinguishes Peter's following at a distance and his going inside the courtyard. Mark uses only one verb: 'Peter followed . . . right into the courtyard' (Mk 14:54). Matthew's emphasis on this going inside *(eiselthōn esō)* creates an inclusion with the end of the denial scene where Peter 'went out *(exelthōn exō)* and wept bitterly' (Mt 26:75).

Matthew also substitutes the phrase 'to see the end' for Mark's reference to Peter's 'warming himself at the fire' (cf. Mt 26:69 and Mk 14:67). Literarily speaking, this phrase prepares for the continuation of Peter's involvement (Mt 26:69). But from the viewpoint of the evangelist's theological interest, it may express a more lively ecclesial interest in the person of Peter, who is here presented as a witness of the events 'until the end'. The end refers here either to the outcome of the trial or to the death of Jesus.

> **Verses 59–60a:** Now the chief priests and the whole council sought false testimony against Jesus that they might put him to death, (60a) but they found none, though many false witnesses came forward.

These verses are a typical example of Matthew's tendency to simplify and clarify the account. He immediately asserts that the Sanhedrin 'sought false testimony against Jesus', whereas Mark mentions the false character of the testimony only after speaking of the Sanhedrin's search for witnesses. Matthew goes straight to the point and then, contrary to Mark, drops the theme of *false* testimony altogether. He is more interested in the *valid* testimony that is given next. According to Matthew, Jesus is judged and condemned on the ground of his messianic claim which is established on the basis of valid testimony (Mt 26:61; compare Mk 14:57, 'And some stood up and bore false witness against him') and the solemn question of the high priest (Mt 26:63).

The accusation by the false witnesses (Mt 26:60b–61)

> **Verses 60b–61:** At last two came forward (61) and said, 'This fellow said, "I am able to destroy the temple of God, and to build it in three days." '

In these verses Matthew considerably alters his Marcan source. The addition of the phrase 'at last' brings about a clear distinction between the false witnesses and these two valid ones, and gives special importance to their testimony. The replacement of Mark's 'some' by 'two' is also to be seen in this light: Deut 17:6 demanded at least two valid witnesses for condemnation: 'On the evidence of two or three witnesses he that is to die shall be put to death'.

The introductory words of the witnesses' deposition are changed from 'We heard him say' (Mk 14:58) into 'This fellow said'. The pejorative use of the demonstrative *houtos* ('this one') is found repeatedly in Matthew (Mt 9:3; 12:24; 13:55) with a connotation of contempt.

The statement attributed to Jesus is very different from that found in Mark:

Matthew	*Mark*
I am able to destroy the temple of God, and to build it in three days.	I will destroy this temple that is made with hands, and in three days I will build another, not made with hands.

The exact purpose of the nuance 'I am able' *(dunamai)* with the infinitive 'to destroy' instead of Mark's 'I will destroy' is not immediately clear. Some have understood it as an attempt to soften Jesus' threat against the 'temple of God'. But others understand it rather as affirming Jesus' power *(dunamis)* over the Temple, which is a very probable interpretation of the phrase in a gospel which avoids any impression of limitation of Jesus' power and tries to emphasize the authority *(dunamis)* and majesty of Jesus in the earlier sections of the passion narrative (cf. Mt 26:17–19; 26:53).

Next Matthew omits Mark's contrast between 'this temple that is made with hands' and 'another not made with hands', and replaces it with a reference to 'the temple of God', i.e., the Jerusalem Temple. Indeed, Matthew is no longer concerned with the building of a spiritualized temple which is different and better than the present one, as in Mark, but is concerned with the Temple of Jerusalem. It is important that 'I am able' refers to both destroying and building. The emphasis is most probably on the latter, for not until this part of the sentence does it become fully clear why it says 'I am able'.

The significance of all these changes is disputed, but it is probable that Matthew introduced them to emphasize the power of Jesus, which would be enhanced if the words deal directly with the destruction and rebuilding of the Jerusalem Temple. This interpretation fits well in a context dealing with Jesus' messianic claims, since contemporary literature mentioned a destruction of the Jerusalem Temple at the beginning of the messianic era and its eventual substitution by a new temple (although it is not clear that this would be done by the Messiah himself). Seen in this light Jesus' words can be understood as a messianic self-affirmation. At any rate, the verse makes clear that Jesus is the Lord and that he is invested with power.

The interrogation, the answer and the reaction (Mt 26:62–66)

> **Verse 62:** And the high priest stood up and said, 'Have you no answer to make? What is it that these men testify against you?'

The changes in this verse are of a purely stylistic character and are entirely obscured by the translation. However, because of the omission of Mk 14:59, 'Yet not even so did their testimony agree', Jesus' alleged claim to power over the Temple is immediately followed by the challenging question of the high priest. The present verse, which should most probably be understood as including one, not two questions, leads us to the decisive issue beginning in Mt 26:63.

> **Verse 63:** But Jesus was silent. And the high priest said to him, 'I adjure you by the living God, tell us if you are the Christ, the Son of God.'

Matthew identifies Jesus as the subject of 'was silent', but omits Mark's 'and made no answer'. The silence of Jesus, which in Mark may have a theological meaning, becomes here a part of the trial: it gives a greater relevance to Jesus' decisive answer which follows.

The evangelist expands the decisive question of the high priest with the addition of the introductory formula, 'I adjure you by the living God, tell us'. An examination of the various elements of the formula leads to the conclusion that it may have been composed by Matthew from Old Testament sources, as e.g., Gen 24:3, '. . . and I will make you swear by the Lord, the God of heaven and of the earth . . .' and I Kgs 22:16, 'How many times shall I adjure you that you speak to me nothing but the truth in the name of the Lord?' The formula is employed here to add solemnity and dramatic emphasis to the question of the high priest. He acts as an 'exorcist' (the Greek verb is *exorkizō*), who mentions the living God by name in order to adjure the man who is questioned.

The core of the high priest's question is left intact except for the change of Mark's 'Son of the Blessed' into 'Son of God'. Since the latter phrase runs parallel with Lk 22:70 it could be traditional. But since the title 'Son of God' plays a much more important role in Matthew's passion narrative than in the other gospels, one cannot be absolutely sure. Matthew again uses the title in Mt 27:40, 43 and 54, of which only the last one has been determined by tradition (cf. Mk 15:39). In his polemic with the Jewish leaders, Matthew may intend to accuse them, in the person of the high priest, of blasphemy, by quoting him as asking Jesus whether he is the Christ, the Son of God. This line of interpretation seems to be confirmed in the following two verses.

Verse 64: Jesus said to him, 'You have said so. But I tell you, hereafter you will see the Son of man seated at the right hand of Power, and coming on the clouds of heaven.'

Although the high priest has asked that he should give 'us' an answer, Jesus addresses himself first to the high priest only *(autōi)*. In a very striking way Matthew changes Mark's unmistakable 'I am' into an apparently ambiguous 'You have said so'. Although the exact interpretation of this phrase may be discussed, it seems clear that it must be understood as an affirmation. The emphasis is on 'you', but this does not mean a total rejection of the words of the high priest; only his particular point of view is rejected. It should be noted that similar replies are found in Mt 26:25 to Judas' question whether he is the betrayer and in Mt 27:11 to Pilate's question whether Jesus is the King of the Jews. All three questions are asked by people who are (in different capacities) opposed to Jesus, and each time Jesus basically confirms what is really expressed in the question.

By the use of the word 'but' *(plēn;* contrast Mark's 'and') Matthew intends to distinguish the continuation of Jesus' answer clearly from what precedes. 'You have said so' basically confirms what the high priest expressed in his question. Now – and this is underlined by the phrase 'I tell you' – we get what Jesus himself has to say about the meaning of his Messiahship. This is confirmed by the fact that, whereas the high priest speaks of the 'Son of God', Jesus uses 'Son of man'.

The phrase 'hereafter', which is also added to Mark (although there are a few manuscripts of Mark in which the expression occurs), is not necessarily to be understood in a chronological sense. In Matthew it usually indicates a clear distinction between the immediate past and a totally different future (cf. Mt 23:39; 26:29). In our present verse the meaning seems to be that Jesus' messianic nature is implicitly acknowledged in the high priest's question, but that it will become clear for all to see in the future.

The change of Mark's 'with the clouds of heaven' into 'on the clouds of heaven' is one of two minor changes, the second of which can be appreciated in the Greek text only, intended to make the quotation concur more closely with the Septuagint text.

What is the overall meaning of Jesus' answer in Matthew? There are on the whole two general lines of interpretation. A first group of scholars understand 'hereafter' in a strongly temporal sense, and give the statement a *polemical* interpretation. The preceding 'but' *(plēn)* is said to have a threatening tone. The outcome is that they give relatively little attention to the first half of the saying, but emphasize the second half, beginning with 'but hereafter', as being a message of threat and judgment. But a closer study of these phrases and the immediate context do not seem to bear out this polemical interpretation.

A second group understand the saying in a *Christological* perspective, i.e., in terms of Jesus' exaltation, rather than polemically. What happens to Jesus now ('hereafter') will lead to future glory ('you will see . . .'). This shows the same kind of foreshortening of perspective which we find in many prophetic statements and also in Jesus' own words (cf. Mt 10:23; 16:28). Matthew basically agrees with Mark, but he emphasizes the connection between Jesus' death and glorification. He will do the same at the end of the crucifixion scene.

Verses 65–66: Then the high priest tore his robes, and said, 'He has uttered blasphemy. Why do we still need witnesses? You have now heard his blasphemy. (66) What is your judgment?' They answered, 'He deserves death.'

Beginning verse 65 with 'then' instead of Mark's 'and', Matthew expresses the close causality between Jesus' self-affirmation and the indignant reaction of the high priest. Matthew clarifies the situation by quoting the high priest as saying first of all, 'He has uttered blasphemy', which explains his gesture.

The addition of 'now' (in Greek *ide nun*, literally, 'see now') draws attention to the key moment in the Jewish trial. Jesus' condemnation is brought about by his messianic self-affirmation and by nothing else. It should also be noted that, because of the addition at the beginning of the high priest's words, the term 'blasphemy' is used twice. It has been suggested that by these changes, together with those noted in the preceding text, Matthew may intend to imply that the high priest and the Sanhedrin, not Jesus, are blaspheming. They would be presented as breaking the Decalogue, not only by seeking 'false witness' (Mt 26:59), but also by their blasphemy (Mt 26:63) which they impute to Jesus. But, as we pointed out in connection with the previous verse, the polemical interpretation of this passage is not convincing.

In verse 66, Matthew changes Mark's related narrative into direct speech, thereby emphasizing the verdict of the Sanhedrin. He also omits 'all', apparently because he considered it superfluous.

The mocking scene (Mt 26:67–68)

Verses 67–68: Then they spat in his face, and struck him; and some slapped him, (68) saying, 'Prophesy to us, you Christ! Who is it that struck you?'

The initial 'then' links the action to the words of the Sanhedrin. Contrary to Mark, Matthew does not mention the covering of Jesus' face with a blindfold, but nevertheless seems to imply that Jesus could not see his assailants. Of the many solutions offered, the most satisfactory is the attempt to resolve the difficulty by recourse to textual criticism. The presence of this feature in Mark may have to be explained as a later interpolation from the Lucan account, and consequently Matthew would not have found it in his Marcan source.

Textual criticism is also employed to solve a second important difference: Matthew's question 'Who is it that struck you?' It is most probably to be attributed to an early harmonization of Matthew with Luke.

While in Mark two groups are clearly distinguished, 'some' of 'all' the members of the Sanhedrin (cf. Mk 14:64) and the 'guards', Matthew refers only to one category of tormentors. This results in a more concise and connected picture of the action.

The address 'Christ' is the most important addition in this verse. The use of this rich Christological title indicates Matthew's true concern in the trial narrative and in the whole passion narrative: the messianic dignity of Jesus. The question of the high priest (Mt 26:63) and the deriding confession of the members of the Sanhedrin who strike him ironically acknowledge Jesus for what he really is. Matthew's main interest is Christology and not polemic, i.e., to show that the trial was fake. We should also note that the title 'Christ' marks the beginning and the end of the hearing before the Sanhedrin: Mt 26:63, 'if you are the Christ, the Son of God' – 'Prophesy to us, you Christ!' (Mt 26:68), thus constituting an inclusion.

The denial of Peter (Mt 26:69–75)

Verse 69: Now Peter was sitting outside in the courtyard. And a maid came up to him, and said, 'You also were with Jesus the Galilean.'

This verse links up with Mt 26:58 in much the same way as Mk 14:66–67a does with Mk 14:54. The main differences between Mt 26:69 and Mk 14:66–67a are to be explained by the differences between Mt 26:58 and Mk 14:54. Other differences are due to Matthew's handling of the immediate parallel of Mk 14:66. Mark's phrase 'was below in the courtyard' is transformed into 'was sitting outside in the courtyard', and 'one of the maids . . . came' is changed into 'and a maid came up to him'. Matthew's conception of the 'courtyard' seems to be quite different from Mark's, and our overall impression is that Matthew succeeds in making a more dramatic use of the movements of his personage.

Taking into account these nuances, it can be said that both in Mark and in Matthew the first challenge takes place in the courtyard and that its basic content is Peter's association with Jesus.

Verse 70: But he denied it before them all, saying, 'I do not know what you mean.'

Adding the phrase 'before them all', and thus extending Peter's audience, Matthew emphasizes the impact of Peter's refusal to admit any association with Jesus. But in the light of texts like Mt 5:16, 'Let your light so shine *before men* . . .' and Mt 6:1, 'Beware of practising your piety *before men* in order to be seen by them', the words seem to connote the concept of making a show of one's behaviour. A comparison with Mt 10:32, 33 is even more impressive: 'So every one who acknowledges me *before men* . . . . but whoever *denies me before men*'. And Mt 26:34, 35 reads: 'Jesus said to him, "Truly, I say to you . . . you will *deny* me three times." Peter said to him, "Even if I must die with you, I will not *deny* you." ' This whole development reaches its culminating point in Mt 26:70, 'But *he denied it before them all*'.

In an effort to simplify Mark's text, but especially to improve his 'crescendo effect', Matthew omits the words 'nor understand' (contrast Mark, where the first reply is more intense than the second).

Verse 71: And when he went out to the porch, another maid saw him, and she said to the bystanders, 'This man was with Jesus of Nazareth.'

Again the description presupposes a different topographical setting from Mark's. Whereas in Mark the second accusation is levelled by the same maid, in Matthew it is 'another maid' who confronts Peter. Instead of Mark's formulation of the second and the third accusation in terms of belonging to the group of disciples (Mk 14:69, 'This man is one of them'; Mk 14:70, 'Certainly you are one of them'), Matthew almost repeats the words of Mark's first accusation, and thus again emphasizes Peter's association *with Jesus*. He thus underlines that Peter denied the Master (cf. Mt 26:34–35).

> **Verse 72:** And again he denied it with an oath, 'I do not know the man.'

In view of his attempt to build up a climax gradually, Matthew reinforces Peter's second denial by the phrase 'with an oath' *(meta horkou)*. A reference has been found to Mt 5:34, 'But I say to you, do not swear at all'. Peter's inconsiderate violation of Jesus' prohibition leads him to apostasy. Another striking passage is the description of Herod's rash promise to the daughter of Herodias in Mt 14:7, 'so that he promised with an oath *(meth' horkou)*'. This probable reference illustrates again how Matthew's treatment of the passion material is in line with ideas found elsewhere in the gospel. It should be noted that both Mt 5:34 and the feature of the promise 'with an oath' in Mt 14:7 are found in Matthew only.

The most important editorial intervention in this verse is the addition of Peter's answer: 'I do not know the man'. With the help of Mk 14:71 (Peter's third denial, parallel with Mt 26:74), Matthew makes explicit the words implied in Mk 14:70. Thus Matthew emphasizes once more that the question under consideration is the confession of Jesus.

> **Verse 73:** After a little while the bystanders came up and said to Peter, 'Certainly you are also one of them, for your accent betrays you.'

The impression of movement which was already given in Mt 26:69, 'And a maid *came up* . . .', is again found in the addition of the phrase 'came up and'. Again Matthew also makes explicit what is implicitly contained in Mark's 'for you are a Galilean', by replacing this clause by 'for your accent betrays you'. Matthew had anticipated the reference to Galilee in Mt 26:69, where instead of Mark's 'the Nazarene, Jesus' (Mk 14:67), we find 'Jesus the Galilean'.

> **Verse 74:** Then he began to invoke a curse on himself and to swear, 'I do not know the man.' And immediately the cock crowed.

Here we reach the culminating point of Peter's denial. In an ultimate attempt to avoid identification as one of 'those with Jesus', he began to curse himself and to swear. Peter, whose oath contributed to his unfaithfulness (cf. Mt 26:72), now 'began to invoke a curse on himself' in denying acquaintance with Jesus.

Matthew omits the superfluous 'of whom you speak', and also the phrase 'a second time', which he also omitted in Mt 26:34, 'before the cock crows' (instead of Mk 14:30, 'before the cock crows twice'). The cockcrow recalls the prophetic word of Jesus.

> **Verse 75:** And Peter remembered the saying of Jesus, 'Before the cock crows, you will deny me three times.' And he went out and wept bitterly.

The prophetic word of Jesus brings Peter to repentance. Jesus' words are quoted exactly as they were expressed in Mt 26:34. The departure of Peter concludes the scene. The phrase 'went out' (*exelthōn exō*, literally, 'going out') forms an inclusion with 'going inside' (*eiselthōn esō*, Mt 26:58). Peter who went inside 'to see the end', now goes out repenting. The emotional implications are emphasized by the addition of the adverb 'bitterly'.

Matthew's version of the denial scene is more refined than Mark's. The circle of challengers is more gradually developed and the dramatic build-up is more harmonious. The redactor's activity stresses the disciples' union with Jesus and the literal fulfilment of his prophetic words. Peter's compunction underlines the paraenetical implications of the pericope.

The conclusion of the Jewish trial (Mt 27:1–2)

> **Verse 1:** When morning came, all the chief priests and the elders of the people took counsel against Jesus to put him to death;

The morning gathering mentioned here should almost certainly be understood as a conclusion to the long session of the Sanhedrin which has continued throughout the night until the early morning, and not as a new session. Matthew's chronological indications correspond with those given in Mark: when it was evening (Mk 14:17/Mt 26:20), the cockcrow (Mk 14:72/Mt 26:74), early in the morning (Mk 15:1/ Mt 27:1). But he rephrases Mark's 'as soon as it was morning' and writes 'when morning came' (*prōias de genomenēs*), bringing the expression in line with the phrase 'when it was evening' (*opsias de genomenēs*; Mt 26:20; 27:57). Thus Matthew emphasizes the beginning of Jesus' last day. The expression should be related to the burial of Jesus, 'when it was evening' (Mt 27:57).

These chronological indications are not decisive, but they are reinforced by other evidence. The phrase 'they took counsel' (*sumboulion elabon*; cf. Mt 12:14/Mk 3:6; Mt 22:15; 27:7; 28:12; see also Mt 26:4) describes a meeting of the Jewish leaders to decide upon a particular course of action. Here in Mt 27:1, they gather 'to put him to death' (*hōste* expresses result). In Mt 26:59 they 'sought false witness against Jesus that they might put him to death'. In Mt 26:66 they proclaim: 'He deserves death' (contrast Mk 14:64, 'they all *condemned* him – literally: judged him – as deserving death' – this is final), but the final decision has not yet been taken. The formal conclusion is noted in Mt 27:1, 'they took counsel . . .', as is confirmed in Mt 27:3, 'when Judas, his betrayer, saw that he was condemned'. It is, therefore, clear that for Matthew, Mt 27:1–2 constitutes the conclusion of the Jewish trial.

He omits Mark's 'and the whole council', but makes up for this by adding 'all' in front of 'the chief priests and the elders of the people'. He adds also 'against Jesus', thus emphasizing the hostile character of the conclusion (cf. Mt 26:59). As has been pointed out, the result of Matthew's editing of Mk 15:1 is a clear inclusion framing the Jewish trial:

Mt 26:59	Mt 27:1
Now the chief priests	All the chief priests
and the whole council	and the elders of the people
sought false testimony	took counsel
against Jesus	against Jesus
that they might put him to death.	to put him to death.

Verse 2: and they bound him and led him away and delivered him to Pilate the governor.

This verse, which is almost identical with Mk 15:1b, directs the narrative towards the Roman trial. Mark's 'Jesus' is replaced by the indefinite 'him' because Matthew has already used the proper name in Mt 27:1. The Greek text has another word for 'led him away' (*apēgagon*) than Mark (*apēnenkan*); the former word is also used in Mk 14:44, 53; 15:16, but Matthew seems to reserve it for passages describing the major transfers of Jesus as a prisoner (Mt 26:57; 27:2, 31). Matthew also adds the title 'the governor' to the name Pilate. Pilate being duly identified, Matthew will from now on use 'Pilate' or 'the governor' as alternatives.

It appears, then, that Mt 27:1–2 fulfils an important role in Matthew's passion narrative. Verse 1 concludes the Jewish trial, and verse 2 directs the narrative towards the Roman trial. Thus the passage constitutes a marked fulfilment of the third prediction of the passion, 'The Son of man . . . they will condemn him to death, and deliver him to the Gentiles . . .' (Mt 20:18–19). It forms an 'editorial bridge' similar to those found in Mt 26:30 (from the place of the Last Supper to the Mount of Olives, or Gethsemane; cf. Mt 26:36) and Mt 27:32–33 (from the governor's palace to Golgotha).

The fate of Judas (Mt 27:3–10)

Before narrating the Roman trial, Matthew inserts the pericope about the fate of Judas. The passage raises a number of questions. Firstly, it is found only in Matthew, and there does not seem to be any trace of the incident in either Mark or Luke. Secondly, even a brief comparison with the only other reference to the death of Judas, i.e., Acts 1:16–20, shows that this passage has nothing in common with our text, except the reference to the buying of a field which was called Field of Blood. Thirdly, historically speaking, the pericope does not belong here. How could Judas possibly find the chief priests and the elders at the Temple? Mt 27:2 says very clearly that they were on their way to deliver Jesus to Pilate!

These three remarks make us raise questions, first, as to the character of this account and, second, why Matthew inserted it here.

First, the pericope has been called a popular story by means of which the author sheds light on questions raised by the passion narrative. It has been said that it adds to factual recollections a rather subtle *midrash* interpretation of different biblical texts. *Midrash* denotes a distinctively Jewish literary genus which we have explained elsewhere.[6] The analysis of the present account will further clarify this notion.

Second, it has been shown that it would be a mistake to presume that this account is a high-handed interruption of the sequence of the passion narrative. The fundamental data of Mt 27:3–10 can be found in Mark (Mk 14:10–11, 21); but its actual position, too, can be clarified. There is a definite parallelism between the prediction–fulfilment pattern in the cases of Peter and Judas. Judas' betrayal is predicted in Mk 14:18–21/Mt 26:21–24. Peter's denial is predicted in Mk 14:30/Mt 26:34. Both predictions take place in the context of the Last Supper, respectively immediately before and after the institution account. The fulfilment of the prediction concerning Peter is extensively described in the account of Peter's denial (Mk 14:66–72/Mt 26:69–75), in close connection with the Jewish trial. But what about Judas? True, Mark refers to Judas at the arrest, but the tragic fate predicted in Mk 14:21 is not fulfilled in Mark. Therefore, the account of Judas' fate in Mt 27:3–10 fills a gap in Mark's account. What we said about the respective predictions applies also here: both the denial of Peter and the final fate of Judas are narrated in the same context, namely in close relation to the Jewish trial.

Verse 3: When Judas, his betrayer, saw that he was condemned, he repented and brought back the thirty pieces of silver to the chief priests and the elders,

The redactor tries in several ways to integrate the following pericope with the overall sequence of the passion narrative. Mt 27:1–2 is to be considered the conclusion of the session of the Sanhedrin which has gone on throughout the night until morning. By the use of the conjunction 'when' (*tote*) Matthew links the Judas account with the 'counsel to put him to death' in Mt 27:1–2. Judas is referred to as 'his betrayer' (*ho paradous auton*, a phrase identical to the one by which he is introduced in this gospel, Mt 10:4). The phrase 'saw' also links Judas' action to the outcome of the Jewish trial: when he saw that Jesus was led to Pilate (Mt 27:2), he concluded that he was condemned. This is confirmed by the expression 'was condemned' (*katekrithē*) which aptly describes the outcome of the trial (cf. Mk 14:64; compare Mt 26:66). Realizing that Jesus was condemned, Judas 'repented' (*metamelētheis*). The same word is used in Mt 21:29, 32 and seems to mean 'to change one's mind' or 'to regret one's decision', but does not imply true repentance or conversion (*metanoia*). The 'change of mind' refers to Mt 26:14–16; there Judas agreed to betray Jesus for thirty pieces of silver, now he brings them back.

Judas tried to appease his regret 'and brought back the thirty pieces of silver to the chief priests and the elders', the most typical Matthean expression to indicate Jesus' opponents. The phrase 'thirty pieces of silver' is a clear sign of the influence of the quotation from Zechariah (cf. Mt 27:9–10) on the narrative part of the pericope. It is a traditional feature that Judas betrayed Jesus for a sum of money (cf. Mk 14:11), but the number 'thirty' comes from the quotation of Zechariah.

The text, also referred to in Mt 27:5–6 and partly quoted in Mt 27:9, reads: 'Then I said to them, "If it seems right to you, give me my wages; but if not, keep them." And they weighed out as my wages thirty shekels of silver. Then the Lord said to me, "Cast it into the treasury" – the lordly price at which I was paid off by them. So I took the thirty shekels of silver and cast them into the treasury in the house of the Lord' (Zech 11:12–13). It is part of a compact literary unit, Zech 11:4–17, which narrates how the prophet, the good shepherd of the flock, performed a symbolic action, involving two staffs, the payment of thirty silver pieces and casting these silver pieces into the treasury. The irony of the scene consists in the fact that the wages demanded by the shepherd for his work was not money but the submission of the sheep, their fidelity to God. The people who, instead of being submissive and faithful, gave the shepherd money, showed themselves unwilling to obey God who had been speaking to them through his spokesman, the prophet. The thirty pieces of silver which they gave to the shepherd were indicative of contempt, and, in the final analysis, of the categorical refusal of the gift of salvation which God was offering them. The prophet, who understood the implication of the monetary recompense made to him, threw the sum into the treasury on God's orders.

The number thirty is usually explained in the light of Ex 21:32, where a slave is valued at thirty shekels. The shepherd's efforts are worth just the price of a menial slave. However, the element of contempt present in Zech 11 is totally lacking in Ex 21:32. Some scholars have referred to passages in Sumerian poetical literature where dealing with a temple as something worth thirty shekels means treating the sanctuary with contempt. The question remains, of course, how the author of Zech 11:12f. came to know the Sumerian tradition. The question has not yet received a satisfactory answer, but it may be pointed out that late Jewish tradition seems to show knowledge of the old Sumerian usage. While Gen 37:28 says that Joseph was sold to Midianites by his brothers for twenty shekels, the *Testament of Gad* 2 states that he was sold for thirty shekels.

Verse 4: saying, 'I have sinned in betraying innocent blood.'
They said, 'What is that to us? See to it yourself.'

Confronting the authorities, Judas admits his guilt: 'I have sinned', which is subsequently contrasted with the heartless attitude of the chief priests and the elders. He describes his sin as betraying 'innocent blood'. A reference to 'innocent blood' is found in Jer 19:4, a text which almost certainly influenced the formulation of Mt 27:9–10. See also Deut 19:10. In Mt 27:24, Pilate, at the close of the Roman trial, will wash his hands to symbolize that he is 'innocent of this man's blood'. The people reply, 'His blood be on us and on our children!' (Mt 27:25), an expression which is to be understood as an admission of responsibility. The theme of responsibility for the 'just blood of the prophets' is the background for the present statement (cf. Mt 23:35 speaking of the blood of the prophets shed from the blood of Abel to that of Zechariah).

We may have to take into consideration here Deut 27:25, 'Cursed be he who takes a bribe to slay an innocent person (literally, innocent blood)'. A man who was cursed lived as an outlaw and was designated for final destruction. Now a curse can only be removed if the object of it is taken away (cf. e.g., II Sam 21:1–9). Judas tried to do so by returning the money, but since this way was barred by the authorities, he had only one possibility left, to do away with himself.

Judas' despair is confronted by the heartless attitude of the chief priests and elders. They refuse to consider the matter ('What is that to us?'), but they will nevertheless dispose of the money (cf. Mt 27:6), and their present refusal to accept the 'blood money' sharply contrasts with their statement, 'His blood be on us and on our children' (Mt 27:25). The expression 'See to it yourself' is paralleled in Mt 27:24 where Pilate refuses to take responsibility and diverts it to the Jews with the words 'see to it yourselves'.

Verse 5: And throwing down the pieces of silver in the temple, he departed; and he went and hanged himself.

Judas threw the pieces of silver into the Temple, another feature of the account most probably inspired by the quotation from Zech 11:13, '... Cast it (the thirty shekels) into the treasury' (Greek text; the Hebrew text refers here to a 'potter'; note that both interpretations could be related to our present text!).

Then 'he went and hanged himself'. Although some have tried to weaken the importance of the parallel, most interpreters see here a clear reference to II Sam 17:23, where we are told that Ahithophel, after betraying David and seeing 'that his counsel was not followed ... went off home ... and hanged himself'. Ahithophel seems to be the only suicide in the Old Testament, as Judas is the only one in the New Testament. These are also the only two places in the canonical writings where the term *apēnxato* ('hanged himself') is used (but see Tobit 3:10). II Sam 17:23 probably provided the background for early Christian reflection on Judas' lot. A similar process took place with Ps 41(40):9, 'Even my bosom friend in whom I trusted, who ate of my bread, has lifted his heel against me', which was understood by the rabbis as referring to Ahithophel's betrayal of David, and was applied to Judas in Jn 13:18. In the composition of Matthew, Judas' suicide constitutes the fulfilment of the prophecy of Mt 26:24, '... but woe to that man by whom the Son of man is betrayed! It would have been better for that man if he had not been born.'

Verse 6: But the chief priests, taking the pieces of silver, said, 'It is not lawful to put them into the treasury, since they are blood money.'

The chief priests took the abandoned money and so implicitly admitted their responsibility. They declared that it was not lawful to put this money into the Temple treasury, most probably thinking of Deut 23:18, 'You shall not bring the hire of a harlot or the wages of a dog (sodomite?) into the house of the Lord your God'. The phrase 'put them into the treasury' is most probably again due to the influence of Zech 11:13 on the narrative.

By saying that the thirty pieces of silver constitute 'blood money' (*timē haimatos*, literally, 'price of blood'; note that *timē* is found in Zech 11:13, whereas 'innocent blood' is found in Jer 19:4), they concur with Judas' statement that he betrayed 'innocent blood'.

Verse 7: So they took counsel, and bought with them the potter's field, to bury strangers in.

Taking counsel, the chief priests decided to buy the 'potter's field'. The phrase does not appear as such in the Old Testament. The combination may be the result of a quotation mixture which Matthew used, although even so the appearance of the 'field' in the context is somewhat surprising. It could point to the existence of a popular tradition which associated the name of a field, 'Field of Blood', or the purchase of a field, with Judas' betrayal or death. Acts 1:18, 19, 'Now this man bought a field . . . so that field was called in their language Akeldama, that is, Field of Blood', supports the existence of such a tradition.

The field was bought 'to bury strangers in'. The detail should again be traced to the Old Testament background of the narrative. Jer 19 which has already provided the reference to 'innocent blood' (Jer 19:4) and speaks of a change of the land's name to 'valley of Slaughter' (Jer 19:6), says also that 'men shall bury in Topheth because there will be no place else to bury' (Jer 19:11 Hebrew text). The field purchased by the chief priests with blood money was the site of the sinfulness of God's people narrated in Jer 18 – 19. Mt 27:3–10 demonstrates that the complete rejection of Jesus by the Jewish leaders fits perfectly into the sinful pattern established in the Old Testament.

Verse 8: Therefore that field has been called the Field of Blood to this day.

In the last verse before the formula quotation of Mt 27:9–10, the author concludes with a redactional comment about the origin of the name 'Field of Blood'. A certain affinity has been noted to a similar remark in Mt 28:15, 'and this story has been spread among the Jews to this day', as has the resemblance to aetiological formulas in the Septuagint, of which the phrase 'until this day' is a typical element (cf. Gen 26:33; 35:20; Deut 11:4, etc.). Both the existence of the field and its name 'Field of Blood' are considered generally known. However, aetiology is not the (main) purpose of this pericope. It is, in a way, rather its starting-point or initial inspiration.

Verse 9a: Then was fulfilled what had been spoken by the prophet Jeremiah, saying,

This clause constitutes the typical introduction to a fulfilment text, so familiar in Matthew (cf. Mt 1:22; 2:15, 17, 23; 4:14; 8:17; 12:17; 13:35; 21:4; 26:56). A comparison with the other introductory formulas shows that the only unusual elements in Mt 27:9a are the first word 'then' (*tote*) and the reference to Jeremiah. 'Then' is used in

Mt 2:17 and 27:9 for two fulfilment texts in which the enemies of Jesus are the main actors. In both cases it may suggest that the acts of Herod and the chief priests respectively are an unconscious fulfilment of scripture.

As to the reference to Jeremiah, the study of Mt 27:9b–10 will show that Matthew has fused Jer 19 and 32 (and maybe 18) with the quotation from Zechariah. Jeremiah being the more important of the two, Matthew may have attributed the whole 'quotation' to him. But beyond that, we can say that just as 'Isaiah' can stand for some general aspects of Isaiah's message, especially its universal redemptive atmosphere, so 'Jeremiah' seems to evoke a context of judgment.

> **Verse 9b:** 'And they took thirty pieces of silver, the price of him on whom a price had been set by some of the sons of Israel,

Almost all exegetes refer here to Zech 11:13, 'Then the Lord said to me, "Cast it into the treasury" – the lordly price at which I was paid off by them. So I took the thirty shekels of silver and cast them into the treasury in the house of the Lord.' Matthew used this passage as his fulfilment text, but adapted it to the context of the pericope in which it is now found. His quotation is closer to the Hebrew text than to the Septuagint.

> **Verse 10:** 'and they gave them for the potter's field, as the Lord directed me.'

This part of the quotation is problematic since it departs considerably from the Old Testament text. The appearance of the word 'field' has especially caused difficulty. Many explain the situation of the text by taking into account allusions to passages in Jeremiah, an idea suggested by the fact that the redactor attributes the whole quotation to Jeremiah instead of Zechariah. Some refer to Jer 32:6–9 which speaks of the buying of a field at Anathoth, but it should be noted that this is the only link with Mt 27:3–10. Others would rather think of or combine the previous text with Jer 18:2–3 in which Yahweh tells Jeremiah to 'go down to the potter's house'. But here again the reference to a 'potter' is the only link with our present pericope. In Jer 32:6–9 we have a field but no potter, in Jer 18:2–3 we have a potter without a field! Finally, there is a third passage, Jer 19:1–13, which contains several themes related to our present pericope: involvement of the chief priests and elders (Jer 19:1), emphasis on a profaned piece of land which is destined to become a burial place (Jer 19:3–6), and allusions to a prophetic action which involves the buying and breaking of a potter's vessel (Jer 19:1, 10–11). Besides, there are also several literary contacts. It has been suggested that Matthew, or the tradition before him, was prompted to fuse the Zechariah text with some of these Jeremiah passages because of the similarity of the Hebrew words *yotser* and '*otsar*, meaning respectively 'potter' and 'treasure/treasury'. All of this seems to support the view that it is mainly Jer 19:1–13 to which Matthew refers.

It seems that Matthew rephrases the first words of Zech 13:11, 'Then the Lord said to me', to attune them to the classical obedience formula found especially in the Pentateuch (cf. e.g., Ex 9:12; 34:4; 36:5, etc.). By this clause Matthew draws our attention to the theme of fulfilment of the will of God as expressed in the scriptures.

A study of Mt 27:9–10, therefore, shows that Matthew has adapted the citation in view of its role in the pericope. The main source of the quotation is Zech 11:13, but it has been influenced by allusions to Jer 19:1–13 and perhaps Jer 32:6–9 (less probably by Jer 18:2–3). This explanation may seem rather subtle, but we should not forget that one of the characteristics of *midrash* is precisely its subtlety.

Summing up, we may say that Matthew's purpose is not to give us accurate information concerning the death of Judas or to explain the origin of the name 'Field of Blood', which would have very little salvific meaning. Rather, by means of a *midrash* combination of quotations and allusions he tries to emphasize the following points:

(1)   The prophetic knowledge of Jesus whose announcement of the fate of the betrayer (Mk 14:21; Mt 26:24) is here fulfilled.

(2)   The innocence of Jesus, one of the important concerns of the passion narrative, which is here admitted by Judas and indirectly by the chief priests and elders. Both this and the previous point enhance Matthew's Christology.

(3)   The question of the responsibility for Jesus' death: Judas turns over the 'blood money' to the chief priests and elders who, by deciding on its use, accept responsibility for the (innocent) blood of Jesus (Mt 27:25).

(4)   The fulfilment of scripture (Old Testament), another of Matthew's interests.

III. Luke 22:54–71; 23:1

Luke's order of events is altogether different from that of Mark and Matthew. He deals successively with:

(1)   The introduction (Lk 22:54);
(2)   Peter's denial and repentance (Lk 22:55–62);
(3)   The mocking by the soldiers (Lk 22:63–65);
(4)   The interrogation by the Sanhedrin in the morning (Lk 22:66–71);
(5)   The delivery of the prisoner to Pilate (Lk 23:1).

Introduction (Lk 22:54)

Verse 54: Then they seized him and led him away, bringing
him into the high priest's house. Peter followed at a distance;

Contrary to Mark and Matthew who mentioned the arrest of Jesus
much earlier (Mk 14:46; Mt 26:50), Luke states it only now, after
Jesus has forbidden any further resistance (Lk 22:51). As Jesus is
brought into the high priest's house, 'Peter followed at a distance'. This
information is also found in Mk 14:54, but the editorial changes suggest that for Luke the clause has a deeper theological meaning than for
Mark. He changes Mark's aorist (*ēkolouthēsen*, 'followed'), denoting a
particular single action in the past, into the imperfect (*ēkolouthei*,
'followed'), denoting *continuous* action. He drops Mark's place reference, 'right into the courtyard of the high priest', so that 'followed' is
used absolutely, denoting following as a disciple. These changes suggest that Luke gives the clause the same theological significance as
Lk 22:28, 'You are those who have continued with me in my trials'.
Peter's present 'following' of Jesus is a continuation of the close
relationship with Jesus which has brought him from Galilee to
Jerusalem. The phrase 'at a distance' occurs again in Lk 23:49, where
'all his acquaintances (including his disciples) . . . who had followed
him from Galilee stood at a distance' and witnessed Jesus' death.

Peter's denial and repentance (Lk 22:55–62)

Verse 55: and when they had kindled a fire in the middle of
the courtyard and sat down together, Peter sat among them.

This verse is very different from Mk 14:54. The most noticeable
addition is the reference to the kindling of a fire in the middle of the
courtyard. This is the only instance in the New Testament where the
phrase *periaptein*, 'to kindle', is found. Those who arrested Jesus made
a big circular fire to give as many people as possible a chance to warm
themselves. Peter joins them.
   Whereas Mk 14:54 is a simple reference to Peter's following and
presence which will be taken up again in Mk 14:66 when the actual
account of the denial begins, Lk 22:55 is the real beginning of the
denial story which follows immediately.

Verse 56: Then a maid seeing him as he sat in the light and
gazing at him, said, 'This man also was with him.'

Luke explains that the maid who first challenged Peter recognized him
in the glare of the fire. Whereas in Mark the maid addresses herself

directly to Peter (Mk 14:67), in Luke she exposes him as a disciple before those gathered around the fire. This construction allows Luke to intensify the pressure in the second confrontation: '*You* also are one of them' (Lk 22:58). The clause 'This man also was with him' denotes discipleship (cf. Lk 8:38; 11:23; 22:59; Acts 4:13).

> **Verse 57:** But he denied it, saying, 'Woman, I do not know him.'

Peter rejects the allegation of discipleship with a denial of any knowledge of Jesus. Luke had previously established the nature of Peter's sin in Lk 22:31–34 where, after speaking of the coming 'sifting' of the disciples (Lk 22:31, plural 'you'), Jesus tells of his prayer that Simon's faith may not fail (Lk 22:32, singular 'you'). This prayer, which is clearly related to Peter's denial, mentioned two verses later, is evidently effective, so that Peter's faith will not fail.

Luke's version of the prediction of Peter's denial (Lk 22:33–34) is in line with Lk 22:32. Peter's sin will be a sin of cowardice but not a loss of faith. Luke has added two words to the prophecy: 'until you three times deny *that you know (mē eidenai) me*'. Thus Peter's sin will consist not in rejecting Jesus as the Christ (cf. Lk 12:9), but in denying his personal acquaintance. The prediction said that Peter would deny that he knew Jesus. This is exactly fulfilled in Peter's words, 'I do not know him'. Luke omits the reference to Peter's departure into the gateway. Apparently he remains in the same place.

> **Verse 58:** And a little later some one else saw him and said, 'You also are one of them.' But Peter said, 'Man, I am not.'

A little later – note Luke's timing – some one else (a man, not the same maid as in Mk 14:69) addresses Peter directly: 'You also are one of them', i.e., you also belong to his disciples. This time Peter denies his own identity as a disciple, 'I am not'. The similarity has been noted between this statement and Jn 18:17, 25 which the fourth evangelist contrasts with Jesus' twofold 'I am' (Jn 18:5, 8). The address 'Man' is typical for Luke (compare Lk 5:20; 12:14; 22:60). In the rest of the New Testament we find it only in Rom 2:1, 3; 9:20; Jas 2:20, but then in the form 'O man'.

> **Verse 59:** And after an interval of about an hour still another insisted, saying, 'Certainly this man also was with him; for he is a Galilean.'

The reference to 'an interval of about an hour' is found in Luke only and may be intended to bring Peter closer to the hour of cockcrow. It has also an effect on the account itself: for quite some time Peter could hope not to be recognized again. Another man accuses Peter of being a disciple of Jesus before those who are assembled around the fire: 'this man also was with him'. While Mark stresses Peter's belonging to the circle of the disciples, Luke is concerned with the fact that Peter belonged to *Jesus'* company and thus knew him. The identification of Peter as a 'Galilean' seems to imply that he might be a Zealot or a rebel.

Verse 60: But Peter said, 'Man, I do not know what you are saying.' And immediately, while he was still speaking, the cock crowed.

Peter answers the third accusation very evasively, 'I do not know what you are saying', without the cursing and swearing found in Mk 14:71, thus considerably toning down the vehemence of Peter's denial. Again, Peter's faith has not really failed. If the mention of two cock-crows is to be considered the original reading in Mark, Luke omits the first of the cockcrows (cf. Mk 14:68 in some manuscripts: '. . . and the cock crowed', as against Lk 22:57). So Luke says here, in keeping with Lk 22:34, 'the cock crowed' (compare Mk 14:72, 'the cock crowed a second time'). But he emphasizes the immediate fulfilment of Jesus' words: 'And immediately, *while he was still speaking*, the cock crowed'.

Verses 61–62: And the Lord turned and looked at Peter. And Peter remembered the word of the Lord, how he had said to him, 'Before the cock crows today, you will deny me three times.' (62) And he went out and wept bitterly.

That 'the Lord turned and looked at Peter' is found in Luke only. Of the three Synoptics only Luke refers to Jesus regularly as 'Lord' (fifteen times, against once in Mark and Matthew; Luke uses the word twice in this verse). The term 'turning' *(strapheis)* is used by Luke in connection with the disciples (Lk 9:55; 10:23) or the crowds (Lk 14:25; 23:28) who follow Jesus on his way to Jerusalem or to Golgotha. It should therefore be understood in connection with the phrase 'followed' in Lk 22:54.

'Peter remembered *the* word of the Lord' *(logos tou Kuriou)*. Except for four passages in I and II Thessalonians, the expression is found only here and in Acts (8:25; 13:49; 15:35; 19:10, 20; 20:35; in some manuscripts also in 13:44, 48; 16:32). It seems to be a technical formula synonymous with 'the gospel'.

The verse cites Jesus' prediction of Peter's denial in Lk 22:34, thus showing its fulfilment. The phrase 'today', not found in Mk 14:72, corresponds to 'this day' in Lk 22:34, where it represents Luke's rewriting of Mark's expression 'this very night' (Mk 14:30).

We should reckon with the possibility that Lk 22:62 is the result of a secondary assimilation of Luke's text to that of Matthew. If Lk 22:62 is not original, the account of Peter's denial reaches a suitable conclusion with the reference to Jesus' look which reminds Peter of the word of the Lord. Luke seems to emphasize Jesus' prophetic knowledge. Indeed, Jesus had not been present at the denial scene.

In summary, we can say that just as Luke did not say that the disciples forsook Jesus and fled, so he does not say that Peter denied Jesus in the real sense of the word. He denies that he knows Jesus, but he does not deny that Jesus is the Messiah. This interpretation is reinforced by the fact that, contrary to Mark and Matthew, Luke tells the 'denial' scene before Jesus' self-affirmation as Messiah. Peter's action is understood as a sign of cowardice, not as apostasy. In Mk 14:29–30 Peter's denial was interpreted as a 'falling away'. But in Lk 22:33–34 it is understood as a refusal to go to prison and death with Jesus.

Mark's treatment placed Peter on the side of the Sanhedrin and those who reviled Jesus. Luke handles the traditional material in such a way that Peter has already repented and is back on the side of Jesus when he is insulted after his affirmation that he is the Messiah. In Luke, Peter is never on the side of those who revile Jesus, neither does Luke expect his Christian readers to be. It is with the attitude of a converted sinner that they should follow the sufferings of their Lord.

But if Lk 22:62 is not original, this interpretation should be modified. In light of the missionary character of Luke's gospel it should be formulated as follows: In Jesus' looking at Peter all should know themselves to be looked at by the good Lord who assumed his passion for each one of them, a sinner. In remembrance of Jesus, and especially of the word of the Lord, they follow the Lord.

The perseverance of the disciples during the passion, which is a necessary basis for the faith of the Church, is assured by Luke's distinction between the *fact* of Jesus' Messiahship, which is never denied, and its *modality*, i.e., that Jesus is a *suffering* Messiah, which is rejected by Peter. The unimpeachable character of the disciples' testimony and the continuity of their faith, necessary for the continuity between the Age of Jesus and the Age of the Church, are warranted by their 'standing by' Jesus from Galilee to Jerusalem, the place of his passion and death (cf. Lk 22:28).

The mocking by the soldiers (Lk 22:63–65)

Verse 63: Now the men who were holding Jesus mocked him and beat him;

The position of the incident in Luke and Mark differs: in Luke the mocking follows the denial of Peter and precedes the hearing before the priests and scribes; in Mark it follows the trial and precedes the denial of Peter. Possibly Luke wants to connect more closely the hearing by the Sanhedrin and the proceedings before Pilate. Thus the mocking no longer appears as a consequence of Jesus' messianic confession, which it now precedes, but rather as a warning. However, it is hard to find a fully convincing reason why Luke does not mention the account of the mocking at the end of the hearing before the Sanhedrin, as in Mark.

The content of the narrative is also different: in Luke the men who mock Jesus are the same as those who arrested him; in Mark they seem to be members of the Sanhedrin, since in contrast to them the 'guards' are mentioned later. Finally, in Luke Jesus is mocked and beaten, whereas in Mark he is spat upon and struck.

Verse 64: they also blindfolded him and asked him, 'Prophesy! Who is it that struck you?'

Mark mentions the blindfold, but omits the question, while Matthew has the question, but does not mention the blindfold! Only Luke's version is clear: the guards blindfolded Jesus, struck him, and then said: 'Use your prophetic powers to tell us who struck you'. Thus they seem to play a brutal version of the guessing game called blind-man's-buff. But it has been pointed out that *enepaizon* should not be thought of as a mere mockery. The cultural history of the game implies the connotation that the one who sees, in this case the soldier mocking Jesus, is blind, and that the one who is blinded, in this case Jesus, sees.

Verse 65: And they spoke many other words against him, reviling him.

This whole verse is peculiar to Luke and is most probably an editorial expansion (compare Lk 3:18). Luke, who has omitted that the guards spat on Jesus and struck him, seems to summarize these cruel details by the phrase 'many other words' or 'many other things'. The use of *blasphēmountes* ('reviling', literally, 'blaspheming'), suggests that these words or things concerned his relationship to God.

Luke's account of the mocking lacks all allusion to the Servant of Yahweh. This is not necessarily due to conscious elimination. Luke may have followed a tradition which did not consider the mocking scene a fulfilment of Isa 50:6. But it is also in keeping with Luke's point of view that individual incidents of the passion are not considered as fulfilment of the scriptures.

The interrogation by the Sanhedrin in the morning (Lk 22:66–71)

Many scholars feel that the difference in order and in time points to the use of a special tradition or source, although others maintain that Luke's dependence on Mark is unmistakable, Lk 22:67–71 being based on Mk 14:61–64 with the usual Lucan editorial changes. Dependence on Mark, they feel, appears clearly in Lk 22:71. Nothing, then, would require a source other than Mark, which Luke reconstructed on the basis of his sense of historical probabilities.

> **Verse 66:** When day came, the assembly of the elders of the people gathered together, both chief priests and scribes; and they led him away to their council, and they said,

The verse is freely written, as often at the beginning of a narrative. The parallel verse is most probably Mk 15:1, where a meeting of the Sanhedrin in the morning is recorded. Apparently Luke says that Jesus was kept a prisoner throughout the night in the house of the high priest, where the Jewish authorities gather in the morning to bring Jesus before their council. Luke refers to the Sanhedrin with an expression that would be familiar to his Greek-speaking readers: 'the elders of the people'. It is not altogether clear whether he means to say that this council of elders is composed of 'chief priests and scribes', or whether he intends to say that the chief priests and the scribes join the elders. According to Lk 20:1 the latter seems the more probable solution.

> **Verses 67–68:** 'If you are the Christ, tell us.' But he said to them, 'If I tell you, you will not believe; (68) and if I ask you, you will not answer.'

Luke omits the reference to the (false) witnesses (Mk 14:55–56) and the saying about the Temple (Mk 14:57–58) and goes straight to the question whether Jesus is the Christ, which is here raised not by the high priest but by the whole Sanhedrin. Mk 14:61 and Mt 26:63 say that the high priest asks whether Jesus is 'the Christ, the Son of God', thus paralleling the two titles, but Luke has separated the two titles, thus apparently intending to give 'Son of God' its full Christian meaning. To Luke and to his readers 'Son of God' is the supreme title of Jesus. In its Lucan form the statement 'If you are the Christ . . .' betrays a striking similarity with the temptations in the desert, 'If you are the Son of God . . .' (Lk 4:3, 9) and the taunts of the rulers and the soldiers at the cross, '. . . if he is the Christ of God . . .' (Lk 23:35) and 'If you are the King of the Jews . . .' (Lk 23:37).

Jesus gives an evasive answer, 'If I tell you, you will not believe . . .'. Jesus' reply is expressed in the style of the prophetical refusal to answer. Compare Jer 45:15LXX (=38:15 in the Hebrew text and in English Bibles), 'If I tell you, will you not be sure to put me to death? And if I give you counsel, you will not listen to me.' A number of manuscripts read in Lk 22:68, 'and if I tell you, you will not release me'. He exposes the insincerity of the question and leaves the problem in the air. Any answer on Jesus' part would be merely superfluous, since they are neither prepared to accept the truth from his lips, nor capable of true faith. Although a Christological interpretation of *pistis* ('faith') may be the best interpretation for Lk 8:25; 22:32 where it designates the faith of the disciples, Lk 22:67 is the only place in the gospel of Luke where 'to believe' (*pisteuein*) has an explicitly Christological meaning, and here it is a question of unbelief rather than of belief. Jesus was unwilling to answer this first challenge by a clear yes or no, because those who put it to him were incapable of faith.

Verse 69: 'But from now on the Son of man shall be seated at the right hand of the power of God.'

The transition from verse 68 to verse 69 is abrupt. Luke entirely 'de-eschatologizes' Jesus' words. The phrase 'from now on' (*apo tou nun*) is characteristic of Luke (cf. Lk 1:48; 5:10; 12:52; 22:18; Acts 18:6; outside Luke-Acts only in Jn 8:11; II Cor 5:16). It indicates that Luke thinks of the reign of Christ, his 'sitting at the right hand', as beginning 'from the present time', i.e., in connection with the death–resurrection–ascension event. The condition described begins now. Luke sets the saying in the context of salvation history.

The phrase 'you will see' (Mk 14:62) is omitted. Luke cannot conceive that the Sanhedrin would see either the parousia or Christ seated at the right hand of God. To see the glorified Lord before the parousia is reserved to the martyrs (Acts 7:56). Seeing the parousia, however, is out of the question for the present generation.

Luke omits also 'coming with the clouds of heaven' (Mk 14:62; a quotation from Dan 7:13) and has to do so, because the heavenly reign of Jesus is invisible. Thus in place of the double response of Jesus in Mark, there is only the citation of Ps 110(109):1, 'the Son of man shall be seated at the right hand of the power of God'. In Mark 'Power' is a Jewish paraphrase for God, but Luke no longer takes it as a paraphrase for the divine name and explains it by adding the possessive 'of God'.

Verse 70: And they all said, 'Are you the Son of God, then?' And he said to them, 'You say that I am.'

Jesus' previous words aroused the interest of the whole Sanhedrin and they *all* ask the second question. The stress on 'all' fits in the context of Luke's emphasis on the guilt of the Jewish leaders. There is no question here of a failure to understand that Jesus was the Messiah. They recognize Jesus for what he is, and so their deliberate rejection is underlined.

For Luke, the Sanhedrin's question seems logically to follow Jesus' answer (cf. 'then'). But the title 'Son of God' cannot so easily be derived from 'Son of man' or from the context of Ps 110(109). Luke's thought rather seems to be the following: He who sits at the right hand of God must claim the dignity of the Son of God. The phrase 'of God' expresses the special nearness and the unique relationship of Jesus to God.

The exaltation of Jesus to the right hand of God is the presupposition for the confession of his divine sonship. Because Jesus is exalted to the right hand of God he is the Son of God. Therefore, Luke's 'then' refers back to verse 69. There is no antithesis here between the titles 'Son of man' and 'Son of God'. Rather, the train of thought of Lk 22:67–70 reaches its climax with the title 'Son of God', which implies here divinity, as it does in Lk 1:35. Elsewhere in Luke-Acts the title 'Son of God' has a messianic connotation.

This time Jesus acknowledges his divine sonship: 'You say that I am'. Although the exact meaning of the statement is not immediately clear, the context shows that it must be taken as an affirmative. The meaning is not 'You say it, not I', but 'You say it, now you have openly answered the question who I am' (cf. Lk 22:67–68). At the height of the gospel, the words express Jesus' explicit confirmation of his divine dignity.

Verse 71: And they said, 'What further testimony do we need? We have heard it ourselves from his own lips.'

Luke speaks of 'testimony' instead of 'witnesses' (Mk 14:63), avoids the word 'blasphemy', replacing the phrase by the vague 'it', and adds the typically Lucan expression 'from his own lips', literally 'from his own mouth' (*stoma*), a noun found nine times in the gospel and twelve times in Acts. Luke also omits the sentence (compare Mk 14:64, 'and they all condemned him').

The Sanhedrin has heard Jesus' affirmation; they do not need any further testimony. In Luke this notice does not have the same function as in Mark and Matthew. There the high priest can conclude with a sigh of relief that they do not need any further witnesses. Jesus' public affirmation has brought the hearing to a 'happy conclusion', after the contradicting witnesses had almost spoiled it. Luke, who did not mention the (false) witnesses, says that Jesus' affirmation has made a trial superfluous; the Jewish leaders have got what they were looking for: a reason to bring Jesus before Pilate.

The omission of any form of sentence may be due to the fact that for Luke the present session is undoubtedly only a hearing, not a trial, or because the Sanhedrin's decision had to be ratified by Pilate; but it could also be in line with a number of other omissions: Jesus is nowhere said to be bound, he is not spat upon, etc. Luke, the loving disciple, passes over in silence these offensive details.

Concluding, we may say that Luke's dependence on Mark is very clear in Lk 22:67a, 69, 71. However, his version differs from that of Mark in its Christological interest, especially in its concentration on the title 'Son of God', and in describing the session of the Sanhedrin clearly as a hearing, not a trial.

The delivery of the prisoner to Pilate (Lk 23:1)

Verse 1: Then the whole company of them arose, and brought him before Pilate.

The verse is apparently based on Mk 15:1b. The 'whole company of them', i.e., the Sanhedrin, leads Jesus before Pilate. Lk 23:4 will speak of 'the chief priests and the multitudes', Lk 23:10 refers to 'the chief priests and the scribes' as Jesus' accusers before Herod, and in Lk 23:13 Pilate calls together 'the chief priests and the rulers and the people'. Clearly, various elements of the Jewish people were involved in the Roman trial.

4   The trial before Pilate

I. Mark 15:2–20

We divide this section into three parts:
(1)   Initial interrogation by Pilate (Mk 15:2–5);
(2)   The Barabbas incident and death sentence (Mk 15:6–15);
(3)   The mocking by the soldiers (Mk 15:16–20).

Though this section is rather loosely constructed, it is not a mere compilation of originally separate items of tradition. The whole scene clearly bears a Marcan stamp and the characteristics of his style are found throughout the section.

The initial interrogation by Pilate (Mk 15:2–5)

> **Verse 2:** And Pilate asked him, 'Are you the King of the Jews?' And he answered him, 'You have said so.'

Pilate asked immediately, 'Are you the King of the Jews?' From an historical point of view several questions could be raised: how could Pilate know this? Has he been previously informed, or did he have a hand in Jesus' arrest? The whole trial is apparently related in a stylized manner and all the details which may be of historical interest but are not essential for the proclamation are omitted. Mark straight away focuses on the central issue of the trial and Pilate's question leads us immediately to its core. The title 'King of the Jews' which has not been found in Mark up to this point is now suddenly used very frequently (cf. Mk 15:2, 9, 12, 18, 26; compare Mk 15:32, 'King of Israel', which should not too easily be identified with 'King of the Jews'). Jesus is identified as king only in his trial. It is as 'King of the Jews', or Messiah, that Jesus is on trial and will be condemned.

Jesus' answer, 'You have said so', has been explained in very different ways which can be classified as follows:
(1)   'You say so', i.e., 'No'.
(2)   'You say so', i.e., 'Yes' (many commentators).
(3)   Jesus gives an indirect answer. He confirms Pilate's words, implying that he would put things differently.

It seems that Jesus accepts the title, while querying the meaning the governor reads into it. Jesus does not wish this to be taken in a political sense. He cannot say that he is 'King of the Jews' in the sense in which Pilate probably understands this designation, yet the statement is correct on another plane.

> **Verses 3–5:** And the chief priests accused him of many things. (4) And Pilate again asked him, 'Have you no answer to make? See how many charges they bring against you.' (5) But Jesus made no further answer, so that Pilate wondered.

The 'many things' of which the chief priests accuse Jesus in verse 3 suggest their efforts to get Jesus condemned to death. Apparently the tradition did not contain any information about the exact formulation of the charges. Pilate's reference to the 'many charges' in verse 4 reinforces the impression we were already given in the previous verse. The imperfect 'asked' in verse 4 matches the imperfect 'accused' of verse 3. The tenses suggest reiteration: the chief priests accused Jesus repeatedly, and Pilate asked him repeatedly whether he had no answer to make. From the narrator's point of view the function of the emphasis on the chief priests' efforts is to make Jesus' silence stand out more clearly.

Indeed, as in the Jewish trial (Mk 14:61), so here Jesus' silence is stressed. This could be an allusion to Isa 53:7, 'and like a sheep that before its shearers is dumb, so he opened not his mouth', but in Mark Jesus' silence seems to play a definite role apart from a hidden reference to Isaiah. In Mk 14:61 and 15:5 this silence is strongly contrasted with an immediately preceding or following self-affirmation of Jesus. A perfect parallel with Isa 53:7 would demand total silence. The emphasis on silence, therefore, may serve a dramatic effect rather than a concern for the fulfilment of scripture.

Jesus' silence appeared so unusual 'that Pilate wondered'. References to amazement abound in Mark. The verb *thaumazō* ('to wonder', 'to be amazed') usually has a religious connotation, as it most probably does in our text. Jesus' enemies, therefore, never respond with amazement, except in Mk 12:17, where it is clearly understood as non-religious, on the same level as their fear of the crowd. The notice that 'Pilate wondered' may also be an allusion to the suffering servant, more specifically to Isa 52:15LXX, 'So many nations shall wonder at him'. It is repeated in Mk 15:44.

The Barabbas incident and the death sentence (Mk 15:6–15)

> **Verse 6:** Now at the feast he used to release for them one prisoner whom they asked.

The evidence for the custom referred to in this verse is limited to the gospels. There is no conclusive proof of a regular amnesty granted to a convict on a festival, and some scholars have gone as far as to say that it is nothing but a figment of the evangelist's imagination. But some traces of a practice of this kind are found in Papyrus Florentinus 61, 59ff. and the Mishnah tractate *Pesahim* VIII, 6a. It is certainly unwarranted to dismiss the whole Barabbas incident as unhistorical. Possibly the present verse is a mistaken inference from the account itself and made to provide the narrative with an introduction.

> **Verse 7:**   And among the rebels in prison, who had committed murder in the insurrection, there was a man called Barabbas.

Barabbas is introduced in a strikingly precise way: he was in prison with the rebels 'who had committed murder in *the* insurrection'. He was apparently known for his part in an act of revolt which assured him a certain popularity. The designation 'a man called Barabbas' (literally, 'the one called Barabbas') is strange. We could expect it to be preceded by a personal name, since Barabbas ('Son of Abba', 'Son of the Father') is a second name. In fact the Caesarean text of Mt 27:16f. reads 'Jesus Barabbas'. At any rate, the fact that others were crucified with Jesus (cf. Mk 15:27) shows that several people appeared together before Pilate on that same day. One of them, 'a man called Barabbas', was acquitted by a single act of clemency, not because of a custom. This was originally reported to form a contrast with the condemnation of Jesus, and may have been developed into an account in which Pilate gave the people the choice between Jesus and Barabbas.

> **Verses 8–9:**   And the crowd came up and began to ask Pilate to do as he was wont to do for them. (9) And he answered them, 'Do you want me to release for you the King of the Jews?'

'The crowd', mentioned now for the first time in the passion narrative, 'came up' (the steps of Pilate's quarters in the Tower of Antonia?) and requested Pilate that he would release a prisoner according to the (alleged) custom. It is not at all necessary to presuppose that this crowd was composed of Barabbas' partisans. Pilate's question seems to imply that the crowd had not asked for any specific prisoner. In actual fact it may be phrased in this way to emphasize the difficult choice which will face them. Jesus is again identified as 'King of the Jews'. The crowd is confronted by the choice whether to accept or reject the Messiah; and so are we.

Verse 10: For he perceived that it was out of envy that the chief priests had delivered him up.

Pilate perceived (*eginōsken; ginōskein* is often employed by Mark as a verb of recognition and penetrating insight; cf. Mk 4:13; 8:17; 13:28, 29) that the chief priests had delivered Jesus up because they were envious of him. He is, therefore, depicted as aware of the innocence of Jesus. Jealousy (*phthonos*) is not mentioned anywhere else in the gospels (Mk 15:10/Mt 27:18; but see Jn 12:19).

'To deliver up' (*paradidonai*) applied to Jesus is found in the second and third predictions of the passion (Mk 9:31; 10:33), seven times in Mk 14 and three times in Mk 15. Here the phrase indicates irreducible facts: the chief priests delivered Jesus up to Pilate (Mk 15:1, 10), and Pilate in his turn delivered him to be crucified (Mk 15:15).

Verse 11: But the chief priests stirred up the crowd to have him release for them Barabbas instead.

This verse shows that the chief priests are responsible for inciting the crowd to reject Jesus. Thus Mark pins responsibility where he believed it belongs. In the Greek text this is even more obvious since verse 10 ends with 'the chief priests' and the present verse begins with the same phrase: the chief priests delivered Jesus up to Pilate and also stirred up the people against him. The verb 'to stir up' (*anaseiein*) is found only here and in Lk 23:5, where Jesus is accused by the chief priests of stirring up the people. Mk 15:11 contains the only unfavourable reference to the crowd (*ochlos*) in the entire gospel of Mark ('the crowd' in Mk 14:43 is clearly a group of armed men), but the verse at the same time explains that if the crowd becomes definitely hostile in Mk 15:13–14 this is only because it has been stirred up by the chief priests.

Verse 12: And Pilate again said to them, 'Then what shall I do with the man whom you call the King of the Jews?'

Again Pilate seeks to influence the crowd. He asks them what he should do with Jesus, who is again identified as 'the King of the Jews', thus reinforcing the kingship motif which sounds all through this stage of the passion narrative. Pilate's question is very strange. One would not expect a Roman governor to ask the people what to do with an accused. It is possible, however, that the phrase 'whom you call the King of the Jews' refers to the chief priests' accusation with which Pilate does not want to go along.

Verse 13: And they cried out again, 'Crucify him.'

The change from '(they) began to ask' (verse 8) to 'they cried out' is very marked. Although the word does not always have a negative meaning (cf. Mk 11:9; Mt 27:50), it is often used to express demonic resistance to Jesus (Mk 1:24; 3:11; 5:5, 7; 9:26). Here the use of the verb may suggest that a more than human power inspires these cries. For the first time the specific punishment to be inflicted on Jesus is mentioned: 'Crucify him'. It should be noted that the whole crowd (the whole nation?) demands crucifixion.

> **Verse 14:** And Pilate said to them, 'Why, what evil has he done?' But they shouted all the more, 'Crucify him.'

Pilate's question again clearly shows Jesus' innocence, while at the same time indicating that he is about to yield to the demand of the crowd. His question provokes an even stronger reaction: 'Crucify him'. For Mark, this is another fulfilment of Jesus' saying that 'the Son of man must . . . be rejected by the elders and the chief priests' (Mk 8:31).

> **Verse 15:** So Pilate, wishing to satisfy the crowd, released for them Barabbas; and having scourged Jesus, he delivered him to be crucified.

This verse is designed to make clear that Pilate was driven to the verdict by Jewish pressure. He yielded to both of their demands: he released Barabbas (cf. Mk 15:11) and delivered Jesus to be crucified (cf. Mk 15:13–14). Pilate had Jesus scourged. A Roman scourging was a terrible punishment. The convict was stripped, bound to a post or thrown to the ground, and was then beaten with the *flagellum* consisting of leather strips tipped with pieces of bone or lead. Roman law did not prescribe a maximum number of strokes, and people frequently died from the scourging. Although scourging could be inflicted as a separate punishment, it was usually administered as a preliminary to execution. The fact that Mark deals with this cruel punishment in so few words (in Greek a single verb!) shows that the early Church did not linger over the physical tortures, but emphasized rather the rejection of the Son of man as his true suffering.

Pilate 'delivered him to be crucified'. This clause, which may have been formulated to call to mind Isa 53:6LXX, 'The Lord delivered him for our sins', implies a condemnation, but nevertheless remains vague. This may be explained by the fact that 'to deliver' had become a kind of technical term to describe Jesus' martyrdom. It is also possible that Mark is trying in this way not to undo the result of his attempts to pin the responsibility for Jesus' death on the chief priests. Therefore the emphasis of Mk 15:15 falls most probably on the first half of the verse, 'So Pilate wishing to satisfy the crowd (stirred up by the chief priests) . . .'.

The mocking by the soldiers (Mk 15:16–20)

Verses 16–17: And the soldiers led him away inside the palace (that is, the praetorium); and they called together the whole battalion. (17) And they clothed him in a purple cloak, and plaiting a crown of thorns they put it on him.

Some scholars have held the pericope of the mocking by the soldiers to be an insertion. However, a similar incident of a mocking of Jesus is found at a somewhat earlier stage of the trial, but also immediately after the scourging, in Jn 19:1–3.

The incident is vividly related (note the historic presents in the Greek text). The soldiers come together and put a 'purple cloak', most probably a soldier's faded scarlet cloak, over Jesus' shoulders. Then they plait a crown of thorns and put it on his head. There are many thorny plants in Palestine and there is no need to think of big thorns. The crown is not primarily intended as a torture but rather as part of a mock attire. The purple cloak and the crown are signs of royal dignity, which are here derisively mimicked.

Verses 18–20: And they began to salute him, 'Hail, King of the Jews!' (19) And they struck his head with a reed, and spat upon him, and they knelt down in homage to him. (20) And when they had mocked him, they stripped him of the purple cloak, and put his own clothes on him. And they led him out to crucify him.

In line with the preparations, the soldiers now greet Jesus with mock royal honours. They salute him, 'Hail, King of the Jews', a greeting which corresponds formally to the Roman acclamation 'Ave, Caesar', 'Hail, Caesar'. At the same time they kneel down before him, imitating an essential element of Hellenistic homage to a king.

A striking parallel has been found in Philo, who records that when Agrippa I, who had just been recognized as 'King of the Jews' by Rome, visited Alexandria, the people staged a mockery, laying hold of an imbecile, named Carabas, whom they gave a crown, a royal robe and a sceptre, and addressed him as lord.

Into this mocking scene Mark has introduced references to strokes and spitting which recall Mk 14:65. The reed with which the soldiers struck Jesus' head may well have been used first to mimic a sceptre, another sign of royal dignity. When the mockery degenerated, they used it to strike Jesus. In Mk 14:65 Jesus was mocked and maltreated as a *prophet*, here he receives the same treatment as a *king*.

The pericope ends with the removal of the mock regalia, the return of Jesus' own clothes, and the departure for the place of execution. We should note the similarity of the phrases 'he delivered him (to the soldiers) to be crucified' (Mk 15:15) and 'they (the soldiers) led him out to crucify him' (Mk 15:20).

Summing up, we may say that in Mk 15:2–20 we are not faced with an eyewitness report but with the result of a choice of traditional materials and editorial activity guided by:

(1)   Christological reflection which is apparent in:
    (a)   the emphasis on the fact that it is as Messiah that Jesus was crucified (cf. the repeated use of 'King of the Jews' in Mk 15:2, 9, 12, 18, 26);
    (b)   the emphasis on Jesus' innocence;
    (c)   the probable associations with the songs of the suffering servant: Jesus' silence (Isa 53:7), Pilate's wondering (Isa 52:15LXX), and Jesus' innocence (Isa 53:9);
    (d)   the contrast between Jesus and Barabbas;
    (e)   the increasing loneliness and rejection of Jesus.
(2)   Emphasis on the responsibility of the Jews (Mk 15:3, 11, 15a), whose envy is so obvious that Pilate easily discerns it (Mk 15:10, 14). The attitude of the Jewish authorities towards the early Christian community is, as it were, projected into the description of the trial.

Mark presents the trial before Pilate as the trial of the King of the Jews. A strange trial, since the Jews are the accusers and the King keeps silent. Pilate is disconcerted. In a second scene, the King of the Jews is compared with Barabbas; Barabbas is set free, and the King is condemned to the cross. In an epilogue, we are told how the soldiers illustrate the verdict in an appropriate *mise-en-scène*: the King of the Jews receives a purple robe, a crown, and homage; but the crown consists of thorns and the homages are mockeries. God's designs are again depicted in disconcerting images.

II. Matthew 27:11–31

In parallel with our treatment of Mark, we divide this section of Matthew into the following parts:
(1)   The initial interrogation by Pilate (Mt 27:11–14);
(2)   The Barabbas incident and the death sentence (Mt 27:15–26);
(3)   The mocking by the soldiers (Mt 27:27–31).

The initial interrogation by Pilate (Mt 27:11–14)

Verse 11: Now Jesus stood before the governor; and the governor asked him, 'Are you the King of the Jews?' Jesus said to him, 'You have said so.'

Because the sequence of events mentioned in Mt 27:1-2 was interrupted by the insertion of the Judas incident (Mt 27:3-10), Matthew begins the trial account with a formal and recapitulating introduction: 'Now Jesus stood before the governor'. The re-introduction of the main characters indicates the beginning of a new phase of the narrative announced in Mt 27:2. Moreover, the addition of the name 'Jesus' is typical of Matthew.

The phrase 'stood before the governor' reminds us of Mk 13:9, 'and you will stand before governors and kings for my sake', and seems to be a typically biblical expression for describing a prisoner facing his interrogators or judges. Here in Matthew the phrase contributes to the picturing of Jesus' greatness in the passion. It seems to be important for the interpretation of the present passage. The editorial character of the verse is clear.

In the second half of the verse Matthew rejoins his Marcan source with the governor's question: 'Are you the King of the Jews?' This question, which precedes the formulation of the charges, and is taken literally from Mark, states the central theme of the whole trial. Of the five instances in which Mark uses the title 'King of the Jews', Matthew retains three (Mt 27:11, 29, 37); in the other two cases he prefers the more explicitly messianic 'Christ' (Mt 27:17, 22). He retains also the title 'King of Israel' (Mk 15:32; Mt 27:42). Many scholars maintain that the title 'King of the Jews', the use of which is reserved to non-Jewish speakers, has more of a political colouring than the title 'King of Israel'.

Again the name Jesus is added. Jesus' answer, 'You have said so', can be compared with the analogous 'You have said so' in Mt 26:25 and 26:64. As in these two passages, Jesus' reply to Pilate confirms what is implied in the latter's question. To Caiaphas' unconscious 'confession' of Jesus as the Christ, Matthew now adds Pilate's unconscious 'confession' of Jesus as the 'King of the Jews'.

Verse 12: But when he was accused by the chief priests and elders, he made no answer.

Matthew expands Mark's 'chief priests' to the stereotyped expression 'chief priests and elders'. Pilate's question 'Have you no answer to make?' (Mk 15:4) presupposes that Jesus remained silent in the face of the accusations, but Mark does not say so explicitly. Matthew makes up for this: 'he made no answer'. The construction of the verse shifts the emphasis from the accusations to Jesus' silence (compare Mk 15:5 and Mt 27:12). Several exegetes state that Matthew's formulation results in a greater emphasis on the silence of Jesus (Mt 27:12 and 14, against Mk 15:5), and therefore a greater emphasis on the suffering servant typology (cf. Isa 53:7).

Verse 13: Then Pilate said to him, 'Do you not hear how many things they testify against you?'

Since Matthew has already said that Jesus 'made no answer', he does not repeat that phrase in Pilate's question (compare Mk 15:4). In fact, in Matthew, Pilate's words are more an expression of amazement than a real question: 'Do you not hear what they say?' It is possible that Matthew changes Mark's phrase 'how many charges they bring against you' into 'how many things they *testify against you*' for the sake of variety (in Greek, Mark has the same verb in verses 3 and 4), but it could also be an echo of Caiaphas' question, 'What is it that these men *testify against you*' (Mt 26:62b), the only other passage in the gospels where the verb *katamarturoun* ('to testify') is used.

Verse 14: But he gave him no answer, not even to a single charge; so that the governor wondered greatly.

The clause 'but he gave him no answer, not even to a single charge' is a plausible translation of a Greek text that causes some difficulty. The verse apparently intends to emphasize that despite the many charges levelled against him, Jesus did not answer any of them. Matthew adds the adverb 'greatly', thus reinforcing the reaction of Pilate, a detail which seems to be part of Matthew's effort to create a more favourable image of Pilate.

The Barabbas incident and the death sentence (Mt 27:15–26)

Verse 15: Now at the feast the governor was accustomed to release for the crowd any one prisoner whom they wanted.

The attention of the narrator shifts from Jesus and Pilate to Pilate and the crowd. In terms very similar to Mark's, Matthew states the issue. As usual, he explicates Mark's vague subject by adding the title 'the governor'. Similarly the vague 'them' is changed into 'the crowd'. Matthew also prefers 'whom they wanted' to 'whom they asked', possibly because he intends to emphasize the theme of a free choice between Jesus and Barabbas in the course of the account (cf. Mt 27:17, 'whom do you want me to release', and Mt 27:21, 'which of the two do you want'). Thus Matthew emphasizes the conscious rejection of Jesus and the choice of Barabbas.

Verse 16: And they had then a notorious prisoner, called Barabbas.

They, i.e., the Romans, had a 'notorious prisoner'. Matthew omits the details of Barabbas' crime, so that it becomes more difficult to see how the leaders and the crowd could prefer Barabbas. All indications of Barabbas' popularity found in Mark disappear. The fact that the Jews choose a 'notorious prisoner' underlines that they were blinded by their envy.

It has been widely discussed whether the text should read 'Barabbas' or 'Jesus Barabbas', as is found in some manuscripts. Most modern scholars seem to prefer the latter reading, because they consider it more probable that the name Jesus would have been omitted for reasons of piety than that it would have been added in some manuscripts. Moreover, Matthew's concern to emphasize the choice between Jesus and Barabbas would be served by a contrast between 'Jesus Barabbas' and 'Jesus who is called Christ'.

> **Verse 17:** So when they had gathered, Pilate said to them, 'Whom do you want me to release for you, Barabbas or Jesus who is called Christ?'

In an effort to reduce the tumultuous impression we get from Mark's account and to emphasize the theme of a deliberate choice, Matthew substitutes 'when they had gathered' for Mark's menacing 'the crowd came up and began to ask' (Mk 15:8). Contrary to Mark, Matthew says that it was Pilate who brought up the issue.

Instead of Mark's one-sided 'Do you want me to release for you the King of the Jews?' (Mk 15:9), Matthew explicitly presents the two possible choices, 'Whom do you want me to release for you, Barabbas or Jesus . . . ?' This idea of choice will be emphasized again in Mt 27:20b and 21.

This is further intensified by the reading already mentioned, 'Jesus Barabbas', and the substitution of 'Christ' for Mark's 'King of the Jews'. It is indeed noteworthy that Matthew takes over Mark's 'King of the Jews' except in this pericope (compare Mk 15:9, 12 and Mt 27:17, 22). This editorial activity may be explained by the attempt to emphasize the theme of choice between 'Jesus (who is called) Barabbas' and 'Jesus who is called Christ'. Moreover, Matthew may want to stress that Jesus is rejected not as a political figure but as the one who to the faith of the Church is 'the Christ' for all men.

> **Verse 18:** For he knew that it was out of envy that they had delivered him up.

Matthew takes over this Marcan parenthesis without any important changes. It apparently fits in with his intention to contrast Pilate's attitude with that of the Jews. Some biblical scholars think that the delivering up of Jesus by his own people should be read in the light of Jewish traditions about the betrayal of Joseph by his brothers.

> **Verse 19:** Besides, while he was sitting on the judgment seat, his wife sent word to him, 'Have nothing to do with that righteous man, for I have suffered much over him today in a dream.'

This verse is peculiar to Matthew. A study of its vocabulary leads to the conclusion that Matthew has given the verse its present form. It is even possible that it was composed by Matthew on the basis of a vague tradition. It has been suggested that the intercession by Pilate's wife for Jesus reflects the intervention of the Memphian woman for the patriarch Joseph in *Testament of Joseph*.

The addition of the verse has been explained as a literary device suspending the course of events and thus giving the Jewish leaders the time to influence the crowd in favour of Barabbas (cf. Mt 27:20), while at the same time preparing for Mt 27:24 where Pilate openly declares Jesus innocent. Thus Matthew's ultimate motive for the addition of the verse would be the question of responsibility for the death of Jesus which is indeed one of the concerns of this section.

But a closer consideration of the content of the verse leads to a theologically more interesting explanation. The phrase 'in a dream' indicates the divine origin of Pilate's wife's insight (cf. Mt 1:20; 2:12, 13, 19, 22). She is divinely inspired to intercede on behalf of 'that righteous man'. By inserting this verse into the account, Matthew creates a contrasting parallel: Pilate's wife speaks on Jesus' behalf, while the Jewish leaders speak for Barabbas. Whereas the profession of Jesus' innocence ('that righteous man') is inspired by God, the attempt to free Barabbas and reject Jesus is inspired by blindness and envy (Mt 27:18).

> **Verse 20:** Now the chief priests and the elders persuaded the people to ask for Barabbas and destroy Jesus.

Again Matthew adds 'and the elders' to 'the chief priests' so as to obtain his standard reference to the Jewish leaders in the passion narrative (compare, e.g., Mk 15:3 and Mt 27:12). He also replaces the rare word 'to stir up' (*anaseiein*) by the more common 'to persuade' (*peithein*). As a result, Matthew again suggests a less tumultuous atmosphere and a more deliberate choice. The crowds, persuaded by the leaders, will consciously reject Jesus.

In line with his previous attempts to emphasize the choice, Matthew does not just take over the request to release Barabbas, but adds 'and destroy Jesus' (compare Matthew's handling of Mk 15:9 in Mt 27:17). Thus we get a double demand. What Mark implied by the word 'instead' (*mallon*) is here made explicit. The overall result of Matthew's editorial changes, but especially of the addition 'and destroy Jesus' (cf. Mk 3:6; 11:18), is in striking contrast with Mt 27:19.

Verse 21: The governor again said to them, 'Which of the two do you want me to release for you?' And they said, 'Barabbas.'

The question of verse 17 is repeated. In fact the whole account is dominated by the double question, 'Which of the two do you want me to release for you?' (Mt 27:17, 21), and it leads to a double stand which is taken in Mt 27:24 and 25, when Pilate's confession of Jesus' innocence causes the people to take full responsibility in Jesus' death.

Once more Matthew makes explicit what is presupposed in Mark's text. Mk 15:12 apparently supposes that the activity of the chief priests has led to a request for Barabbas (suggested by 'again' in Mk 15:12, 13), but it is not said explicitly. Matthew fills this lacuna by the question 'Which of the two do you want me to release for you?', taken from the dominating verse 17. The proper names of Jesus and Barabbas are replaced by the phrase 'which of the two', since they have just been mentioned at the end of Mt 27:20. Matthew then makes the people explicitly ask for Barabbas.

Verse 22: Pilate said to them, 'Then what shall I do with Jesus who is called Christ?' They all said, 'Let him be crucified.'

Since this verse is the continuation of Matthew's expanded conversation between Pilate and the people, and the latter have just requested Barabbas, Matthew adds here, 'Pilate said to them'. Pilate's question has also undergone some editing. The addition of the name 'Jesus' is typical for Matthew, but here it may have been inspired especially by the following 'who is called Christ'.

In the second half of the verse Matthew adds 'all', thus emphasizing the collective element. All ask for Jesus' crucifixion. The phrase 'all' should be related to 'all the people' in Mt 27:25. Some scholars have interpreted the change of 'crucify him' (Mk 15:13) into 'Let him be crucified' as an attempt to dissociate Pilate from the crucifixion. But Matthew almost always uses the verb 'to crucify' in a passive (or impersonal) form (cf. Mt 20:19; 26:2; 27:22, 23, 26, 31, 38; 28:5; exceptions: Mt 23:34; 27:35), and may simply have followed his preference here.

Verse 23: And he said, 'Why, what evil has he done?' But they shouted all the more, 'Let him be crucified.'

This verse is practically the same as in Mark except for the change of 'crucify him' into 'let him be crucified', but in Matthew it serves as a preamble to verses 24–25, the most important addition in Matthew's version of the Roman trial.

> **Verse 24:** So when Pilate saw that he was gaining nothing, but rather that a riot was beginning, he took water and washed his hands before the crowd, saying, 'I am innocent of this righteous man's blood; see to it yourselves.'

A study of this verse's vocabulary leads to the conclusion that Matthew constructed it by blending Old Testament elements with his own stylistic preferences.

In the introduction, especially by the phrase 'that he was gaining nothing', Matthew conveys that, according to his opinion, Pilate has done everything possible to set Jesus free. We learn also 'that a riot was beginning (*thorubos ginetai*)', a phrase which reminds us of Mt 26:5, 'lest there be a tumult (*thorubos genētai*)'. Mt 26:5 and 27:24 are the only two instances where Matthew uses the word *thorubos*.

The main statement consists of two elements: a symbolic gesture and an explanatory word. The meaning of the gesture is usually sought in the Old Testament, especially in Deut 21:1–9, where we are told that as symbol of their profession of innocence, the elders of a city wash their hands (Deut 21:6). While doing this, they explain their gesture: 'And they shall testify, "Our hands did not shed this blood . . ." ' (Deut 21:7). The significance of the practice is to show freedom from religious guilt, as confirmed in the following prayer, 'O Lord, . . . set not the guilt of innocent blood in the midst of your people Israel; but let the guilt of blood be forgiven them' (Deut 21:8). The purpose of it all is that 'you shall purge the guilt of innocent blood from your midst, when you do what is right in the sight of the Lord' (Deut 21:9). Similar expressions of innocence are found in Ps 26(25):6, 'I wash my hands in innocence' (literally, 'among the innocents'), and Ps 73(72):13, 'I . . . washed my hands in innocence' (again literally, 'among the innocents'). Pilate's words 'I am innocent of this man's blood' are similar to II Sam 3:28, 'I and my kingdom are for ever guiltless (*athōios*, 'innocent') before the Lord for the blood of Abner the son of Ner'. Some authors have also referred to Susanna 46 (Theodotion; = Dan 13:46). This Old Testament background shows that by his gesture and statement Pilate declares his innocence before God. That he did this also 'before the crowd' underlines the public character of the gesture.

We know already that the word 'innocent' (*athōios*) plays an important role in Matthew's assessment of responsibility for the death of Jesus. We think especially of Mt 27:3–10 with its theme of 'innocent blood'. In the decisive confrontation between Pilate and the Jews,

Matthew is again mainly concerned with establishing the responsibility for the innocent blood of Jesus.

In what is most probably an attempt to harmonize the present verse with Mt 27:19, some manuscripts add the phrase 'righteous' to Pilate's statement, 'I am innocent of this *righteous* man's blood' (found in the translation of RSV and NAB, but not in JB and NEB). Most commentators reject this longer reading as a later harmonization.

It has been pointed out that Mt 27:3–10 and 27:24–25, both found in Matthew only, share two expressions ('innocent blood' and 'see to it yourself/yourselves') and recount actions (throwing down the silver coins and the washing of hands) which involve the Jewish people. We have already noted the affinity of this present verse with Mt 27:3–10. This opinion is also supported by the last part of the verse, 'see to it yourselves'. In Mt 27:4 the chief priests rejected Judas' return of the blood money, which symbolizes his admission of responsibility, with the abrupt 'see to it yourself'. Here Pilate uses exactly the same words to indicate the transfer of responsibility to the Jewish people. It is possible that Matthew intends to suggest that the fate of Judas is the prefiguration of the fate awaiting the Jewish people.

Verse 25: And all the people answered, 'His blood be on us and on our children!'

Pilate's self-ablution has its counterpart in the words of the people. Again the verse seems to be the result of Old Testament symbolism blended with Matthew's redactional activity.

Most commentators agree that 'all the people' (*pas ho laos*) does not just mean 'the whole crowd', but rather 'the Jewish people', 'the Jewish nation'. The phrase represents the standpoint of the early Church on the question of responsibility for Jesus' death: the people present at the praetorium represented a nation which rejected its Messiah.

The answer of the people, 'His blood be on us and on our children', should be interpreted in the light of its Old Testament background, especially texts like I Kgs 2:33, 'So shall their blood come back upon the head of Joab and upon the head of his descendants for ever', and Jer 26:15, 'Only know for certain that if you put me to death, you will bring innocent blood upon yourselves and upon this city and its inhabitants'. We could also think of Deut 19:10, 'lest innocent blood be shed in your land which the Lord your God gives you for an inheritance, and so the guilt of bloodshed be upon you', a text already referred to for the interpretation of Mt 27:3–10. In this latter passage we discussed the role of the theme of 'innocent blood' in assessing the responsibility for the death of Jesus. It seems to have its roots in Mt 23, especially in the theme of the 'righteous/innocent blood' of the prophets: 'that upon you may come all the righteous blood shed on

earth from the blood of innocent Abel to the blood of Zechariah . . .'
(Mt 23:35). This saying finds its realization in the words of the Jewish
people in Mt 27:25.

I Kgs 2:32, 'The Lord will bring back his bloody deeds on his own
head', shows that such words are addressed to God. And so we discover the perfect parallel between the gesture and word of Pilate and
the people's statement: the governor proclaimed his innocence before
God; the Jewish nation proclaim their responsibility for Jesus' blood
before God. The phrase 'his blood' seems to be the link between verse
25 and verse 24. Thus Matthew confronts us in Mt 27:24–25 with a
decisive turning point in salvation history.

The phrase 'on our children' has sometimes been understood as
referring to the following generation and the fact that it was this
generation which bore the horrors of the events of A.D. 66–70, culminating in the destruction of Jerusalem. But, in the light of Mt 21:43,
'the kingdom of God will be taken away from you and given to a nation
producing the fruits of it', it seems preferable to understand it in a
wider sense as referring to all future generations. However, Matthew
should definitely not be understood as cursing generations unborn. His
is a perspective of salvation history, not of revenge. Because of their
rejection of the Messiah, the risen Christ will send the disciples not to
the house of Israel (cf. Mt 10:6) but to 'all nations' (Mt 28:19).

Verse 26: Then he released for them Barabbas, and having
scourged Jesus, delivered him to be crucified.

Matthew omits Mk 15:15a, 'So Pilate, wishing to satisfy the crowd'.
Thus the release of Barabbas and the crucifixion of Jesus are more
exclusively the result of the deliberate choice of the people mentioned
in Mt 27:24–25, to which our present verse is causally linked by means
of the added 'then'.

The mocking by the soldiers (Mt 27:27–31)

Verse 27: Then the soldiers of the governor took Jesus into
the praetorium, and they gathered the whole battalion before
him.

By the addition of 'then' (cf. Mt 26:67, 'Then they spat in his face . . .')
and the identification of the soldiers as 'of the governor', Matthew
links the mocking scene more closely to the Roman trial. Matthew's
'took' (*paralabontes*) corresponds better to 'delivered' (*paredōken*;
Mk 15:15; Mt 27:26) than Mark's 'led away' (*apēgagon*). As usual,
the name 'Jesus' is preferred to 'him'. The use of 'they gathered . . .

before him' instead of 'they called together' is a minor change but may add to the threatening character of the scene.

Verse 28: And they stripped him and put a scarlet robe upon him,

Matthew's description is more complete than Mark's, which mentions only the clothing with a purple cloak. At the same time Matthew forms an inclusion:

Mt 27:28 they stripped him and put . . . upon him. . . .
Mt 27:31 they stripped him . . . and put . . . on him. . . .

He also replaces Mark's 'purple cloak' with a 'scarlet robe'. The 'purple cloak' is undoubtedly intended as a parody of the purple garment worn by the emperor. But it is probable that the soldiers had at their disposition only a scarlet robe, a common soldier's cloak. This change at the same time intensifies the caricatural character of the scene.

Verse 29: and plaiting a crown of thorns they put it on his head, and put a reed in his right hand. And kneeling before him they mocked him, saying, 'Hail, King of the Jews!'

Matthew is again more precise in his description. Instead of 'on him' he writes 'on his head'. He expands the symbolism inherent in Mark by adding 'and put a reed in his right hand', thus parodying the imperial sceptre. Finally, he improves the sequence of action found in Mark:

Mark	*Matthew*
robing	robing
crowning	crowning
—	sceptre
acclamation	genuflection
striking with reed	acclamation
spitting	spitting
genuflection	striking with reed

The change of sequence explains a number of minor changes in the text.

The acclamation 'Hail, King of the Jews' controls the entire pericope. We note also the striking parallel between the mockery following the Jewish trial (Mt 26:67–68) and the mockery by the soldiers of the governor. In the former, Jesus is addressed as 'Christ' and mocked in connection with his prophetic and messianic prerogatives; in the latter, Jesus is addressed as 'King' and subjected to a parody of royal homage. The titles 'Christ' and 'King' are both inspired by the preceding dialogue in the trial scenes (respectively Mt 26:61–64 and Mt 27:11), to which Matthew has carefully linked the mocking scenes (cf. 'then' in Mt 26:67 and Mt 27:27). This results in an inclusion (in both Mark and Matthew) framing the Roman trial: Mt 27:11, 'Are you the King of the Jews?' – Mt 27:29, 'Hail, King of the Jews!' Similarly, the title 'Christ' marks the beginning and the end of the hearing before the Sanhedrin (cf. Mt 26:63, 68).

> **Verse 30:** And they spat upon him, and took the reed and struck him on the head.

By rearranging the sequence of action Matthew succeeds in presenting a picture of surging violence: the most violent action of the soldiers, spitting and striking with the reed, concludes the mockery. Matthew's addition 'they took the reed' is consistent with Mt 27:29 where we were told that the soldiers 'put a reed in his right hand'. Thus Matthew's reference to the reed is more consistent than its sudden appearance in Mk 15:19.

> **Verse 31:** And when they had mocked him, they stripped him of the robe, and put his own clothes on him, and led him away to crucify him.

This verse is almost identical with Mk 15:20, except for the fact that, in line with Mt 27:28, Matthew replaces the 'purple cloak' with the '(scarlet) robe', and that he substitutes the almost technical 'they led him away' for Mark's 'they led him out'. The verb 'to lead away' was already used in Mt 27:2, after the Jewish trial, to indicate the progression of events as Jesus was led before Pilate. Here it takes up again the progression of events indicated in Mt 27:26, 'delivered him to be crucified', but delayed by the intervening mockery scene.

Summing up, we may say that, although Matthew follows Mark very closely in this section of the passion narrative, his treatment of the traditional material is nevertheless distinctive on several counts:

(1)   The main emphasis is again on the confession of Jesus as the Christ: 'Jesus who is called Christ' (Mt 27:17, 23).

(2)   He also emphasizes the deliberate choice between Jesus and Barabbas.

(3)   He plays up the contrasting role of Pilate and his wife who testify to Jesus' innocence, and the Jewish leaders and people who reject Jesus by choosing Barabbas.

(4)   There is a strong suggestion that all the events are controlled by the divine will (Mt 27:19, 24–25).

(5)   In the mocking scene, Matthew completes the picture of a mock royal coronation (Mt 27:29) and intensifies the atmosphere of violence which surrounds it (Mt 27:27, 29, 30).

III. Luke 23:2–25

In Luke the narrative of the trial before Pilate consists of the following parts:
(1) The initial interrogation by Pilate (Lk 23:2–5);
(2) The examination before Herod (Lk 23:6–12);
(3) The examination before Pilate resumed and concluded (Lk 23:13–25).

The most important difference between Mark's and Luke's composition is the insertion of the pericope narrating Jesus' appearance before Herod.

The initial interrogation by Pilate (Lk 23:2–5)

> **Verse 2:** And they began to accuse him, saying, 'we found this man perverting our nation, and forbidding us to give tribute to Caesar, and saying that he himself is Christ a king.'

Whereas in Mark and Matthew the trial before Pilate starts abruptly with the governor's question, 'Are you the King of the Jews?' (Mk 15:2; Mt 27:11), Luke clarifies the course of events by having Pilate reply to the accusations expressed by the Jewish leaders. He does not just say that they accused Jesus of many things (cf. Mk 15:3; Mt 27:12), but indicates clearly the content of the charges. The Jewish leaders try to convince Pilate of the political danger emanating from Jesus by a threefold accusation: (1) Jesus perverts the nation. This expression could have a religious meaning (cf. Lk 9:41; Acts 13:8, 10), but it must have been understood by Pilate as referring to incitement to revolt (compare Lk 23:14; see JB translation of Lk 23:2: 'We found this man inciting our people to revolt'). (2) Jesus forbids people to pay taxes to Caesar. This is a political accusation which ranks Jesus with the Zealots. (3) Jesus says that he himself is Christ a king. He claims to be a political leader of the Jews, which makes him a direct opponent of the Roman authorities.

The description of the charges betrays a typical interest of Luke's. This appears from the striking similarities with the charges levelled against Paul in the Acts of the Apostles. There too the charges are intended to brand him as an insurgent and rebel (cf. Acts 17:7; 24:2–5; 25:7–8). The similarity – even in vocabulary and formulation – makes it probable that in Lk 23:2, 5 Luke is stressing the political element.

Luke first establishes the political character of the accusations, and then shows that they are false. (1) Jesus has not perverted the nation; it already was perverse (Lk 9:41). (2) The second charge is a patent lie when compared with Lk 20:20–26, especially 25, 'Then render to Caesar the things that are Caesar's, and to God the things that are God's'. (3) Jesus did not accept the messianic title as the Sanhedrin intended it, i.e., politically. We must note, however, that Luke has laid the foundation for such a possible accusation by having the people acclaim Jesus not just as he 'who comes in the name of the Lord' (Mk 11:9), but as 'the *King* who comes in the name of the Lord' (Lk 19:38).

In the hearing before the Sanhedrin Luke omitted the reference to false witnesses. Here it is not witnesses who are the liars, but the leaders of the people, who declare their real nature by their lie.

Verse 3: And Pilate asked him, 'Are you the King of the Jews?' And he answered him, 'You have said so.'

This verse is almost identical with Mk 15:2, but in Luke it is to be read as a reaction to the accusations formulated in Lk 23:2, and thus seems to have a more explicitly political twist than in Mark and Matthew. Contrary to Mark and Matthew, Luke has already referred to Jesus as King at the entry into Jerusalem (Lk 19:38, 'Blessed is the King who comes in the name of the Lord!'; compare Mk 11:9; Mt 21:9). Now when he repeats the title it is a matter not of a first disclosure but of a repetition of what has already been professed before the whole of Jerusalem. Of the three charges, the governor takes up the basic one, the accusation that Jesus claimed to be the Christ, a king.

Since the governor is thinking in purely political terms, Jesus cannot give an unqualified answer to his question. But he will not give up all messianic-royal claims either. Jesus is the Christ; he is the Messiah and a king, but in a different way.

Verse 4: And Pilate said to the chief priests and the multitudes, 'I find no crime in this man.'

It is impossible that this verse is dependent on Mk 15:14, 'Why, what evil has he done?' Pilate's reaction, 'I find no crime in this man', to the enigmatic reply of Jesus presupposes a longer interrogation similar to that of Jn 18:35-38. Luke emphasizes Pilate's testimony to the innocence of Jesus: the governor three times expresses his conviction that the prisoner is no criminal and offers no threat to Roman rule (Lk 23:4, 14, 22). Throughout the Acts of the Apostles, Luke carefully shows that the Roman authorities have always acquitted Paul of the charges brought against him (cf. Acts 16:35-39; 18:12-15; 19:31-41; 24:22-23; 25:18, 25-26; 26:31-32); here he presents the Roman governor declaring that Jesus is not guilty of the political charges.

We should also pay attention to the remarkable association of 'the chief priests and the multitudes'. The Jewish people as a whole, but especially their leaders, are responsible for Jesus' death. While the Roman governor insists on Jesus' innocence, they continue to repeat the charges (Lk 23:5, 10), to reject Jesus (Lk 23:18), and finally to demand his crucifixion (Lk 23:21, 23) until their voices prevail and Pilate reluctantly grants their demand (Lk 23:23–24).

Verse 5: But they were urgent, saying, 'He stirs up the people, teaching throughout Judea, from Galilee even to this place.'

After Pilate's declaration that Jesus is innocent, the Jewish leaders insist and repeat their political accusation: 'He stirs up the people'. Nowhere in his gospel has Luke mentioned anything that looks like stirring up the people, and thus the accusation is again implicitly branded as a gross misrepresentation (cf. e.g., Lk 4:18–21; 19:28 – 21:38).

The present statement is a kind of summary of Jesus' ministry in Galilee and Judea. Emphasis is placed on Jesus' teaching. Luke's record of this teaching has clearly shown that Jesus is not a threat to the Roman empire. 'Judea' should be understood here as referring to the whole of Palestine. The mention of 'Galilee' is part of the political character of the charge, since Galilee was the hot-bed of revolutionary action; it also provides the connection with the account of the hearing before Herod. Jesus exerts his influence 'from Galilee even to this place', i.e., Jerusalem.

The examination before Herod (Lk 23:6–12)

This account is peculiar to Luke and there is little to suggest the use of a source: its vocabulary and style are typically Lucan. Scholars do not agree whence Luke derives the account. While several have defended its historicity, many refer for its origin to Acts 4:25–27, which should undoubtedly be considered as a traditional passage integrated by Luke in his composition. This passage, the only one in the New Testament where Pilate and Herod are mentioned together as involved in the death of Jesus, cites Ps 2:2, 'The kings of the earth set themselves, and the rulers take counsel together, against the Lord and his anointed'. The quotation is followed by the identification of the 'kings' and 'rulers' as Herod and Pilate. Once this interpretation of Ps 2:2 was accepted in the early Christian community it would easily lead to the association of these two names with the actual passion narrative. However, it should be admitted that this explanation is not without difficulties.

Verses 6–7: When Pilate heard this, he asked whether the man was a Galilean. (7) And when he learned that he belonged to Herod's jurisdiction, he sent him over to Herod, who was himself in Jerusalem at that time.

These verses link on to verse 5 and should be considered as a redactional transition to the hearing before Herod. When the chief priests mentioned Galilee as the beginning of Jesus' ministry, Pilate decided to turn Jesus over to Herod, the tetrarch of Galilee and Perea (cf. Lk 3:1, 19; 9:7; Acts 13:1), who had jurisdiction over Jesus (cf. Lk 13:31). Luke then adds 'who was himself in Jerusalem at that time' (Lk 23:7b), which is a necessary clarification since the evangelist had previously connected Herod with Galilee.

Why did Pilate send Jesus to Herod? Five theories have been advanced:
(1) Pilate may have wanted to rid himself of a difficult case.
(2) Pilate sought to placate Herod for the massacre of Galileans in Jerusalem.
(3) Luke may have had contacts with the house of Herod from which he drew this special information (Luke is the only New Testament writer to mention Joanna, the wife of Chuza, Herod's steward; Lk 8:3).
(4) Perhaps Pilate was legally bound to send Jesus to Herod under some law of *forum domicilii*.
(5) The above four hypotheses assume that Luke is reporting what he considered to be a historical event, but Martin Dibelius and Henry J. Cadbury suggest that Luke himself worked up the story from Ps 2:1–2.

Verse 8: When Herod saw Jesus, he was very glad, for he had long desired to see him, because he had heard about him, and he was hoping to see some sign done by him.

The description of Herod is consistent with previous references to the tetrarch, especially the clause 'for he had long desired to see him, because he had heard about him' which refers to Lk 9:9, ' "Who is this about whom I hear such things?" And he (Herod) sought to see him.' Now Herod's wish is fulfilled. He hopes to see something special ('some sign'). Luke may have thought here of other instances in which Jesus' enemies asked for signs (cf. Lk 11:16, 29–30). Although 'to see' can have eschatological connotations (cf. Lk 2:30; 10:23; 17:22; 21:27), Herod's seeing is without perceiving (cf. Lk 8:10), a looking for miracles rather than for salvation. The verb 'to hope' (*elpizein*) is often used in Luke-Acts with a negative meaning (cf. Lk 6:34; Acts 24:26). In our present text, too, a nuance of moral reprehension or of unfoundedness is clearly present.

Verse 9: So he questioned him at some length; but he made no answer.

The curiosity of Herod who wishes to 'see' Jesus is not satisfied: Jesus 'made no answer' (*ouden apekrinato*). The expression used indicates dependence on Mark, who mentions this silence of Jesus at Mk 14:60–61 and 15:4. Luke does not include this feature in his account of the hearing before the Sanhedrin and before Pilate, because of his different concept of these scenes. It is understandable that this motif of the silence of Jesus, which is so important in the context of the suffering servant typology, is now fitted into the hearing before Herod.

Verse 10: The chief priests and the scribes stood by, vehemently accusing him.

Referring to the 'chief priests and the scribes' as Jesus' opponents, this verse too ties the hearing before Herod to the preceding context (cf. Lk 22:66; 23:2). The content of the charges is not described, but the mere repetition of the reference to the accusations underlines the negative role of the Jewish leaders.

Verse 11: And Herod with his soldiers treated him with contempt and mocked him; then, arraying him in gorgeous apparel, he sent him back to Pilate.

Verses 11–12 are the only two verses in the pericope which contain definite information and cannot have been derived from other passages. The present verse is usually interpreted as a reaction of Herod to Jesus' refusal to perform a sign, and the mockery is understood as directed against Jesus' claim to royal dignity. 'Arraying him in gorgeous apparel' would be part of this mockery of Jesus as 'king'. But this interpretation is questionable if looked at from the point of view of Lk 23:15, where we are told that even Herod considered Jesus innocent. Most probably Luke had in his traditional material a reference to a hearing before Herod, during which the tetrarch mocked Jesus by, among other things, 'arraying him in gorgeous apparel'. In its present context, however, this mocking should be seen as a preparation for Lk 23:15 where it appears that Herod considers Jesus innocent. In that context the 'gorgeous apparel' may have a positive meaning. Applied to garments, *lampros* may mean 'white', 'radiant'. Thus by giving this white garment, Herod pronounces a positive verdict on Jesus.

Verse 12: And Herod and Pilate became friends with each other that very day, for before this they had been at enmity with each other.

The original meaning of this statement was undoubtedly that Pilate and Herod were common enemies of Jesus. The previous conflict between Pilate and Herod should be understood in the light of the information, found in Philo and Josephus, that Herod accused Pilate in Rome of offensively placing Roman standards in the palace at Jerusalem. Following this accusation Pilate was reprimanded. Moreover, Lk 13:1 mentions a mass murder of Galileans, Herod's subjects, by Pilate. It is therefore understandable that Pilate decided to consult Herod in this case.

We are told that Pilate and Herod became reconciled in their common action regarding Jesus. This is formulated in a way strongly reminiscent of Prov 15:28LXX, which corresponds to Prov 16:7 in the Hebrew text and most translations, 'When a man's ways please the Lord, he makes even his enemies to be at peace with him'. However, in the Septuagint, the verse is found in a different context and can be paraphrased, 'and through them (the righteous) enemies become friends (towards them)'. But in Luke the meaning shifts considerably. He says that 'Herod and Pilate became friends *with each other* that very day' by their common attitude towards Jesus; both consider him innocent. Thus the former enemies form a common front against the Jewish leaders who demand Jesus' death.

An alternative interpretation holds that Luke probably knew that both Pilate and Herod were deposed at about the same time and that the trial of Jesus occurred only a few years before their downfall. It is said in that connection that Luke may have shared the view of the Fourth Gospel that Pilate was on his way toward being 'no friend of Caesar's' (cf. Jn 19:12). Luke would add that Herod Antipas was also on the way down. By A.D. 38 both ex-rulers may have been 'friends' of each other, but they were no longer friends of Caesar.

Summing up, we may say that Luke must have known a tradition which attributed to Herod a negative role in the trial of Jesus. Luke took this up from the point of view that, as a Galilean, Jesus had to appear before Herod. However, he entirely changed the scene by presenting Herod as testifying to Jesus' innocence. The historical situation seems to be better preserved in Acts 4:25–27, by way of the interpretation of Ps 2:1–2.

The examination before Pilate resumed and concluded (Lk 23:13–25)

Verse 13: Pilate then called together the chief priests and the rulers and the people,

That 'Pilate then called together the chief priests . . .' seems to imply a recess before the convening of the final session. Apparently 'the people' are included at this point in the passion narrative in order to emphasize that the Jewish people are to quite an extent responsible for Jesus' death. Previously we were told that the entire assembly led Jesus before Pilate (Lk 23:1), becoming 'the chief priests and the multitudes' in Lk 23:4, 'the chief priests and the scribes' as accusers in Lk 23:10, and finally now 'the chief priests and the rulers and the people'. However, Luke never presents an altogether negative picture of the whole people (cf. Lk 23:27, 35–36).

> **Verse 14:** and said to them, 'You brought me this man as one who was perverting the people; and after examining him before you, behold, I did not find this man guilty of any of your charges against him;

Having called together the chief priests and the rulers of the people, Pilate proceeds to repeat part of the charge, 'You brought me this man as one who was perverting the people' (cf. Lk 23:2, 'We found this man perverting the nation') and to make clear that he examined Jesus 'before' them. So in their presence he had a good look at the charges, which in Luke are considerably more specific than in Mark and Matthew, and concludes a second time that Jesus is 'not . . . guilty of any of your charges against him'. Luke again strongly emphasizes Jesus' innocence.

> **Verse 15:** 'neither did Herod, for he sent him back to us. Behold, nothing deserving death has been done by him;

This verse expresses the meaning of the hearing before Herod. By sending Jesus back arrayed in gorgeous apparel, Herod establishes that Jesus is politically innocent. Indeed, in a new attempt to set Jesus free, Pilate states that Herod did not find Jesus guilty of any of the charges. The beginning of the verse should be translated: 'Even Herod did not . . .'. To Luke and his readers Herod was a bad king (cf. Lk 3:19–20; 9:9; 13:31–32), but even he had to admit Jesus' innocence. Herod's dismissal of Jesus is understood as an acquittal on the charge of sedition. Pilate's and Herod's conclusion is: 'Behold, nothing deserving death has been done by him'.

> **Verse 16:** 'I will therefore chastise him and release him.'

The word 'chastise' (*paideuein*) used here of Jesus' scourging is never used in this sense outside the Bible. Because of the verb's connotation of educating or teaching, we could paraphrase: 'I will teach him a lesson'. Some think that Luke is speaking here of a light beating or whipping accompanied with a severe warning (cf. Acts 16:22–24; 22:24), but it is very possible that he uses the word here as a euphemism for the brutal scourging. It should not be overlooked that he says nowhere that Jesus was actually chastised or scourged! Note also that in Mk 15:15 Pilate has Jesus scourged *before* delivering him to be crucified. Here in Luke it is proposed to inflict a punishment *instead* of the death penalty.

It remains possible that Luke, who is concerned to show an entirely different perspective from Mark's, has more in mind than just a light word to express the terrible *flagellatio*. For Luke there never really was a criminal trial. Pilate was prepared to let Jesus go with only a warning, though a firm one, which often consisted of a lesson by the rod when the governor felt that no further legal action was necessary.

(Verse 17: Now he was obliged to release one man to them at the festival.)

Here (or after Lk 23:19) some manuscripts add verse 17, which seems to be an explanatory note based on Mk 15:6; Mt 27:15. It is apparently a later copyist's attempt to explain the outcry for Barabbas (cf. Lk 23:18).

Verse 18: But they all cried out together, 'Away with this man, and release to us Barabbas' –

Since Luke omits Mk 15:6–11, the sudden reference to Barabbas compels him to explain who this man is. According to Luke, it is the Jews themselves who bring the name of Barabbas into the discussion. The figure of Barabbas loses much of its importance in Luke's composition: Barabbas is mentioned three times in Mark, five times in Matthew, and only once in Luke. Luke dislikes the comparison between Jesus and a murderer, and since he cannot leave him unmentioned, he insists on the contrast by emphasizing the enormity of the dreadful choice (compare Lk 23:25 and Mk 15:15b). The phrase 'away with this man' is reminiscent of Isa 53:8, 'by oppression and judgment he was taken away'.

Verse 19: a man who had been thrown into prison for an insurrection started in the city, and for murder.

The verse may be based on Mk 15:7, but Luke adds that the 'insurrection started in the city', i.e., in Jerusalem. The extensive description of Barabbas' crime underlines the blindness of the people of Jerusalem and their leaders: they choose an insurgent and a murderer. Luke bitterly repeats this description at Lk 23:25. They asked for a murderer to be granted to them, and killed the author of life (cf. Acts 3:13–15).

Verse 20: Pilate addressed them once more, desiring to release Jesus;

'Desiring to release Jesus', Pilate did not give up immediately. Thus Luke continues his favourable description of the governor's role in the trial. But he omits the question, 'Then what shall I do with the man whom you call the King of the Jews?' (Mk 15:12b; compare Mt 27:22a). Instead Luke immediately relates the violent reaction of the crowd.

Verse 21: but they shouted out, 'Crucify, crucify him!'

The Jews insistently demand Jesus' death; note the twice-repeated 'Crucify, crucify' against the single 'Crucify him' (Mk 15:13) and 'Let him be crucified' (Mt 27:22b). In accordance with Mk 15:13, this is the first time this word occurs in the gospel. In Matthew, the verb has occurred already in the third prediction of the passion (Mt 20:19), the indictment of the scribes and Pharisees (Mt 23:34), and the conspiracy against Jesus (Mt 26:2).

Verse 22: A third time he said to them, 'Why, what evil has he done? I have found in him no crime deserving death; I will therefore chastise him and release him.'

The threefold proclamation of Jesus' innocence is due to Luke's conscious editorial activity, as can be seen from the introduction of this verse, 'A third time he said to them'. This brings out the significance of the official confirmation of Jesus' innocence. 'Why, what evil has he done?' agrees with Mk 15:14, while 'I will therefore chastise him and release him' forms a doublet with Lk 23:16. These two clauses frame the third proclamation of Jesus' innocence, 'I have found in him no crime deserving death.'

Verse 23: But they were urgent, demanding with loud cries that he should be crucified. And their voices prevailed.

Here we reach the climax of a carefully orchestrated intensification of the demands: 'But they were urgent, saying' (Lk 23:5) – 'but they all cried out together' (Lk 23:18) – 'but they shouted out' (Lk 23:21) – 'but they were urgent, demanding with loud cries' (Lk 23:23). Luke apparently developed what is found on a smaller scale in Mark (Mk 15:13–15, 'And they cried out' – 'But they shouted all the more'). For the third time Pilate bears witness to the innocence of Jesus, while the Jews insistently demand his death. 'And their voices prevailed (*katischuon*).' Outside this passage the verb is found only in Lk 21:36, 'that you may *have strength* to escape all these things that will take place', and Mt 16:18, 'and the powers of death (the gates of Hades) shall not prevail against it'. The verb therefore seems to have an eschatological connotation.

Verse 24: So Pilate gave sentence that their demand should be granted.

By omitting the words 'wishing to satisfy the crowd', Luke softens the picture of political cowardice found in Mark. To the phrase 'that their demand should be granted' corresponds 'but Jesus he delivered up to their will' (Lk 23:25). We cannot miss the emphasis on the Jews' responsibility for Jesus' death. Luke's account almost seems to say that it was the Jews who crucified Jesus! In fact no Roman soldiers have been mentioned in the whole account, and Luke now omits the mockery by the Roman soldiers (Mk 15:16–20; Mt 27:27–31). In Luke, it was Herod and his soldiers who treated Jesus with contempt (cf. Lk 23:11).

Luke uses the technical phrase for the passing of a sentence. Yet the specification of punishment is totally unexpected. Luke has omitted the most important aspect of a capital trial, namely that Jesus was sentenced to scourging and crucifixion (cf. Mk 15:15), and replaced it with the very vague 'but Jesus he delivered up to their will' (Lk 23:25). Luke cannot mention the pre-crucifixion scourging because he does not consider this case to have been a regular Roman trial.

Verse 25: He released the man who had been thrown into prison for insurrection and murder, whom they asked for; but Jesus he delivered up to their will.

Pilate released the man for whom they kept asking (this is the force of the imperfect, which may be intended to recall 'whom they asked' in Mk 15:6). Luke repeats that Barabbas had been imprisoned for insurrection and murder (cf. Lk 23:19; but note that he does not repeat the name Barabbas), thus intensifying the contrast with the innocent Jesus. He has the expression 'delivered up' (*paredōken*) in common with Mark, but contrary to the latter who attributes to Pilate the order to crucify Jesus, here Pilate makes no final decision, but turns Jesus over to the Jews to deal with as they wish.

Summing up, it may be said that the main theme of Luke's redaction is the innocence of Jesus, three times attested by Pilate (Lk 23:4, 14, 22) and confirmed by Herod (Lk 23:11b, 15). As a faithful disciple Luke untiringly insists on Jesus' innocence. This motif is paralleled by a similar concern in the Acts of the Apostles to exonerate the Christians of all charges levelled against them.

The governor three times expresses his intention to release Jesus

(Lk 23:16, 20, 22). To this Luke opposes the outcries of the Jewish leaders and the people of Jerusalem (Lk 23:5, 18, 21, 23). Thus he lays the blame squarely on the Jews while he minimizes the responsibility of Pilate and the Romans. However, Luke specifies that he pins the responsibility not on the whole people, but rather on the leaders and Jerusalem (cf. Lk 13:31–35; 23:27–32; Acts 13:27). This theme serves polemic and apologetic purposes, but it is also used in the preaching to the Jews (Acts 3:17–19): they acted out of ignorance (cf. Lk 23:34), and it was 'necessary that the Christ should suffer' (Lk 24:26; cf. 24:44). The emphasis on guilt is repeatedly intended as a serious call to conversion (cf. Acts 2:37).

5 Crucifixion and Death

Most scholars agree that a brief basic account underlies this part of the passion narrative, though they do not agree on the extent of this basic account. Mk 15:20b–24a, 'And they led him out to crucify him. . . . And they crucified him', which Vincent Taylor assigns to narrative A (see Chapter One above), is apparently very old. This brief foundation story attached to itself various items of tradition.

I. Mark 15:21–41

Mark's account can be subdivided into the following six scenes:
(1) The requisition of Simon of Cyrene (Mk 15:21);
(2) The crucifixion (Mk 15:22–27);
(3) The mockery (Mk 15:29–32);
(4) The darkness (Mk 15:33–36);
(5) The death of Jesus and its repercussions (Mk 15:37–39);
(6) The mention of the women (Mk 15:40–41).

The requisition of Simon of Cyrene (Mk 15:21)

Verse 21: And they compelled a passer-by, Simon of Cyrene, who was coming in from the country, the father of Alexander and Rufus, to carry his cross.

The soldiers led Jesus to the place of execution which was outside the city walls. The way in which the name of Simon of Cyrene is introduced, i.e., with reference to his sons and not, as one would expect, to his father, suggests that Alexander and Rufus were known to Mark's readers. Had they become Christians (cf. the Rufus mentioned in Rom 16:13)?

The note, 'who was coming in from the country', has figured in the celebrated discussion as to whether the event took place on the eve of the Passover or the feast day itself. But, as the discussion itself shows, very little can be derived with certainty from this phrase.

'They compelled' him, i.e., exercised the right to enlist 'a passer-by' for forced labour, 'to carry his cross'. For the carrying of the cross Mark uses the same verb (*airein*, 'to take up') as in the saying about discipleship, 'let him take up his cross and follow me' (Mk 8:34). Simon thus becomes a model for the Christian reader (Jn 19:17 omits this feature and says, in accordance with Johannine Christology, that 'they took Jesus, and he went out, bearing his own cross'. But see also Plutarch, *Moralia* 554 A, 'Each of the condemned bore his own cross'.)

The condemned person usually did not carry a complete cross, but only the transverse beam or the 'crossbeam' (cf. Lk 23:26 in NAB), which formed the top of the cross. The vertical or upright beam stood permanently on the place of execution.

The crucifixion (Mk 15:22–27)

Verse 22: And they brought him to the place called Golgotha (which means the place of a skull).

Probably the place owed its name to the shape of the hill on which the executions were performed, but later legend connected it with the burial place of Adam: Jesus was crucified on the place where Adam, or his skull, was buried. Golgotha means 'skull' in Aramaic. Calvary, the better-known name, is from the Latin translation, *calvaria*, 'a skull'.

Verse 23: And they offered him wine mingled with myrrh; but he did not take it.

According to an old custom, which was begun in response to the directive given in Prov 31:6–7, 'Give strong drink to him who is perishing, and wine to those in bitter distress . . .', respected women of Jerusalem provided a stupefying drink to those condemned to crucifixion in order to lessen their sensitivity to the torturing pain.

'But he did not take it', and this in the evangelist's view certainly indicates that Jesus willed consciously to endure his sufferings and death.

Verse 24: And they crucified him, and divided his garments among them, casting lots for them, to decide what each should take.

The crucifixion itself could not be told more concisely. Jesus' real suffering did not consist in physical pain, but was caused by his rejection which began with Mk 3:6, 'The Pharisees went out, and immediately held counsel with the Herodians against him, how to destroy him', and reaches its culmination in the passion narrative where Jesus is rejected by the Sanhedrin and denied by the last disciple who still 'followed him at a distance' (Mk 14:54), but has not appeared since Mk 14:72. Jesus' real suffering is the solitude of the Son of man.

The soldiers 'divided his garments among them', in keeping with Roman legal texts confirming that the executioners could claim the minor possessions of an executed man. This was a common feature in any crucifixion, but in Jesus' case it reminded the early Church of Ps 22(21) which in general seemed to express Jesus' passion. Ps 22(21) became for the early Church the principal biblical description of Jesus' passion and death, and occupied a place in its worship similar to that which the passion narrative has for us today.

Ps 22(21) is form-critically classified as an individual lament (verses 1–21), followed by an individual song of thanksgiving (verses 22–31). The individual lament falls into three specific laments (verses 1–2, 6–8, 12–18) rising in intensity, accompanied in the first two instances by affirmations of confidence (verses 3–5, 9–10), and in the last two by petitions (verses 11, 19–21).

Here the evangelist thinks especially of Ps 22(21):18, 'they divide my garments among them, and for my raiment they cast lots'. It is hard to say how far the actual events made the early Church think of the Old Testament passage, and to what extent the Old Testament passage determined the description of the incident. We will have to refer again to Ps 22(21) in our explanation of Mk 15:29, 34 and 36(?).

Verse 25: And it was the third hour, when they crucified him.

It is impossible to reconcile this time indication (nine o'clock in the morning) with Jn 19:14 where we are told that Jesus was condemned to death at 'about the sixth hour' (twelve o'clock noon). Mark does not intend to give us the precise time of the crucifixion, but simply states this to indicate that the different stages of the crucifixion happened in accord with God's plan, according to divine schedule (see Mk 15:33–34, 'And when the sixth hour had come. . . . And at the ninth hour . . .'). Every hour of this day was under God's control. John, on the other hand, wants to emphasize that Jesus was condemned and died at the time when the Passover lamb was slaughtered. If we exhaust ourselves in attempts to reconcile these two statements of time, we fail to listen to the real affirmation which both Mark and John intend to make.

Verse 26: And the inscription of the charge against him read, 'The King of the Jews.'

According to Roman custom, the delinquent carried a wooden board with the specification of his crime to the execution site. After the execution this board was attached to the cross.

This is the fifth and last mention of the title 'King of the Jews' (cf. Mk 15:2, 9, 12, 18, 26; but see also Mk 15:32, 'King of Israel'). We discussed its meaning previously. Here it seems to function as a 'silent proclamation' of the Messiah.

Verse 27: And with him they crucified two others, one on his right and one on his left.

All four gospels mention that Jesus was crucified between 'robbers', a derogatory term most probably first given by Herod the Great to those involved in insurrection. In Josephus it is repeatedly used for the Zealots who committed themselves to armed resistance against the Romans. Luke speaks here of 'criminals'.

(Verse 28: And the scripture was fulfilled which says, 'He was reckoned with the transgressors.')

In some manuscripts the mention of the two robbers crucified with Jesus is followed by this fulfilment text, which is considered as a spurious addition derived from Lk 22:37, and is lacking in the best manuscripts. Apparently, later copyists inserted this verse to indicate that the event fulfilled Isa 53:12, '. . . and (he) was numbered with the transgressors' (RSV and JB give the text in a footnote).

The mockery (Mk 15:29–32)

This passage raises several historical questions. To what extent is it influenced by Ps 22(21):7–8 and Lam 2:15? How do verses 29–30 and verses 31–32, describing two different mockings, each mentioning 'saving himself' and 'coming down from the cross', relate to each other? Would this double mockery be due to Ps 22(21):6, 'scorned by men, and despised by the people?'

Verse 29: And those who passed by derided him, wagging their heads, and saying, 'Aha! You who would destroy the temple and build it in three days,

Mark makes use of psalms and other Old Testament texts to describe the attitude of those who were present at the crucifixion: Ps 22(21):7, 'All who see me mock at me, they make mouths at me, they wag their heads'; Lam 2:15, 'All who pass along the way clap their hands at you; they hiss and wag their heads . . .'; Jer 18:16, 'making their land a horror, a thing to be hissed at for ever. Everyone who passes by it is horrified and shakes his head.'

The phrase 'wagging their heads' recalls the mockery to which the poor but just sufferer of the psalms is subjected (Ps 22[21]:7;

109[108]:25), and the abusive words hurled at Jerusalem in her hour of deepest humiliation (Lam 2:15; cf. Jer 18:16).

The passers-by quote Jesus' words about the destruction of the Temple mentioned by the false witnesses during the hearing before the Sanhedrin (Mk 14:58). Mark thus attributes to the mockers an incorrect understanding of Jesus' passion and an incorrect eschatology. They do not know the necessity for Jesus to take the way of the cross to the end before he can be vindicated by God. In the context of the composition of the gospel they represent an eschatology and Christology which Mark rejects throughout his writing.

The connection between the present verse and Mk 14:58 and 15:38 should be emphasized. The redactional character of Mk 15:29 in relation to Mk 14:58 has been widely recognized, and Mk 15:38 is seen by many as due to Mark either in its composition or in its present location. Taken together these three passages assert the following: in spite of the challenge to come down from the cross, Jesus does not do so. Instead, he dies on the cross. At the precise moment that Jesus dies the old Temple loses its significance, i.e., is destroyed. His very death also makes the centurion *see* that he will build a new eschatological community in God's presence.

Verse 30: 'save yourself, and come down from the cross!'

The words 'save yourself' may be understood as an allusion to the healings Jesus performed to save people. In fact, 'to save' is one of the two key words found in many healings of Jesus (the other one is 'belief'). Now it is time for Jesus to save himself. But previously Jesus had stated that God looks at things in a different way: 'For whoever would save his life will lose it, and whoever loses his life for my sake and the gospel's will save it' (Mk 8:35). The challenge addressed to Jesus to save himself is thus specified in the words 'come down from the cross'.

Verse 31: So also the chief priests mocked him to one another with the scribes, saying, 'He saved others; he cannot save himself.'

The presence of the chief priests and the scribes is surprising and may be the result of Mark's editorial attempt to find room for those who throughout the gospel are referred to as Jesus' opponents. In fact, the vocabulary is very Marcan and, as we pointed out, the words attributed to them are to quite an extent a duplicate of the mocking related in Mk 15:29–30. But there is also a certain development. In Mk 15:30 'save' is most probably to be taken in the sense of 'preserve your life' and could express an original comment of a passer-by, but in the present verse we may discover a modification or creation by the early

Church: we may have here a Christian comment on the crucifixion attributed to his opponents. Jesus saves other men, but the divine necessity demands that he does not save himself.

Verse 32: 'Let the Christ, the King of Israel, come down from the cross, that we may see and believe.' Those who were crucified with him also reviled him.

This is one of the four places where 'Christ' is used as a title (Mk 1:1; 8:29; 14:61; 15:32). For the last time, Mark emphasizes Jesus' kingship, but this time clearly in a religious, messianic context. This may explain the use of 'King of Israel' instead of 'King of the Jews'. It should not too easily be assumed that the two titles are synonymous. 'King of Israel' refers to Jesus as the King of the eschatological Israel.

The phrase 'that we may see and believe' has a Johannine ring (cf. Jn 6:30). As always, the request for a miracle, understood as a proof, is clearly rejected by Mark.

The two 'robbers' who were crucified at the same time as Jesus (the verb *sunstauroumai* is clearly not used in the sense of being *crucified with* Christ, as is the case in Rom 6:6; Gal 2:20) also 'reviled' him. The same verb is used in Ps 69(68):9, 'For zeal for your house has consumed me, and the insults of those who insult (=revile) you have fallen on me'.

The darkness (Mk 15:33–36)

Verse 33: And when the sixth hour had come, there was darkness over the whole land until the ninth hour.

The darkness which begins at noontime, lasts until three o'clock, and extends over the whole land suggests the cosmic effect of Jesus' death. What happens is similar to what will accompany the Day of Judgment according to Mk 13:24, 'But in those days, after that tribulation, the sun will be darkened ...'. The death of Jesus is compared to that event. We are also reminded of Amos 8:9, ' "And on that day", says the Lord God, "I will make the sun go down at noon, and darken the earth in broad daylight".' For the idea of the passion and death understood in terms of judgment, see Jn 12:31, 'Now is the judgment of this world'. Again, if we spend all our energy debating whether or not darkness was possible, e.g., because of a sandstorm, we will miss the real message of the passage, because of our wrong approach.

Verse 34: And at the ninth hour Jesus cried with a loud voice, 'Eloi, Eloi, lama sabachthani?' which means, 'My God, my God, why have you forsaken me?'

Again three hours have passed, and we now reach the hour of fulfilment. Most scholars consider the (inarticulate) cry of Jesus one of the basic historical data of the passion narrative (cf. Mk 15:37). However, it seems that the evangelists have filled out this cry in their own way. Both Mark and Matthew cite Ps 22(21):1, 'My God, my God, why have you forsaken me?' Luke quotes Ps 31(30):5, 'Into your hand I commit my spirit' (Lk 23:46). John's words, 'It is finished', do not refer to any one Old Testament passage, although we may have here an allusion to such texts as Ps 22(21):30–31; Isa 41:20; 42:16.

Mark quotes Ps 22(21):1 in what has been called 'Hebraized Aramaic'. The text very appropriately states both aspects of what is happening here. On the one hand, it is a radical expression of the loneliness of Jesus' suffering and death. But on the other hand, it is a radical expression of dedication to God which is not affected by adverse experience. The latter part of the psalm from which these words are quoted, Ps 22(21):22–31, is a prayer of thanksgiving expressing certainty of God's protection.

Jesus' death is veiled in the language of Ps 22(21). It may be held on good grounds that Jesus reflected and expressed himself in its words. But it is equally possible that the saying has its origin in early Christian reflection on the psalm and that its situation in life is the *todah* ceremony, when a group gathers to remember a friend's deliverance, recalling his sufferings (cf. Ps 22[21]:1–21) and proclaiming what God has done for him (cf. Ps 22[21]:22–31). In either case, Jesus appears as the 'just, vindicated sufferer' of the psalms.

Verse 35: And some of the bystanders hearing it said, 'Behold, he is calling Elijah.'

This and the following verse constitute a rather obscure passage which Matthew tried to clarify and Luke omitted. The misunderstanding could hardly occur if the psalm was quoted in Aramaic as Mark's formulation (*Elōi*) suggests. Matthew's form (*Ēli*) better accounts for the confusion that follows over whether Jesus calls for *Elias* (Elijah). For reasons now more or less unintelligible to us, Jesus was thought to be calling Elijah. Elijah was the recognized forerunner of the Messiah (Mal 3:23[4:5]), but this is most probably of little importance in this passage. More importantly Elijah, who was taken up by a chariot of fire (II Kgs 2:11), was believed to come to the rescue of the just in need.

Verse 36: And one ran and, filling a sponge full of vinegar, put it on a reed and gave it to him to drink, saying, 'Wait, let us see whether Elijah will come to take him down.'

One of the people present (a soldier? cf. Lk 23:36–37) offered Jesus some sour wine vinegar (cf. Num 6:3; Ruth 2:14), apparently to prolong his life, a practice known from Roman sources. This was then described in terms reminiscent of Ps 69(68):21, 'They gave me poison for food, and for my thirst they gave me vinegar to drink'. The present interpretation is reinforced if the accompanying saying means: 'Don't let him die, Elijah is coming!' We should also note that thirst is mentioned in Ps 22(21):15, 'my tongue cleaves to my jaws'.

The death of Jesus and its repercussions (Mk 15:37–39)

Verse 37: And Jesus uttered a loud cry, and breathed his last.

To die on the cross with a loud cry is certainly extraordinary, since anyone who was crucified died of exhaustion. Perhaps for that reason this cry impressed those present and so was specially noted. But it is not excluded that the emphasis is to be explained by the fact that it was regarded as fulfilling such texts as Ps 31(30):22, 'But you did hear my supplications, when I cried to you for help', or Ps 39(38):12, 'Hear my prayer, O Lord, and give ear to my cry'.

We should pay special attention to the fact that Mark does not say that Jesus *died* but that he 'breathed his last' (*exepneusen*, 'he expired'). In itself this is not so remarkable, but the other evangelists explicate what is implied in this verse. 'And Jesus . . . yielded up his spirit' (Mt 27:50). 'Then Jesus . . . said, "Father, into your hands I commit my spirit". And having said this he breathed his last' (Lk 23:46; *exepneusen*, 'he expired'). 'He said, "It is finished"; and he bowed his head and gave up his spirit' (Jn 19:30). The later apocryphal *Gospel of Peter* and the Syrian translation of the gospel of Matthew go one step further and add after Mt 27:50, 'And his spirit went up'. None of the evangelists says 'Jesus died'; this is said only by outsiders who do not believe (cf. Mk 15:44–45). The least we can say is that the gospels stress the personal character of Jesus' death: Jesus was not killed, his life was *not taken*, but he *gave* it out of his own free will. His death is an act of free obedience and love.

Verse 38: And the curtain of the temple was torn in two, from top to bottom.

The interpretation of this verse involves several difficulties. Firstly, this event which, if it really happened, would have had a tremendous impact, to be compared, e.g., to the blowing up of the Vatican, is mentioned in the three synoptic gospels only, although Josephus gives us a detailed description of the Temple including that of the Temple curtain. It should also be noted that while Mark and Matthew record the rending of the curtain after Jesus' death, Luke records it before Jesus' death. Secondly, there are two Temple curtains. An *outer curtain* separated the sanctuary from the forecourt (Ex 26:37; 38:18; Num 3:26), while the *inner curtain* separated the Holy Place from the Holy of Holies, to which the high priest alone had access on the Day of Atonement (Ex 26:31–35; 27:21; 30:6; Lev 16:2, 12–15; 21:23; 24:3). It is not clear whether Mark's reference is to the inner or to the outer curtain. In either case, its rending at the very moment when Jesus died symbolizes the effect and implications of his death. Thirdly, one may wonder whether immediately after recording Jesus' death, Mark had nothing more important to talk about than the rending of a Temple curtain, unless this had for him and his readers a deeper, symbolic meaning.

Taking into account the two possibilities (inner and outer curtain), there are three principal interpretations:

(1)   The destruction of the inner curtain would announce that the Temple service is practically abolished and that the destruction of the Temple is near.

(2)   The rending of the inner curtain can also signify the removal through Christ's death of the barrier between God and man (cf. Heb 9:1–12, 24–28; 10:19–25).

(3)   In view of Eph 2:11–22, especially verses 14–16, the rending of the outer curtain could be a reference to the removal of the barrier between Jews and Gentiles. In Eph 2:14–16 we read: 'For he is our peace, who has made us both one, and *has broken down the dividing wall of hostility*, by abolishing in his flesh the law of commandments and ordinances, that he might create in himself one new man in place of the two, so making peace, and might reconcile us both to God in one body *through the cross*, thereby bringing the hostility to an end'. In Eph 2:11–22, the situation of discrimination in the Temple, whose material expression was the outer curtain, beyond which Gentiles were not allowed to go, becomes a contrast picture by means of which Paul states the universal, non-discriminatory effect of Jesus' death which actualizes God's redeeming, saving presence for all, Jews and Gentiles. This means the end of the old order, the end of the ancient people of God of which the Temple cult was the heart; but it is at the same time the beginning of a new order, of the new people of God, of which Christ's death and resurrection is the heart, as the final manifestation of God's purifying and unifying presence.

This event, therefore, is not to be taken literally. Rather, a profound theological meaning is hidden in this detail. It has been recorded in order to teach us that religion and salvation have become universal.

Verse 39: And when the centurion, who stood facing him, saw that he thus breathed his last, he said, 'Truly this man was the Son of God.'

The centurion 'who stood facing him' as the official witness of the Roman governor and as such, as it were, represented the Roman empire, is described as giving a spontaneous testimony because he was struck by the way in which Jesus died. The loud cry accompanying Jesus' death impressed the centurion as a revelatory sign of power and of voluntary acceptance of death. Having been granted an epiphany of Jesus, the centurion characterizes the whole life of Jesus up to his death as that of God's Son (compare Mk 1:1 and 15:39). If Mk 15:38 represents the significance of Jesus' death as it affected the Jewish people, Mk 15:39 expresses the Gentile acknowledgement of that significance.

But there may be yet another dimension to this verse. It says that the centurion *saw* that (crying out) in such a way, 'he breathed his last'. 'Seeing' may have been preferred to the more expected 'hearing' because Mark wants to relate the centurion's confession to the 'seeing' of Jesus at the parousia (cf. Mk 14:62, 'you will see . . .').

The title 'Son of God' is not meant here in the sense in which we understand it now as 'second Person of the Trinity'. Even if we take into account the Christian overtones given to the phrase by Mark (and Matthew), we should not read into it what was, not without difficulty, to be defined by the Council of Nicaea in A.D. 325, i.e., more than 250 years after the composition of Mark's gospel. In the Old Testament the people of Israel is referred to as son of God, as we can see, e.g., in Hos 11:1, speaking of the Exodus: 'When Israel was a child, I loved him, and out of Egypt I called my son'. The king as the representative and embodiment of the people is referred to as 'son' of God (II Sam 7:12–16). In this light we should also understand Ps 2:7, according to which the king of Israel is 'begotten', i.e., installed, as son of God on the day of his enthronement. This indicates that 'Son of God' should first of all be understood as a messianic title. Post-Easter reflection gradually led to a still deeper understanding of the application of this title to Jesus, and finally to the definition of Nicaea.

There is no doubt that in its present form this statement is a typically Christian profession of faith as it would be professed after Easter and Pentecost. For Mark it certainly echoes the theme of his gospel, announced from the very beginning in the title verse of the gospel, 'The beginning of the gospel of Jesus Christ, the Son of God' (Mk 1:1). Thousands of people, after listening to the gospel, responded in faith, saying, 'Truly this man was the Son of God'. The representative confession of the centurion surpasses that of Peter (Mk 8:29, 'You are the Christ') and asserts what the high priest considered blasphemy (Mk 14:64). The evangelist, therefore, regards it as of the highest significance. That Jesus is the Son of God or Messiah entirely by virtue of his suffering and death is a conclusion which Mark wants to impress on his reader. It is only when Jesus is 'seen' as the one who suffered, died and will come again, that he can be called Son of God in the proper sense.

The mention of the women (Mk 15:40–41)

Verses 40–41: There were also women looking on from afar, among whom were Mary Magdalene, and Mary the mother of James the younger and of Joses, and Salome, (41) who, when he was in Galilee, followed him, and ministered to him; and also many other women who came up with him to Jerusalem.

The section, which reached its climax in the confession of the centurion, closes with the somewhat abrupt appearance of a group of women. Mary Magdalene is distinguished from other women named Mary by the surname Magdalene, which refers to her birthplace Magdala, a fishing village on the western shore of the Sea of Galilee. We know hardly anything of Mary the mother of James and Joses, but apparently her sons were well known to Mark's readers (compare Mk 15:21). Although these women are described as following Jesus and ministering to him, it is not self-evident that they were disciples of Jesus, since, in Mark, neither following nor ministering is sufficient in itself as a definition of discipleship.

These women are apparently introduced here to prepare for their role in the account of the burial (Mk 15:47) and the finding of the empty tomb (Mk 16:1–8). It may be that they are also mentioned as eyewitnesses of the crucifixion.

Summing up, we may say that Mark's account of Jesus' crucifixion and death is controlled by the following aims:

(1)   The reference to Simon of Cyrene and to the women at the cross intends to show that the Christian Church had trustworthy sources of information about the events proclaimed (Mk 15:21, 40–41).
(2)   Mark emphasizes once again the implacable opposition of the Jewish leaders (Mk 15:29–32).
(3)   Mark's main aim is to establish that everything took place according to the scriptures, i.e., according to the will of God as expressed in the scriptures. This he does especially by quoting 'passion *testimonia*', especially Pss 22(21) and 69(68), and Isa 53.

(4)   The evangelist also stresses that Jesus' passion and death was a conscious and free act (Mk 15:23, 37).
(5)   The real suffering of Jesus is constituted by the loneliness of the Son of man (Mk 15:34), who can be properly called Son of God only when he is recognized as the one who suffered, died and will come again (Mk 15:39).

II. Matthew 27:32–56

Matthew follows Mark very closely. The additions and changes are thus the more important. This account can also be subdivided into six scenes:
(1)   The requisition of Simon of Cyrene (Mt 27:32);
(2)   The crucifixion (Mt 27:33–38);
(3)   The mockery (Mt 27:39–44);
(4)   The darkness (Mt 27:45–49);
(5)   The death of Jesus and its repercussions (Mt 27:50–54);
(6)   The mention of the women (Mt 27:55–56).

The requisition of Simon of Cyrene (Mt 27:32)

> **Verse 32:**   As they were marching out, they came upon a man of Cyrene, Simon by name; this man they compelled to carry his cross.

This verse serves as a transition between the Roman trial and the mocking by the soldiers on the one hand, and the crucifixion scene on the other. The added expression, 'As they were marching out', picks up the action initiated in Mt 27:31, 'and led him away to crucify him'. 'As they were marching out (of the city)' is related to Mt 21:39, 'they took him and cast him out of the vineyard and killed him', which is the Matthean rewriting of Mk 12:8, 'And they took him and killed him, and cast him out of the vineyard'. In Matthew the son is killed after having been cast out of the vineyard, while in Mark he is killed first. Matthew's verse is formulated in close relationship with the passion.

The incident involving Simon of Cyrene is introduced by the phrase 'they came upon a man'. In Mark, on the contrary, there is no introduction whatsoever. Instead of 'a passer-by, Simon of Cyrene', Matthew has 'a man of Cyrene, Simon by name'. He omits 'who was coming in from the country' as well as 'the father of Alexander and Rufus', which he must have considered without importance for his readers. At this point Matthew returns to his source; after adding 'this man', he takes the expression 'they compelled' from the beginning of Mark's verse and joins it to the last phrase 'to carry his cross'. 'They compelled' or 'they pressed into service' (NEB) describes the Roman method of requisitioning (cf. Mt 5:41, 'and if anyone forces you to go one mile [i.e., carrying his luggage], go with him two miles').

The crucifixion (Mt 27:33–38)

Verse 33: And when they came to a place called Golgotha (which means the place of a skull),

'And when they came', instead of 'and they brought him', completes the transition from the place of the Roman trial to the place of execution. The place was most probably called 'the skull' because of the shape of the hill, but a legend said that the skull of Adam was buried there.

Verse 34: they offered him wine to drink, mingled with gall; but when he tasted it, he would not drink it.

What was only implied in Mark's 'they offered' is made explicit by the addition of 'to drink'. The change from 'wine mingled with myrrh' to 'wine mingled with gall' is intended to bring about a closer parallel with Ps 69(68):21, 'They gave me poison (Greek, 'gall') for food', and exemplifies again Matthew's concern with 'fulfilment'. Mark's vague expression, 'he did not take it', is clarified in terms of tasting and drinking.

Verse 35: And when they had crucified him, they divided his garments among them by casting lots;

Jesus was laid down on the crossbeam, his hands were nailed to each end, and then the crossbeam with Jesus attached to it was lifted and fixed to the vertical beam, after which the feet were nailed to the latter.
  Mark had already dealt very soberly with the crucifixion itself, but he still gave it some emphasis by repeating Mk 15:24, 'and they crucified him', in Mk 15:25, 'when they crucified him'. In Matthew there is no such repetition; and in the present verse the reference to the crucifixion is found in a subordinate clause. Thus all the emphasis is on the implicit citation of Ps 22(21):18, 'they divide my garments among them, and for my raiment they cast lots'. The phrases 'for them' and 'to decide what each would take' are apparently considered superfluous and therefore omitted.

Verse 36: then they sat down and kept watch over him there.

Mark's time indication, 'and it was the third hour' (Mk 15:25), is omitted and replaced by a redactional verse which may have a certain importance in Matthew's composition. In Mt 26:58 we were told that Peter 'sat with the guards to see the end'; in Mt 26:69–75 he shows up again in the denial scene. In Mt 27:61 we will read that some women 'were there, sitting opposite the sepulchre'; later in Mt 28:1 the same women 'went to see the sepulchre', and are the first to experience the resurrection joy (Mt 28:8). Similarly, the soldiers 'sat down and kept watch over him there'. Since in the other two cases mentioned those who sit down to watch the subsequent events take part in the further action, we may suppose that the present verse refers to the role of the soldiers ('the centurion *and those who were with him*, keeping watch over Jesus' instead of 'the centurion' in Mk 15:39) at the moment of Jesus' death, where they confess the true identity of the Son of God (Mt 27:54). In connection with Mt 27:62–66 and 28:11–15, the notice may also serve an apologetic purpose. Jesus was really crucified and buried, and his body was not taken away by his disciples. The adverb 'there' stresses the presence of the guards at the crucifixion (cf. Mt 27:55, 61).

Verse 37: And over his head they put the charge against him, which read, 'This is Jesus the King of the Jews.'

To Mark's forthright mention of the content of the inscription, Matthew adds the description of the act of fixing, 'and over his head they put the charge'. The inscription itself is more solemnly formulated. Both the emphatic 'this is' and the name 'Jesus' are typically Matthean additions. The result of these editorial changes is a more solemn statement of the title 'the King of the Jews', betraying Matthew's special concern for the Christological aspects of the passion narrative (cf. Matthew's addition of the title 'Son of God' in Mt 27:40, 43).

Verse 38: Then two robbers were crucified with him, one on the right and one on the left.

In Matthew, as in Mark, this verse informs us that the crucifixion of Jesus was but one of three, which took place at the same time. But Matthew's typical use of 'then' (*tote*) enables him to shift our attention from the crucifixion of Jesus to that of the two 'robbers'. In line with his previous use of the verb, 'crucify' is put in the passive. The mention of the two 'robbers' may be inspired by Isa 53:12, 'and (he) was numbered with the transgressors'.

The mockery (Mt 27:39–44)

Verse 39: And those who passed by derided him, wagging their heads

Following Mark closely, Matthew introduces the mockery scene by a reference to Ps 22(21):7, 'All who see me mock at me, they make mouths at me, they wag their heads'. See also Lam 2:15, 'All who pass along the way clap their hands at you; they hiss and wag their heads at the daughter of Jerusalem'.

> **Verse 40:** and saying, 'You who would destroy the temple and build it in three days, save yourself! If you are the Son of God, come down from the cross.'

The most important addition in the present pericope is the title 'Son of God' here and in Mt 27:43. For Matthew the title expresses Jesus' messianic dignity and his special relationship with the Father.

The addition of this title in the context of a mockery reminds us of two other important passages in this gospel. First, the hearing before the Sanhedrin with its enquiry concerning Jesus' identity, 'tell us if you are the Christ, the Son of God' (Mt 26:63). But, second, the present scene also recalls the temptation scene (Mt 4:1–11), especially the introduction to the first two temptations (Mt 4:3, 6), 'If you are the Son of God'. The devil's challenge to Jesus' power and integrity is echoed in the final words of the present verse, 'If you are the Son of God, come down from the cross'. The use of the title 'Son of God', repeated in Mt 27:43, leads to the climactic proclamation of faith in the 'Son of God' in the confession of the centurion (Mt 27:54).

> **Verses 41–42:** So also the chief priests, with the scribes and elders, mocked him, saying, (42) 'He saved others; he cannot save himself. He is the King of Israel; let him come down now from the cross, and we will believe in him.'

Verse 41 is taken entirely from Mark except for the omission of the ambiguous 'to one another' and the addition of 'and elders' to form Matthew's stereotyped description of Jesus' opponents.

The words pronounced by the Jewish leaders are very similar to those of the passers-by. Matthew reduces Mark's 'Christ, the King of Israel' to the simple 'the King of Israel'. The words become more insulting: '*he is* the King of Israel'. Again Matthew focuses on the issue of faith. As often, also elsewhere in the gospel, he underlines the personal object of belief, 'we will believe *in him*.'

> **Verse 43:** 'He trusts in God; let God deliver him now, if he desires him; for he said, "I am the Son of God." '

This verse is found in Matthew only. The words which Matthew puts on the lips of the Jewish leaders are a quotation from Ps 22(21):8, but its formulation has been influenced by Wis 2:12–20. Ps 22(21):8 reads:

'He committed his cause to the Lord; let him deliver him, let him rescue him, for he delights in him!' Matthew has edited this verse carefully, under the influence in particular of the Book of Wisdom, which practically cites Ps 22(21):8 in Wis 2:18–20, 'for if the righteous man is *God's son*, he will help him, and will deliver him from the hand of his adversaries. Let us test him with insult and torture, that we may find out how gentle he is, and make trial of his forbearance. Let us condemn him to a *shameful death*, for according to what he says, he will be protected.'

Though its vocabulary is rather different, this Wisdom passage shares several themes with the mocking scene, especially that of the testing and mocking of the righteous man and the ironic reference to his claim that God will protect him. The addition of the adverb 'now' to the quotation heightens the mocking effect and promotes the blending of the text with its setting in the passion narrative. The final words, 'for he said, "I am the Son of God" ', once again refer to the hearing before the Sanhedrin and express the real issue of the passion: Jesus' self-affirmation as Son of God and the importance of confessing one's faith in him (cf. Mt 27:40).

> **Verse 44:** And the robbers who were crucified with him also reviled him in the same way.

Matthew follows Mark very closely. As usual, he identifies the subject, changing 'those' into 'the robbers'. He adds that they insult Jesus 'in the same way' as the previous two groups, the passers-by and the Jewish leaders, whose taunts were very similar. Thus Matthew again fills in a lacuna of Mark's text. As in Mark, the phrase 'reviled' reminds us of Ps 69(68):9, 'and the insults of those who insult (=revile) you have fallen on me', where the same word is used in Greek.

Summing up, we may say that Mt 27:32–44 is more theologically charged than Mk 15:21–32, especially by its insistence on the Son of God title and the theme of belief in Jesus as the Son of God (Mt 27:40, 43).

The darkness (Mt 27:45–49)

> **Verse 45:** Now from the sixth hour there was darkness over all the land until the ninth hour.

Matthew emphasizes the duration of the darkness: 'from . . . until'. He also changes Mark's 'the whole land' into 'all the land'. Mk 15:33 already showed some similarity to Ex 10:22, 'and there was thick darkness in *all the land* of Egypt three days'. Matthew may have intended a closer parallel by changing 'whole' into 'all'. The plague of darkness in Ex 10:22 makes one think of God's initiative and judgment, which are also very prominent in the crucifixion scene. This does not, of course, exclude a reference to the Day of Yahweh suggested by Amos 8:9, ' "And on that day", says the Lord, "I will make the sun go down at noon, and darken the earth in broad daylight" '.

> **Verse 46:** And about the ninth hour Jesus cried with a loud
> voice, 'Eli, Eli, lama sabachthani?' that is, 'My God, my God,
> why have you forsaken me?'

Matthew changes Mark's precise time indication 'at the ninth hour' into the vaguer 'about the ninth hour'. He emphasizes the phrase 'cried' (in Greek, *aneboēsen* instead of Mark's *eboēsen*) by using a compound verb which in the Old Testament frequently expresses a loud shout of prayer or anguish, as e.g., Ez 11:13, 'Then I fell down upon my face, *and cried with a loud voice*, and said, "Ah Lord God! will you make a full end of the remnant of Israel?" ' (see also Gen 27:34; I Sam 28:12; Isa 36:13).

Matthew's more Hebraized version *Ēli* provides a better explanation than Mark's *Elōi* for the confusion with the name Elijah found in the following verse. Both Mark and Matthew provide a Greek translation, but the original citation as well as the translation differ in the two versions.

In most attempts at an explanation of this quotation the role of the entire content and meaning of Ps 22(21) is emphasized. But whatever interpretation is given to this citation, justice should be done to the theme of abandonment and dereliction expressed in it. This theme belongs to the Old Testament theology of the 'just man' who is tested by God to the point of abandonment, but goes on trusting in God who is faithful and will ultimately deliver him. Pss 22(21) and 69(68) are typical expressions of this theology.

> **Verse 47:** And some of the bystanders hearing it said, 'This
> man is calling Elijah.'

Matthew follows Mark closely, but the scornful character of the words is emphasized by the phrase, 'this man' (*houtos*), which stands in stark contrast with Mt 27:54, 'Truly this (*houtos*) was the Son of God'. Elijah is closely associated with the Messiah. Mark and Matthew identify John the Baptist with the role of Elijah (cf. Mt 11:14; 17:13). Here Elijah is referred to as coming to the rescue of the just in need.

> **Verses 48–49:** And one of them at once ran and took a
> sponge, filled it with vinegar, and put it on a reed, and gave it
> to him to drink. (49) But the others said, 'Wait, let us see
> whether Elijah will come to save him.'

Contrary to what might be thought at first glance, there is little substantial difference between Mk 15:35–36 and Mt 27:48–49. Matthew's changes apparently seek to clarify the movement of the action by describing the respective roles more clearly: 'some of the bystanders' (Mt 27:47) – 'one of them' (Mt 27:48) – 'the others', i.e., the rest of the bystanders (Mt 27:49).

Mt 27:48 contains another allusion to Ps 69(68):21, 'They gave me poison (gall) for food, and for my thirst they gave me vinegar to drink'. The first part of the verse was used in Mt 27:34. Now Matthew uses the second half. Through Matthew's editorial activity the words of the rest of the bystanders become clear (in Mk 15:36 the man offering the vinegar seems to be talking to himself!): 'Do not give him the sour vinegar – let us see whether Elijah will come to save him instead'.

It should still be noted that Mark's 'to take him down' is changed into 'to save him'. The change may be due to the influence of Ps 22(21) where the idea of 'saving' is repeatedly expressed in the Greek text in verses 2, 6, 9, 22, translated in RSV by different words in verses 1 ('helping'), 5 ('saved'), 8 ('rescue') and 21 ('save'). Mt 27:50–54 will describe the end of Jesus' suffering and God's saving intervention expressed in the cosmic signs and the confession of the centurion and the soldiers, which counter the unbelief of the Jews.

The death of Jesus and its repercussions (Mt 27:50–54)

Verse 50: And Jesus cried again with a loud voice and yielded up his spirit.

By adding 'again', contrary to his usual practice, Matthew places the cry in meaningful relationship with Mt 27:46, where Jesus' first cry is mentioned. Thus he indicates that this second cry is also related to the dramatic prayer of Ps 22(21):1. Mark's 'uttered a loud cry' is changed into '*cried* with a loud voice (*kraxas*)', the word used three times in Ps 22(21) to indicate the cry of the just man (Greek text, verses 3, 6, 25; RSV verses 2, 5, 24). The inarticulate cry, therefore, seems to be interpreted as another prayer to the Father for deliverance.

In place of Mark's 'he breathed his last', Matthew has 'he yielded up his spirit', thus stressing the voluntary character of Jesus' death. Jesus does not simply expire but gives up his spirit as an act of voluntary and active surrender of his life to God. This emphasis on the voluntary character of Jesus' death is in tune with the whole of Matthew's passion narrative, which repeatedly emphasizes Jesus' knowledge of what is going to happen, the divine will, and Jesus' intimate relation to the Father as obedient Son. This is also expressed in Mt 26:52–54, a text found in Matthew only, especially Mt 26:54, 'But how then should the scriptures be fulfilled, that it must be so?'

While in Mk 15:37, Jesus' cry may leave some room for discussion, Mt 27:50 clearly understands it as a dramatic prayer of victory.

> **Verse 51a:** And behold, the curtain of the temple was torn in two, from top to bottom;

The verse is taken from Mark, except for the addition of 'behold' which introduces the effects of Jesus' death more dramatically. We discussed the different opinions about the meaning of this incident under Mk 15:38. As far as Matthew is concerned, we should note that the rending of the Temple curtain is no longer an isolated sign as in Mark but becomes part of a series of cosmic events. But notwithstanding this development – especially the sign of the raising of the 'holy ones' – the basic meaning of the rending of the Temple curtain remains the same as in Mark: the death of Jesus brings to an end the Old Testament dispensation and opens the way to salvation to all peoples.

> **Verses 51b–53:** and the earth shook, and the rocks were split; (52) the tombs also were opened, and many bodies of the saints who had fallen asleep were raised, (53) and coming out of the tombs after his resurrection they went into the holy city and appeared to many.

To the rending of the Temple curtain (compare Mt 27:51a and Mk 15:38) Matthew adds a series of events surrounding the death of Jesus. While some scholars maintain that Matthew depended on a written source which he thoroughly reworked and fitted into the crucifixion account adapted from Mark, others think that Matthew himself constructed the passage by drawing upon the apocalyptic motif of a resurrection as part of the coming messianic age. The latter point out that a rich fund of imagery – earthquake, splitting of rocks, opening of tombs, resurrection of those who sleep in death, and victorious return to the holy city – was available through biblical and intertestamental texts and traditions inspired by Ez 37.

Whereas the word 'earth' occurs often in Matthew, Mt 27:51b is the only instance where it is found in the sense of the earth's surface. Mt 27:51b is the only instance in the New Testament where 'earth' is the subject of 'shake' (but see Heb 12:26, a free translation of Hag 2:6, for the combination of 'earth' and 'shake'). The frequent use of 'earth' in the Book of Revelation suggests that it belongs to the established vocabulary of Jewish apocalyptic.

In the Old Testament the earthquake – as well as the other signs mentioned – is considered not only as a sign of the last day, but as an indication of theophany. We are especially reminded of Joel 3:15–16 (Hebrew, 4:15–16), 'The sun and the moon are darkened, and the stars withdraw their shining. And the Lord roars from Zion, and utters his voice from Jerusalem, and the heavens and the earth shake.' Note the combination of darkness, loud cry and earthquake as here in the passion narrative. In post-exilic texts there are also instances where earthquake is understood as a sign of salvation. The prophet Haggai proclaims that God 'will shake the heavens and the earth and the sea and the dry land' (Hag 2:6) as sign of his new salvific action in which he will fill the Temple with new splendour and install Zerubbabel as his anointed (Hag 2:21). In rabbinical and apocryphal literature, God uses earthquakes and other natural phenomena to realize his final, irrevocable coming.

While in Mt 24:7, taken over from Mk 13:8, the earthquake is probably to be understood as a sign of the return of Christ and the end of the world (see Mt 24:3), in all other passages, which all stem from Matthew's special material or from his redaction, the earthquake is a sign of God's presence (Mt 8:24; 21:10; 28:2, 4 all contain the word *seismos* or the related verb *seisthai*). The earthquake at Jesus' death should be interpreted in this latter sense. In this connection it has been pointed out that Matthew altered his empty tomb narrative, especially Mt 28:2–5, to co-ordinate it with the eschatological flavour of his death-scene.

Beside its ordinary use, the verb 'to split' occurs in the Old Testament in very meaningful contexts. Through Moses God 'splits' (RSV: 'divides') the water to free his people from Egypt (Ex 14:61, 21). The verb is also found in prophetic announcements of God's future intervention. Second Isaiah promises the exiles that God will again make water flow in the desert (Isa 48:21, '. . . he cleft the rock and the water gushed out'). Divine action is repeatedly associated with the splitting of rocks. See, e.g. Nahum 1:5–6, 'The mountains quake before him . . . and the rocks are broken asunder by him'. Note the combination of earthquake and splitting of rocks in an eschatological setting. In *Testament of Levi* 4:1 the splitting of the rocks is one of the cosmic events which signal the expected change of the times. In all these texts, as well as in Mt 27:51b, the splitting of the rocks is understood as a powerful act of God.

As a result of the earthquake, 'the rocks were split', which, in turn, prepares for the opening of the tombs. The rending of the Temple curtain and the splitting of the rocks constitutes a transition from the earthquake to the opening of the tombs.

Except for Ps 5:9, where the expression is used metaphorically, the combination of the words 'open' and 'tombs' is in the Old Testament found only in Ez 37:12f. As in the Old Testament and the Book of Revelation, the verb 'to open' represents for Matthew a motif of theophany, especially where it is found in a theological passive form suggesting divine activity.

In the Septuagint the word 'many', applied to persons, appears often in the context of God's saving activity, while in the New Testament it characterizes the circle of those who are affected by Jesus' saving work (e.g., Mt 20:28; 22:14; 26:28). The twofold appearance of the term in the present text may suggest that the related events are explicitly placed in the context of God's saving activity. As elsewhere in the Bible, 'body' refers here not to a part of a human being but to the whole person.

The plural 'saints' occurs relatively seldom in the Old Testament. In the Psalms it refers to the saints of Israel (Ps 34[33]:9). In Dan 7:21f., 25 it is used as a synonym for 'faithful'. The rabbis call people who keep God's commandments, especially the pious of the Old Testament, 'saints'. In apocalyptic literature the term has an eschatological connotation. Here in Mt 27:52 'saints' most probably refers to prominent figures of the Old Testament and may also point to the eschatological character of the events mentioned in connection with the saints.

Faith in the resurrection imposes itself only slowly in the Old Testament writings. Especially in post-exilic times the growing understanding of the limitlessness of God's power led to faith in the full restoration of human beings after death. Older texts, like Hos 6:1–3 and Ez 37:1–14, use the resurrection terminology in a metaphorical sense as an image for the renewal of Israel. Many commentators consider Dan 12:2 the first explicit statement of faith in an individual resurrection. Fully developed presentations of the resurrection of the dead appear first in the inter-testamental period. These presentations are unanimous in affirming that God raises the dead to a life in bodily form, but the descriptions of this body vary considerably. Resurrection is an act and gift of God, the Lord over life and death. It is a demonstration of his faithfulness. The risen life is a fully human life in all dimensions of existence: in bodiliness, as a member of God's people, in communion with God. The resurrection of the dead also means the inauguration of the final consummation, God's eschatological saving act by excellence.

The verb 'to go into' is often used in the Old Testament in theologically meaningful contexts. To go into the sanctuary, into the Temple is a technical term for the cultic service of priests. In Ex 14:22 the crossing of the Reed Sea is described as a going into the sea. The most interesting passages, however, are those in which the verb is combined with 'land'. In Deuteronomy, 'going into the land' is praised as an exquisite gift of God, in which Israel can be itself as a people before God. The land belongs to the foundations of Israel's faith. No wonder then that Ezekiel's promise of a bright future for Israel reaches its climax in the announcement that God will prove himself as 'Yahweh' by letting his people go again into the land: 'Thus says the Lord God: Behold, I will open your graves, and raise you from your graves, O my people; and I will bring you home into the land of Israel. And you shall know that I am the Lord, when I open your graves, and raise you from your graves, O my people. And I will put my Spirit within you, and you shall live, and I will place you in your own land; then you shall know that I, the Lord, have spoken, and I have done it, says the Lord' (Ez 37:12–14). To go into the land means, therefore, to enter into the fullness of salvation which God offers to his people. Similarly in the New Testament, and especially in Matthew, the verb is most of the time used for entering into the kingdom of God (e.g., Mt 5:20; 7:21; 18:3) or entering into life (Mt 18:8f.; 19:17).

In Mt 27:53 the verb 'to go into' is combined with 'the holy city'. In the Old Testament 'the holy city' is Jerusalem, the place God has chosen to cause his name to dwell there. Because of the unfaithfulness of its citizens there are constant prophetic declarations of judgment on the city, but throughout there remains a confident expectation of a new and better Jerusalem. This new Jerusalem is already prepared in heaven and will come down from there to earth at the beginning of the endtime. In rabbinical literature the new Jerusalem will be the capital of the messianic kingdom. The resurrection of the dead will take place in Jerusalem. The New Testament too speaks of Jerusalem as the 'holy city' (Mt 4:5; 27:53), The expression is also used for the heavenly Jerusalem (Heb 11:10, 16; 12:22; 13:14; Rev 3:12; 21:2, 10; 22:19). From these texts it is clear that Matthew cannot mean that those who were raised entered the earthly Jerusalem, but the heavenly Jerusalem, the new centre of the new people of God, the fullness of life of their God.

It is obvious that Mt 27:51b–53 is not a record of an actual incident. In fact, the phrase 'after his resurrection' takes the description out of the chronological sequence of the passion narrative. If all this were taken literally we would have to account, for instance, for the fact that the dead rise at the moment of Jesus' death and start walking after his resurrection, i.e., three days later! Did they wait in their tombs or did they hide somewhere outside Jerusalem? This and other difficulties disappear when one considers these signs as Matthew intended them, i.e., as theological affirmations formulated by means of Old Testament materials and traditional apocalyptic imagery and aimed at bringing out the meaning of Jesus' death.

The whole ensemble refers to the time of the consummation of God's saving activity, ushered in by the death of Jesus. The rending of the Temple curtain means the end of the old order and the beginning of the new. The raising of the saints, i.e., the holy ones of the Old Testament, like Abraham, Moses and David, means that the hopes of the just of the Old Testament are fulfilled through Jesus' death. But Matthew safeguards the priority of Jesus' resurrection by adding the phrase 'after his resurrection'. There does not seem to be any cogent reason for attributing this phrase to a post-Matthew insertion as some have tried to do. In brief, the resurrection of the saints described in Mt 27:52–53 is a proclamation of Christian faith in Jesus' death as a victory over death.

In the death and resurrection of Jesus God is manifested as acting on behalf of humanity, saving it totally from death, forming a new people and offering a new beginning in salvation history and inviting this community to confess its Lord (most of these themes reflecting a christianized version of Ezekiel 37). Thus the end-time has begun in Jesus and one encounters in his personal history, especially his death and resurrection, the saving Lord. As R[iedl] notes, OT 'theophany has now become christophany' (p. 78), without, however, erasing the distinctions between Father and Son maintained throughout the Gospel of Matthew.[7]

Verse 54: When the centurion and those who were with him, keeping watch over Jesus, saw the earthquake and what took place, they were filled with awe, and said, 'Truly this was the Son of God!'

The preceding 'mute' events are given voice in the confession of the centurion and the soldiers who were with him. In fact, Matthew extends the reaction of the centurion to all those who kept watch over Jesus, thus heightening the effect of the action. They were already mentioned in Mt 27:36, where 'they sat down and kept watch over him there'. Now they play their part in the final stages of the drama.

Matthew changes 'when (he) saw that he thus breathed his last' into 'when (they) saw the earthquake and what took place'. The clause is probably to be understood as an explicitation of Mark's 'thus', since it effectively relates Matthew's interpolation, Mt 27:51b–53, beginning with an earthquake and continued in a series of happenings (*ta genomena*), to the rest of the context.

Matthew also adds that 'they were filled with awe', a phrase denoting people's reaction to a manifestation of divine power (cf. Mt 9:8; 17:6). The divine power manifested in the signs which mark Jesus' death with approval leads to a solemn confession of faith on the part of the centurion and those who were with him.

Their confession, 'Truly this was the Son of God', is the most important statement of the passion narrative. Mark's 'this man' is simplified to 'this' (*houtos*) and constitutes a strong contrast with the previous words of mockery (cf. Mt 26:61; 27:37, 47). The confession, already found in Mark where the Christological title 'Son of God' is used for the first time in the passion narrative in Mk 15:39, is enhanced by the emphasis on the Son of God title in this section of Matthew's passion narrative (Mt 27:40, 43). Thus, while in Mark the title appears as a kind of revelation, in Matthew it is rather a confirmation of Jesus' identity. In fact, the present confession is formulated in almost exactly the same terms as the confession of the disciples in Mt 14:33, 'Truly you are the Son of God', at the end of a scene which contains several features paralleled in our present text (divine manifestation, reaction of fear, confession of faith).

The centurion and his soldiers act as mouthpieces for the Christian community, and confess their faith in the Son of God. Already at a much earlier stage of the gospel a centurion had expressed his faith in Jesus and was addressed by him, 'Truly, I say to you, not even in Israel have I found such faith. I tell you, many will come from east and west and sit at table with Abraham, Isaac, and Jacob in the kingdom of heaven, while the sons of the kingdom will be thrown into the outer darkness' (Mt 8:10–12). Here again it is a centurion, a Gentile, who expresses his faith. All the others reject Jesus; he and his companions are the only ones to confess their faith in him. Thus the promise for the Gentiles is reaffirmed above the rejection of Israel. The kingdom will be taken away from Israel and given to a new nation called from the Gentiles producing the fruits of it (cf. Mt 21:43). Matthew's account is marked by a strongly ecclesial and doctrinal orientation.

The mention of the women (Mt 27:55–56)

> **Verses 55–56:** There were also many women there, looking on from afar, who had followed Jesus from Galilee, ministering to him; (56) among whom were Mary Magdalene, and Mary the mother of James and Joseph, and the mother of the sons of Zebedee.

Matthew's formulation of these verses is simpler but more compact than Mark's. Mk 15:40a and Mt 27:55a are the same except for Matthew's addition of 'there' (cf. Mt 27:36), and the conflation of the 'women' mentioned here and the '*many* other women' in Mk 15:41b. Mark's final clause 'who came up with him to Jerusalem' is, as such, omitted, but its substance is found in the added 'here', i.e., in Jerusalem, and 'from Galilee', indicating from where they 'came up'. As usual, Matthew identifies 'Jesus' instead of writing 'him'. While we hesitated to describe Mark's reference to 'following and ministering' as an intended 'definition' of discipleship, it seems that Matthew has real discipleship in mind and describes it as following Jesus from Galilee to Jerusalem.

While Mary Magdalene appears in both Mark and Matthew as the first in the list of three women, the other two are referred to in a somewhat different way. Matthew omits 'the younger' which Mark may have included to distinguish this James from James the son of Zebedee. He also uses 'Joseph' instead of the alternative spelling 'Joses', and seems to identify Salome with the mother of the sons of Zebedee.

Matthew's crucifixion narrative ends with this reference to the faithful presence of these women. Together with the confession of the centurion and his companions the presence of the women expresses faith in the Son of God.

Summing up, we can say that in this section again Matthew remains consistent with his particular treatment of the traditional material, while his special material emphasizes the same tendencies:

(1)   He heightens the Christological impact of this section by his insistence on the title Son of God (cf. Mt 27:40, 43, 54, against Mk 15:39 only). He also insists on belief in the Son of God.

(2)   His presentation is also markedly ecclesial: Jesus' death constitutes the end of the old dispensation and the beginning of the new people of God (Mt 27:51–54).

(3)   Once again Matthew also emphasizes the implacable opposition of the Jewish leaders and their responsibility for Jesus' death (Mt 27:39–43).

III. Luke 23:26–49

Luke's treatment of this sequence is highly characteristic. It can be divided into the following scenes:
(1)   The requisition of Simon of Cyrene (Lk 23:26);
(2)   The multitude and the women of Jerusalem (Lk 23:27–32);
(3)   The crucifixion (Lk 23:33–34);
(4)   The mockery (Lk 23:35–38);
(5)   The two criminals (Lk 23:39–43);
(6)   The darkness and rending of the Temple curtain (Lk 23:44–45);
(7)   The death of Jesus and its repercussions (Lk 23:46–48);
(8)   The mention of the acquaintances and women (Lk 23:49).

The requisition of Simon of Cyrene (Lk 23:26)

Verse 26: And as they led him away, they seized one Simon of Cyrene, who was coming in from the country, and laid on him the cross, to carry it behind Jesus.

This verse is clearly derived from Mk 15:20b–21, 'And they led him out to crucify him. And they compelled a passer-by. . . .' Since Luke has omitted the mocking scene (cf. Mk 15:16–20), the present verse follows immediately after the concluding words of the Roman trial, 'but Jesus he delivered up to their will' (Lk 23:25), i.e., the will of the Jewish leaders. The same people seem to lead Jesus away, although Luke refers to the presence of soldiers in Lk 23:36, 47. The overall impression is that Luke is suggesting that the Jewish leaders crucified Jesus.

Luke omits the detail 'the father of Alexander and Rufus', which probably made sense only to Mark's readers. The clause '(they) laid on him the cross, to carry it behind Jesus' presents Simon of Cyrene as the model of the Christian disciple, and consciously refers to Lk 14:27, 'Whoever does not bear his own cross and come after me, cannot be my disciple', and Lk 9:23, 'If any man would come after me, let him deny himself and take up his cross daily and follow me'. Discipleship seems to be described here as willingness to identify with Jesus.

The multitude and the women of Jerusalem (Lk 23:27–32)

This passage is peculiar to Luke. After mentioning Simon of Cyrene, Luke amplifies the picture: a large crowd and mourning women also followed Jesus. Luke is fond of crowds and their devotion. At the same time this Lucan passage emphasizes the guilt of Jerusalem. Luke shows a special interest in the fate of Jerusalem and its interpretation.

Verse 27: And there followed him a great multitude of the people, and of women who bewailed and lamented him.

The great multitude seems to be distinguished from the women. Luke repeatedly singles out women for special mention. Just as Luke mentions the presence of a multitude at the beginning of the way to the cross, so he will again add a reference to 'all the multitudes who assembled to see the sight' in Lk 23:48. Thus it is suggested that these events take place in the presence of a great anonymous crowd which eventually also included Gentiles. The sympathy of the multitude with Jesus is expressed three times in Luke's report of the crucifixion (Lk 23:27, 35, 48), while Jesus' opponents are specified as the rulers (Lk 23:35), the Roman soldiers (Lk 23:36), and one of the criminals (Lk 23:39).

Deut 21:22f. forbade a public lamentation for anyone who was executed. Yet Jesus was lamented. The women who mourned over him bore courageous witness that Jesus was no criminal (though he allowed himself to be reckoned among criminals, Lk 22:37), in other words, that he was innocent. The scene, especially the mourning and the separate mention of the women, may have been suggested by Zech 12:11–14, 'On that day the mourning in Jerusalem will be as great as the mourning for Hadadrimmon in the plain of Megiddo. The land shall mourn, each family by itself; the family of the house of David by itself, and their wives by themselves. . . .' The phrase 'and their wives by themselves' is mentioned five times in the whole passage.

Verse 28: But Jesus turning to them said, 'Daughters of Jerusalem, do not weep for me, but weep for yourselves and for your children.'

Moved by the thought of the sufferings which lay ahead of them, Jesus, the merciful and compassionate Messiah, even as he goes out to execution, does not think of himself but of them. The phrase 'daughters of Jerusalem (Zion)' is found in Isa 3:16 as part of a threat to the women of Jerusalem.

> **Verses 29–30:** 'For behold the days are coming when they will say, "Blessed are the barren, and the wombs that never bore, and the breasts that never gave suck!" (30) Then they will begin to say to the mountains, "Fall on us"; and to the hills, "Cover us." '

This 'speech' takes up some expressions from the Old Testament and from the gospel. The beginning of verse 29 reminds us of Jesus' words spoken when he drew near the city (Lk 19:41), 'For the days shall come upon you . . .' (Lk 19:43), and may also echo Amos 4:2, 'behold the days are coming upon you, when they shall take you away with hooks'. 'Blessed are the barren, . . . and the breasts that never gave suck' clearly resembles a passage of Luke's apocalyptic discourse, 'Alas for those who are with child and for those who give suck in those days!' (Lk 21:23). To Jewish women barrenness was a disgrace, but in the coming disasters it will be considered a blessing. The childless women will pray for deliverance from these disasters by a violent death, but at least they will not see their children suffer.

Verse 30 practically quotes Hos 10:8, 'and they shall say to the mountains, Cover us, and to the hills, Fall on us'. In the same context Hosea speaks of Israel's critical situation of being without a king (Hos 10:3). Does Luke intend this to reflect his understanding of Israel's situation now (cf. Lk 23:37, 'If you are the King of the Jews')? In contrast to, e.g., Lk 4:16–21, where a prophetic statement is described as having been fulfilled 'today', the present verse implies that the prophecy of Hosea still remains to be fulfilled. What happens at the crucifixion does not yet constitute the final judgment. But the quotation from Hosea makes clear that Jesus' death is closely connected with the last day.

> **Verse 31:** 'For if they do this when the wood is green, what will happen when it is dry?'

The translation of NAB expresses more clearly the contrast between two different kinds of wood, not the same wood at two different moments: 'If they do these things in the green wood, what will happen in the dry?', i.e., If the green wood (=the innocent Jesus) suffers so, what will happen to the dry (=the guilty Jews)? The text can be compared with Ez 20:47 (Greek text = Ez 21:3 in the Hebrew text): 'Behold, I will kindle a fire in you, and it shall devour every green tree in you and every dry tree'. In the phrase 'if they do this', the word 'they' is best understood as referring to God. The meaning of the verse then is: 'If God permits this to happen to one who is innocent, what will happen to the guilty?' For indeed, the fire of God's judgment is paradoxically ignited on the green and not on the dry wood, that is to say on Jesus, in whose passion and death judgment has already begun. The whole passage, therefore, is a call to repentance.

> **Verse 32:** Two others also, who were criminals, were led away to be put to death with him.

Already here, much earlier than in Mark and Matthew, where the robbers appear rather abruptly, Luke tells us that there were two criminals with Jesus. A literal translation of the verse reads: 'And two other criminals, who were led away to be finished off'. While Mark and Matthew speak of 'robbers' (*leistai*), Luke speaks repeatedly of 'criminals' (*kakourgoi*, Lk 23:32, 33, 39). According to recent research, the term 'criminals' seems to have its situation in life in the Christian communities in the Roman empire after the fall of Jerusalem (A.D. 70), in which some Christians called Jews who took up arms against the Romans 'criminals to be finished off', even if these Jews happened to be fellow-Christians. Luke's use of the term 'criminal' should be understood in relation to Lk 22:35–38, the concluding conversation of Luke's farewell discourse, in which Jesus is quoted as telling some people to sell their mantle and buy a sword. To this the disciples answer that they have *two* swords (certainly related to the *two* 'criminals'). In this context Jesus is said to apply to himself the text of Isa 53:12, 'he was numbered with the transgressors' (*anomoi*, literally, 'lawless').

We cannot discuss this matter in detail here, but apparently Lk 22:35–38, which is a Lucan composition, is addressed as a warning to contemporary Roman Christians not to condemn Jewish Christians (the poor among them) for their participation in the armed struggle against the Romans, because Jesus is on the side of these people who have no other choice, or, in other words, that Jesus died *with* and *for* them. The use of the term 'criminal' instead of 'robber' is related to the same situation in life.

The crucifixion (Lk 23:33–34)

> **Verse 33:** And when they came to the place which is called The Skull, there they crucified him, and the criminals, one on the right and one on the left.

This verse is a combination of Mk 15:22, 24a, 27. Luke omits the Aramaic name 'Golgotha', the statement that the sour vinegar wine was rejected by Jesus, and the reference to the time of the crucifixion (cf. Mk 15:25, 'it was the third hour'). He changes 'robbers' into 'criminals'. Being crucified in between the two other 'criminals', Jesus almost appears as their leader! At any rate, the description accords with Isa 53:12, 'he was numbered with the transgressors', quoted almost literally in Lk 22:37, 'And he was reckoned with transgressors'.

> **Verse 34:** And Jesus said, 'Father, forgive them; for they know not what they do.' And they cast lots to divide his garments.

This prayer is peculiar to Luke. It is omitted by Codex Vaticanus and other important manuscripts, but it is well attested by other manuscripts, and most modern textual critics accept it as genuine.

Some scholars take this prayer for forgiveness to refer to the Roman soldiers or to all who were responsible for the crucifixion. In the light of Acts 3:17, 19 and Acts 7:59–60, the prayer of Stephen which is surely intended as a parallel, it is probable that Luke himself understood it as a prayer for forgiveness for the Jews. To the contemplating disciple Jesus gives an example of forgiveness, final accomplishment of his precept of love on which Luke has particularly insisted (Lk 6:27–36; 17:3). Jesus' prayer is in harmony with the spirit of Luke's gospel and his picture of Jesus, and it exemplifies the statement of Isa 53:12 that the servant 'made intercession for the transgressors'. The first martyr, Stephen, will generously follow this example (Acts 7:60). In fact, Stephen's trial and death are closely parallel to those of Jesus in Luke's gospel; but there are also important differences.

Luke follows Mark in quoting Ps 22(21):18, 'they divide my garments among them, and for my raiment they cast lots'. On his journey to Jerusalem (Lk 9:51 – 19:27) Jesus had often laid stress on poverty. Now everything is taken from him.

The mockery (Lk 23:35–38)

> **Verse 35:** And the people stood by, watching; but the rulers scoffed at him, saying, 'He saved others; let him save himself, if he is the Christ of God, his Chosen One!'

In this and the following verse, Luke divides the onlookers into three categories: (1) 'The people' stood there without taking part in mocking Jesus. They were watching. (2) 'The rulers', i.e., the members of the Sanhedrin, the Jewish leaders engaged in the mocking. (3) 'The soldiers' also mocked Jesus (cf. Lk 23:36). Since Luke did not mention the accusation about the destruction of the Temple, the corresponding mockery is also omitted and Luke immediately quotes the words, 'He saved others . . .'.

The words used in the mocking sum up all that is contained in Jesus' different titles, 'Saviour', 'God's Anointed', 'Messiah', 'Chosen One of God'. If Jesus were all that these titles claimed, he must demonstrate the power they express here and now and save himself. The formulation of the mocking is reminiscent of Wis 2:17–20 and Ps 22(21):7–8. Some of the words are also similar to the temptation in the desert: 'If you are the Son of God . . .' (Lk 4:3, 9). There they stand at the beginning of Jesus' public ministry; now they mark the end of Jesus' earthly journey. Jesus had to make a final, definitive choice between demonstrating his power or surrendering himself in complete obedience to God.

> **Verses 36–37:** The soldiers also mocked him, coming up and offering him vinegar, (37) and saying, 'If you are the King of the Jews, save yourself!'

Luke adds here that the soldiers also mocked Jesus. The mocking is not positively designated as Jewish, but it is not designated as Roman either. Using the detail about the vinegar, which comes later in Mark and Matthew (cf. Mk 15:36; Mt 27:48), he composes his picture of the scene. The change from Mark's 'wine mingled with myrrh' to 'vinegar' is probably due to Ps 69(68):21. The offer of vinegar is here, in keeping with Ps 69(68):21, explicitly designated as part of the mocking.

While until now Luke has used the title 'King of the Jews' only once (Lk 23:3; compare Mk 15:2, 9, 12, 18), now he uses it twice in two consecutive verses, Lk 23:37, 38. The title is therefore clearly emphasized in this passage.

> **Verse 38:** There was also an inscription over him, 'This is the King of the Jews.'

The inscription attached to the cross is the climax of this mockery. The addition of 'this' (*houtos*) enhances the irony of the description. Compared to Mark's 'The King of the Jews', Lk 23:38 reads literally, 'The King of the Jews (is) this', making the statement more emphatic. By this inscription Pilate is made to proclaim that Jesus dies as the King of the Jews, or Messiah. In fact, Jesus was never more King than on the cross.

The two criminals (Lk 23:39–43)

Except for the notice that two criminals/robbers were crucified with Jesus this passage is proper to Luke.

Verse 39: One of the criminals who were hanged railed at him, saying, 'Are you not the Christ? Save yourself and us!'

While Mark stated that 'those who were crucified with him also reviled him' (Mk 15:32b), Luke says that only one did so. He shares the other mockers' misunderstanding: Jesus cannot save himself *and* them. If the Christ is to save the lost (cf. Lk 19:10), he has to give himself up. Luke says also that they were 'hanged', which may be a reference to Deut 21:23, 'for a hanged man is accursed by God', where exactly the same Greek word is used.

Verses 40–41: But the other rebuked him, saying, 'Do you not fear God, since you are under the same sentence of condemnation? (41) And we indeed justly; for we are receiving the due reward for our deeds; but this man has done nothing wrong.'

The other 'criminal' is made to express Luke's theology. Again Jesus' solidarity with these 'criminals' is stressed: he is 'under the same sentence of condemnation'. The 'criminal' goes on to say that he and his companion are punished justly. Not so Jesus: 'but this man has done nothing wrong'. 'This man' (*houtos*) may echo the inscription of Lk 23:38. Thus one of the 'criminals' confesses Jesus' innocence. Though innocent, Jesus was 'numbered with the transgressors; yet he bore the sin of many, and made intercession for the transgressors' (Isa 53:12).

Verse 42: And he said, 'Jesus, remember me when you come in your kingly power.'

Turning to Jesus, he said repeatedly (this is the force of the imperfect tense): 'Jesus, remember me when you come with kingly power'. This translation, which refers more clearly to the parousia, is to be preferred to the RSV translation, since it accords better with Luke's tendency not to identify the kingdom geographically. According to Lk 17:21, 'the kingdom of God is in the midst of you', or 'within you'.

Verse 43: And he said to him, 'Truly, I say to you, today you will be with me in Paradise'.

Jesus assures the 'criminal' that his prayer will be answered more promptly than he could ever have dreamed. All three parts of the answer are important, but the phrase 'today' carries most of the weight. Sharing prevalent Jewish notions, the 'criminal' thinks of a world to come, and asks Jesus to remember him at that later date. In place of this futuristic hope Jesus substitutes a present happiness: The 'criminal' will be blessed today! This mention of 'today' is the last of a whole series: 'for to you is born this day in the city of David a Saviour, who is Christ the Lord' (Lk 2:11); 'Today this scripture has been fulfilled in your hearing' (Lk 4:21); 'Today salvation has come to this house' (Lk 19:9). The eschatological time of salvation is 'today'; it is 'now', but at the same time it is also still future. This statement responds to the expectation of *future* salvation with salvation that is experienced *today*. With the advent of Jesus a new time has begun. Salvation is not linked exclusively with the resurrection but with the entire Jesus event.

The 'criminal' will be with Jesus 'in Paradise'. Jewish belief in an afterlife had evolved so that the lot of individuals after death had become clearer. Paradise, a Persian word meaning 'garden' or 'park', is used in the Septuagint to render 'the garden of Eden' (Gen 2:8). It reflects the imagery of Jewish apocalyptic and rabbinic writings, and occurs also in the New Testament, e.g., in the story of the Rich Man and Lazarus (Lk 16:19–31). In the *Testament of Levi* 18:10 it is used for the place reserved after death for the just. When Jesus speaks of Paradise, he implicitly alludes to his resurrection and subsequent glory.

'You will be with me.' In both the Old and New Testaments, the essence of happiness is being with God. After Jesus' resurrection the just are with him from the moment of death, though we cannot say where or under what conditions this mysterious experience takes place. By juxtaposing two phrases, one mythical ('in Paradise') and one existential ('with me'), Luke has interpreted his mythical language.

It should be pointed out that Lk 23:39–43 is similar to other Lucan stories about forgiveness for people who repent (cf. Lk 7:36–50; 18:9–14; 19:1–10). Thus we are also told how Luke wants his readers to follow the unfolding of the gospel message, especially the passion narrative: as repenting sinners.

It should also be noted that Luke, who does not exactly eliminate the early Church's expectation of the end, but nevertheless situates it in a far future, emphasizes 'individual eschatology'. He shows indeed a special interest in the fate of individuals immediately after death. Our present verse seems to be a clear example of this particular interest of Luke.

Jesus is confronted by a threefold challenge (Lk 23:35, 37, 39). Messianic dignity and saving power are inseparably related to each other. Jesus, therefore, can prove his messianic dignity only by the exercise of his saving power. This is the meaning of the episode of the repentant 'criminal'. First he states Jesus' innocence (Lk 23:41). Then he prays: 'Jesus, remember me when you come in your kingly power' (Lk 23:42). He hereby confesses Jesus' Messiahship as well as his saving power, but in an exclusively eschatological perspective. Indeed, his request refers to the moment of the parousia.

Jesus' answer does not refer to the man's condition during an alleged waiting period for the full revelation of the final kingdom. It means rather that salvation, which the repentant 'criminal' prayed would be his in the endtime, will be his at the moment of death. This individual perspective does not eliminate or contradict the traditional collective eschatology, but it is also clear that the human condition after death is not understood by Luke as a provisional situation (cf. Lk 12:16–20; 16:19–31).

The darkness and the rending of the Temple curtain (Lk 23:44–45)

Verses 44–45: It was about the sixth hour, and there was darkness over the whole land until the ninth hour, (45) while the sun's light failed; and the curtain of the temple was torn in two.

Luke follows Mark very closely in the description of the darkness that covered the land. We are again reminded of the traditional imagery of the Day of Yahweh as found, e.g., in Amos 8:9, ' "And on that day", says the Lord God, "I will make the sun go down at noon, and darken the earth in broad daylight" '. Similarly, Joel 2:10b, 'The sun and the moon are darkened, and the stars withdraw their shining', and Joel 2:31 (Greek text = 3:4 Hebrew text), 'The sun shall be turned to darkness, and the moon to blood, before the great and terrible day of the Lord comes'. See finally Zeph 1:15, 'A day of wrath is that day, . . . a day of darkness and gloom, a day of clouds and thick darkness'. In the understanding of the early Church the day of Jesus' death is the day of God's judgment and the beginning of the eschatological age.

The rending of the Temple curtain, placed after the death of Jesus by Mark and Matthew, is here connected with the darkness. In Mark the darkness and the rending of the Temple curtain are mentioned in different parts of the account, the rending following the reference to the death of Jesus. In Luke, on the contrary, the two incidents have been brought together, and both immediately precede the dying cry of Jesus.

If we keep in mind the general meaning of the Temple curtain, the meaning of the Lucan sequence becomes clear: Jesus promises to the repentant 'criminal' that right now he is going to enter with him into Paradise; upon this the curtain of the Temple is rent, i.e., the gate to Paradise (which is 'to be with God') is opened (cf. *Testament of Levi* 18:10, where we are told that the priestly messiah will open the gates of the abode of the just!); then Jesus expires recommending his spirit to the Father. Thereupon Jesus enters into Paradise, into God's presence, and the repentant 'criminal' apparently with him. This is perfectly in

accordance with the theology of the gospel of Luke in which not only
the salvation of the Gentiles is stressed, but also the fact that the less
fortunate, the outcast, the sinners and publicans will be first. Therefore
this 'criminal' is the first to enter.

The death of Jesus and its repercussions (Lk 23:46–48)

Verse 46: Then Jesus, crying with a loud voice, said, 'Father,
into your hands I commit my spirit!' And having said this he
breathed his last.

Luke omits the citation of Ps 22(21):1, possibly because he found it
mysterious and liable to misunderstanding. Instead he cites
Ps 31(30):5, 'Into your hand I commit my spirit . . .'. He gives this
quotation with the address 'Father' prefixed. Thus the crucifixion
scene is, as it were, framed by two prayers to the Father: 'Father,
forgive them; for they know not what they do' (Lk 23:34) and 'Father,
into your hands I commit my spirit!' (Lk 23:46). Both these passages
are missing in the other gospels, but they are perfectly in accordance
with the tendency of the Lucan passion narrative and with a gospel
characterized by its emphasis on prayer. Jesus, who died at the ninth
hour (three o'clock in the afternoon), recited this prayer at the
moment the trumpets were sounded for the evening prayer, the end of
which was precisely 'Into your hands I commit my spirit . . .'. Joining
the people in their evening prayer, Jesus expressed his confidence and
certainty that his death was only a 'going to sleep', and therefore the
beginning of life with the Father. This is suggested by the one
significant change in the quotation. Jesus says, 'Abba – Dear Father',
the babbling sound of a small child speaking to its Father, which no Jew
would have dared to use; but Jesus always addresses his Father in that
way.

By this prayer Luke's passion narrative strongly brings to the fore
the relationship of Jesus to the Father. Together with Jesus' prayer for
those who crucify him (cf. Lk 23:34), it is an example of love of
enemies and trust in God. This is confirmed by the account of Stephen
(Acts 7:59f.). Thus paraenetic motives are at work in Luke's passion
narrative.

The word for 'breathed his last' literally means 'he gave out his
spirit'. None of the evangelists says 'Jesus died', but all emphasize that
Jesus' death was an act of free and conscious surrender to God. This is
expressed here in the accompanying quotation of Ps 31(30):5.

Verse 47: Now when the centurion saw what had taken
place, he praised God, and said, 'Certainly this man was
innocent!'

Pilate and the penitent 'criminal' have declared Jesus innocent; now the centurion adds his testimony. According to Mark he said, 'Truly this man was the Son of God' (Mk 15:39), but the version given here fits better in Luke's perspective. While Mark made the centurion comment on the way in which Jesus died, and Matthew on the extraordinary phenomena which followed Jesus' death, in Luke he seems to be commenting on the whole series of events. The text intends to suggest that this responsible Roman official had witnessed the whole process from the beginning and that he finally came to the conclusion: this man was innocent, he did not have the political ambitions with which the Jewish authorities charged him (cf. Lk 23:2). The specific apologetic theme of Luke–Acts clearly breaks through: neither Jesus nor Christianity had any political ambitions. They did not, therefore, constitute any danger for the Roman empire.

The fact that it is said that the centurion 'praised God' indicates that Luke goes beyond the apologetic meaning of the centurion's statement and points to a kerygmatic aspect of his declaration. In fact, in Luke, bystanders seeing something or hearing something are often said to glorify or to praise God. The term *doxazein* is used once in Mark, four times in Matthew, nine times in Luke, and eighteen times in the Fourth Gospel. This indicates that we are dealing here with the influence of Christian faith on the description of the reaction of audiences to the words and deeds of Jesus. Generally speaking, 'to praise God' means to give due recognition to the fact that God has intervened in human history, that God has taken another step in his saving history, which fills men with feelings of gratitude, joy and praise. It is especially ascribed to those who believe that God has now finally and decisively intervened in salvation history in the person of the Lord who passed through death to life (e.g., Lk 17:15; 18:43). This is also the real background of what Luke ascribes to the centurion under the cross when he says that 'he praises God'. With feelings of joyful recognition and gratitude he expressed his faith in the fact that God had really taken the decisive step in salvation history.

The adverb *ontōs* (translated here by RSV as 'certainly' and in Lk 24:34 as 'indeed') signals an unexpected state of affairs brought about by God, for which he is here praised by the centurion. Considering that Jesus' last words are taken from Ps 31(30), the prayer of the faithful sufferer who ultimately celebrates his vindication as 'righteous one' (see Ps 31[30]:18), one may say that the centurion's *dikaios* refers to the messianic victor about to be vindicated by God in spite of the human attacks on him (see Acts 3:14–15, 'the Holy and Righteous One').

As can be seen in Acts 3:14; 7:52 and 22:14, *dikaios* ('just'; RSV translates 'innocent' in Lk 23:47) is certainly a Christological title. As such it goes back to Isa 53:11, 'By his sufferings my servant, *the just one*, will justify many, taking their faults on himself' (translation of the

Hebrew text). However, for a full understanding of Luke's use of the term 'just' we should realize that, during the centuries which followed after Second Isaiah, reflection on the person referred to as 'the just one' continued. The title acquired a deeper meaning as expressed, e.g., in Wis 2. There the just ones are the poor, oppressed people who are persecuted by wealthy, powerful and godless oppressors, who at the same time laugh at the faith of these poor in God. There the 'just ones' are the *anawim* ('little ones', 'poor ones') in Israel who have no power and no voice in this world and who are at the mercy of the godless, powerful oppressors. The rich and powerful speak thus in Wis 2:19–20: 'Let us test him with insult and torture, that we may find out how gentle he is, and make trial of his forbearance. Let us condemn him to a shameful death, for, according to what he says, he will be protected (by God).'

In this light, the use of 'just' in Lk 23:47 means that Jesus died and went to a life beyond for the liberation of the poor and the oppressed. This is illustrated by the 'criminal' who, before anyone else, entered with Jesus into God's presence. This is the climax of one of Luke's prominent themes: Christ is the Christ of the poor in the widest sense of the word: all the oppressed, all those discriminated against, all those in prison. Thus Luke presented Jesus in the inaugural discourse at Nazareth (Lk 4:16–30, especially 4:18–21) and he remains consistent with that presentation up to this conclusion in the crucifixion scene.

Verse 48: And all the multitudes who assembled to see the sight, when they saw what had taken place, returned home beating their breasts.

Just as he described a large crowd following Jesus and Simon of Cyrene, Luke now again 'amplifies' the picture by adding a moving description of the repentant crowd. Luke's words are reminiscent of Zech 12:10, 'And I will pour out on the house of David and the inhabitants of Jerusalem a spirit of compassion and supplication so that, when they look on him whom they have pierced, they shall mourn for him, as one mourns for an only child, and weep bitterly over him as one weeps over a first-born'. However, this lament took place against a background of hope for forgiveness of sins (cf. Zech 13:1). So here, the lament of the multitudes may be understood to foreshadow the gift of the spirit and forgiveness of sins as described in Acts 2:37–38, '. . . Repent, and be baptized every one of you in the name of Jesus Christ for the forgiveness of your sins; and you shall receive the gift of the Holy Spirit'.

By the abundant use of words of seeing ('to see the sight, when they saw') Luke undoubtedly intends to emphasize the multitudes' function as eyewitnesses. Like the tax collector in the Temple (Lk 18:13), they beat their breasts as a sign of repentance.

The mention of the acquaintances and the women (Lk 23:49)

Verse 49:   And all his acquaintances and the women who had followed him from Galilee stood at a distance and saw these things.

Mark referred only to women who were looking on from afar (Mk 15:40), but in Luke, 'all his acquaintances', the Eleven therefore included, appear together with the women as witnesses of Jesus' death, since they 'saw these things'. The formulation of the verse reminds us of Ps 38(37):11, 'My friends and companions stand aloof from my plague, and my kinsmen stand afar off', and of Ps 88(87):8, 'You have caused my companions to shun me; you have made me a thing of horror to them'.

Together with Luke's omission of the flight of the disciples at Jesus' arrest (cf. Mk 14:50), the notice in Lk 22:54 that 'Peter followed at a distance', and Luke's special treatment of Peter's denials, the presence of the acquaintances at the cross, though again 'at a distance', is a clear expression of the fact that their fellowship with Jesus has not been broken.

Luke is not introducing the women here for the first time. He has already mentioned them in Lk 8:2–3, 'and also some women who had been healed of evil spirits and infirmities: Mary, called Magdalene, from whom seven demons had gone out, and Joanna, the wife of Chuza, Herod's steward, and Susanna, and many others, who provided for them out of their means'. The women are mentioned almost as a separate group. It is emphasized that they 'saw these things' in view of the important role they will play at the burial (Lk 23:55–56) and the finding of the empty tomb (Lk 24:1–11).

Summing up, we may say that Lk 23:26–49 is mainly based on Mark, but that his highly typical treatment has given a different flavour to the account. Especially typical are Jesus' love for the sinner, powerful now as during his public ministry, and his unwavering confidence in the Father's protection.

The following are the most distinctive features of Luke's account:

(1)   Besides Simon of Cyrene, Jesus is followed to the place of execution by a great multitude of people and women who bewailed him and whom Jesus tells to weep rather for themselves and their children (Lk 23:27–31).

(2)   Instead of two reviling robbers, Luke tells of one impenitent and one penitent 'criminal'. The latter is told that he will be with Jesus in the presence of God (Lk 23:39–43).

(3)   Instead of the citation from Ps 22(21):1, 'My God, my God, why have you forsaken me', Luke fills in the loud cry with a citation from Ps 31(30):5, '(Father), into your hands I commit my spirit'.

Luke does not so much evoke the replacement of the old order by the new era; he does not give the same importance to the theme of the Temple as Mark and Matthew do, and does not show so much interest in the eschatological aspects. But he pays special attention to the *interior* repercussions of the events and to all that touches the personal relationship with Jesus. In this sense, Luke's account reaches its climax in the centurion's confession (Lk 23:47) and in the picture of the crowds beating their breasts when they saw what happened (Lk 23:48).

6 The Burial of Jesus

In all four gospels the narrative of Jesus' death is followed by the report of his burial. The accounts show a remarkable degree of agreement on the events which took place late Friday afternoon or evening. We may assume that Matthew and Luke are basically dependent on Mark. It is obvious that the Johannine tradition is closely related to the synoptic tradition, but direct literary dependence on Mark cannot be demonstrated.

I. Mark 15:42–47

> **Verse 42:** And when evening had come, since it was the day of Preparation, that is, the day before the sabbath,

While most scholars consider the clause 'when evening had come' redactional, they are divided over 'it was the day of Preparation', but a good case can be made for its traditional character. The clause, 'that is, the day before the sabbath', is probably also traditional.

Friday evening had come and there was little time left for carrying out the burial, 'since it was the day of Preparation'. The latter phrase has important implications since, beside informing us of the day of the week on which these events took place, it was originally intended to give their motivation as well: *since* it was Friday. The sabbath would have been profaned if the bodies had not been taken down. There was, however, also Deut 21:22f., 'And if a man has committed a crime punishable by death and he is put to death, and you hang him on a tree, his body shall not remain all night upon the tree, but you shall bury him the same day'. In the next verse we will see how Mark brought about a shift in the description of this motivation.

> **Verse 43:** Joseph of Arimathea, a respected member of the council, who was also himself looking for the kingdom of God, took courage and went to Pilate, and asked for the body of Jesus.

Joseph of Arimathea is characterized in a threefold manner: (1) he hails from Arimathea; (2) he is an important member of the council; (3) he is expecting the kingdom of God.

In Mark's source it was not really clear why Joseph should have undertaken to bury Jesus. A Jew might have wanted to bury the condemned man because of Deut 21:22f., but this does not explain why *Joseph*, 'a respected member of the council', wanted to do so. This made Mark add the personal touch, 'who was also himself looking for the kingdom of God', thereby describing Joseph as sympathetic to Jesus' cause and perhaps open to his message, without explicitly making him a Christian.

This description of Joseph stands somewhat in tension with Mk 14:64, 'And they all (=the whole council) condemned him as deserving death', and Mk 15:1, 'and the whole council held a consultation; and they bound Jesus and led him away and delivered him to Pilate'. Luke, who has already either omitted or rewritten the two Marcan verses mentioned, adds here in Lk 23:51, 'who had not consented to their purpose and deed'. Matthew, who did not rewrite Mk 16:64 and 15:1 so extensively (cf. Mt 26:66; 27:1, 2), may also have felt the difficulty and therefore omitted here 'a respected member of the council'.

But does Mark really intend to describe Joseph as a member of the Sanhedrin? Because of Luke's interpretation of Mark's *bouleutēs* ('councillor'), most exegetes hold Joseph of Arimathea to be a member of the Sanhedrin. But Mark usually refers to particular groups within the Sanhedrin (chief priests, scribes, elders) and not to the Sanhedrin as a whole, and Mk 15:43 is the only instance where *bouleutēs* is used in this gospel. It seems also that 'councillor' was not a technical expression current among the Jews. Moreover, in the two passages of the Septuagint where *bouleutēs* is used (Job 3:14; 12:17) the word does not mean a member of the Sanhedrin. In both passages the term seems to refer to V.I.P.s. The word occurs at least eight times in the writings of Flavius Josephus, but only in one instance is he probably referring to members of the Sanhedrin, and it certainly cannot be considered a technical expression. We should conclude, therefore, that a 'councillor' could be a member of the Sanhedrin, but also e.g., a member of any local court.

The term *euschēmōn* is usually translated by 'respected' or a similar word, but most probably it should be understood as referring to a rich landowner. This is the case in the papyri, and Matthew too has understood the word in this way.

Verses 44–45: And Pilate wondered if he were already dead; and summoning the centurion, he asked him whether he was already dead. (45) And when he learned from the centurion that he was dead, he granted the body to Joseph.

These verses are not found in Matthew and Luke. They have been suspected of being a later gloss, but it seems more probable that they are Mark's own addition to the tradition which both Matthew and Luke omitted for parallel reasons. The fact that the number of probably redactional terms in these verses is impressive supports this view.

Mark stresses that Jesus died quickly and, as Pilate's wondering shows, that his death was 'amazing'. Thus he draws the readers' attention to the fact that the outcome of the crucifixion and the death of Jesus were not 'normal', but, as Mark's chronology (Mk 15:25, 33, 34) may also intend to show, unusually quick. By Pilate's question, Mark may also remind us of the centurion's confession at the moment of Jesus' death.

This interpretation does not exclude the possibility that for apologetic reasons Mark may have intended to heighten the importance of the last pericope before Jesus' resurrection: the latter would never be beyond doubt if it were not first established that Jesus was dead. This explains the emphasis on the thrice-repeated 'dead'. The same emphasis may also be found in Mark's use of the word *ptōma*, 'corpse' (not 'body' as RSV translates). But why did Mark then use *sōma*, 'body', in verse 43? Do we have here an indication of two separate traditions? Or should we say with some scholars that *sōma* in Joseph's request leaves open the possiblity of resurrection, whereas *ptōma* in Pilate's reply does not?

> **Verse 46:** And he bought a linen shroud, and taking him down, wrapped him in the linen shroud, and laid him in a tomb which had been hewn out of the rock; and he rolled a stone against the door of the tomb.

This verse belongs again to the pre-Marcan tradition, except perhaps for its final clause. This is indicated by, among other things, the fact that 'him' has no real antecedent in verses 44–45, where only 'body' and 'corpse' are used. It refers back to 'Jesus' in verse 43. Verses 44–45 appear therefore as redactional.

The present verse stands somewhat in tension with the rest of the pericope and the rest of Mk 15, which leaves very little time for carrying out the burial (cf. Mk 15:1, 25, 33, 34, 42), as well as with the implication from Mk 16:1 that there had been no time on Friday to buy spices and to anoint the body. In our present verse there seems to be plenty of time, the atmosphere is dignified and there is no trace of hurried action. Apparently Mk 15:46 and 16:1 did not originate together.

Originally, that is before the insertion of Mk 15:44–45 by Mark himself, the present verse 46 may have been intended as a confirmation of Jesus' death, but in its present context it loses this sense of finality which made it quite clear that Jesus was dead.

Notwithstanding certain difficulties raised against this opinion, a number of scholars defend the dependence of the clause 'and laid him in a tomb which had been hewn out of the rock' on Isa 22:16, '. . . that you have hewn here a tomb for yourself, you who hew a tomb on the height, and carve a habitation for yourself in the rock?' Matthew's text is closer to Isa 22:16 than Mark's. Dependence on this text suggests that Jesus received the burial of an important man.

The final clause, 'and he rolled a stone against the door of the tomb', is certainly related to the question which the women put to themselves in Mk 16:3, 'Who will roll away the stone for us from the door of the tomb?' It is not clear which verse prompted the other, but since Mk 16:3 is more closely related to its context than the final clause of Mk 15:46, we are inclined to think that Mark himself added the clause to prepare the reader for Mk 16:3. The mention of the rolling of a stone against the door of the tomb seems to conclude the account. But then we have yet another verse.

It is not the burial as such which is emphasized but rather the fact that the tomb was firmly sealed. From this it can be concluded that already at this point the ensuing account of the angel's message at the opened tomb is the centre of interest. The whole account of Jesus' burial leads on to the episode of the opened tomb, and is leading up to it as its ultimate climax. This objective is served by the added remark about the women in Mk 15:47. They are witnesses not of the burial proceedings but of the location of the tomb. So it may be said that the account of Jesus' burial intends to describe the setting of the Easter account narrated next. This, in its turn, focuses on the raising from the dead which the angel proclaims by calling attention to the change which had occurred at the tomb: the stone has been rolled away from the entrance (Mk 16:4), and the body of Jesus is not there (Mk 16:6).

Verse 47: Mary Magdalene and Mary the mother of Joses saw where he was laid.

The difficulties which beset this verse will appear as soon as we compare it with Mk 15:40f. and Mk 16:1.

Mk 15:40f.	*Mk 15:47*	*Mk 16:1*
There were also women looking on from afar, among whom were		And when the sabbath was past,
	Mary	
Mary Magdalene	Magdalene	Mary Magdalene
and Mary the mother	and Mary the (mother)	and Mary the (mother)
of James the younger		of James
and of Joses	of Joses	
and Salome		and Salome,

Mk 15:40f.	*Mk 15:47*	*Mk 16:1*
who, when he was in		
Galilee, followed him,		
and ministered to him;		
and also many other		
women who came up with		
him to Jerusalem.		
	saw where he	bought spices, so
	was laid.	and they might go
		and anoint him.

Did the redactor of Mk 16:1 understand Mk 15:40f. as 'Mary, the wife of James the younger and the mother of Joses'? Did he then decide to mention her only in reference to her husband and to omit 'the younger' since James was no longer known in the community? (The latter is hard to prove.) Was the second Mary of Mk 15:40 the wife of James (the younger) and the mother of Joses (Joseph), did she have two sons called James and Joses, or was she the daughter of James the younger? All questions which can legitimately be raised.

All three lists of women start with Mary Magdalene, add another Mary, and the first and third lists end with Salome. Without discussing here all the difficult problems raised by these verses, we would support the opinion that Mk 15:40f. is a conflation of Mk 15:47 and Mk 16:1, composed to solve the problem posed by the different male names, Joses and James, used in Mk 15:47 and Mk 16:1, and to clarify the genitives *Jōsētos* and *Jakōbou* which would normally have been understood as referring to a father or husband, but which are explained in Mk 15:40 to refer to sons: the other Mary is the mother of James and Joses.

In its present position Mk 15:47 forms a bridge to Mk 16:1–8. The women 'saw where he was laid', and so they knew where the right grave was to be found. The verse, therefore, has an apologetic interest. It is necessary that they 'saw', since otherwise they could not know where Jesus was buried. The clause '(they) saw where he was laid' may also be understood in relation to what some have called the aetiological-cultic character of Mk 16:1–8 (cf. especially Mk 16:6, 'see the place where they laid him'). It is more difficult to say what the verse meant before its combination with Mk 16:1–8. It may have been the introduction to an alternative resurrection narrative, but this answer is no more than an unproven hypothesis.

In summary, we may say that a study of tradition and redaction in Mk 15:42–47 leads to the conclusion that Mark received the following traditional account: Since it was the day of Preparation (that is, the day before the sabbath), Joseph of Arimathea, a respected member of the council, took courage and went to Pilate, and asked for the body of

Jesus. And he bought a linen shroud, and taking him down, wrapped him in the linen shroud and laid him in a tomb which had been hewn out of the rock.

By the redactional introduction, 'when evening had come', Mark inserted this account into his passion chronology. It is this insertion into a chronological framework which creates the impression of a hasty burial. There is no trace of haste in the pre-Marcan tradition.

The traditional account based Joseph's action on the character of the following day. Although Mark still retains this feature, he brings about a shift of attention to Joseph's personal motivation.

The addition of verses 44–45 may be explained by Mark's intention to stress the 'amazing' character of Jesus' death as well as by apologetic reasons: Jesus was really dead, a necessary foundation for later belief in the resurrection.

The redactional clause, 'and he rolled a stone against the door of the tomb', serves as preparation for the finding of the empty tomb, especially Mk 16:3. Verse 47, which is most probably traditional, but did not belong to the earliest stratum of the tradition, forms another bridge to Mk 16:1–8.

II. Matthew 27:57–61

Matthew has ironed out some of the difficulties of Mark's account and made it into a better introduction to the resurrection narratives.

> **Verse 57:** When it was evening, there came a rich man from Arimathea, named Joseph, who also was a disciple of Jesus.

The clause 'since it was the day of Preparation, that is the day before the sabbath', which in Mark, but especially in the pre-Marcan tradition, seems to motivate Joseph's action, but in fact raises a lot of questions, is omitted.

In calling Joseph 'a rich man', Matthew may have correctly interpreted the meaning of Mark's words, 'a respected member of the council', but very likely this formulation is also influenced by Isa 53:9, 'And they made his grave with the wicked and with a rich man in his death, although he had done no violence, and there was no deceit in his mouth'.

Matthew's description of Joseph as one 'who was also a disciple of Jesus' goes beyond Mark's 'who was also himself looking for the kingdom of God', which does not necessarily imply that Joseph was a disciple of Jesus. Compare the description of Simeon as a man who was 'righteous and devout, looking for the consolation of Israel' (Lk 2:25). Matthew may have been moved by a sense of what would have been fitting: Jesus was buried by a disciple.

Verse 58:   He went to Pilate and asked for the body of Jesus. Then Pilate ordered it to be given to him.

In the first half of the verse, Matthew follows the text of Mark almost literally. Then he omits Mk 15:44–45. Although some scholars think that verses 44–45 were not present in the Marcan text which Matthew and Luke knew, we think with others that it is at least equally possible that both Matthew and Luke *omitted* the verses for parallel redactional reasons. Possibly Matthew takes care of the apologetic reasons which prompted Mark to insert the verses 44–45 (to prove that Jesus was really dead) by his addition of Mt 27:62–66 and 28:11–15, the account of the guards at the tomb. Right after the omission, Matthew takes up his source again stating that 'Pilate ordered it (the corpse) to be given him'.

Verses 59–60:   And Joseph took the body, and wrapped it in a clean linen shroud, (60) and laid it in his own new tomb, which he had hewn in the rock; and he rolled a great stone to the door of the tomb, and departed.

Matthew follows Mark very closely. He omits the reference to the *buying* of the linen shroud, but makes up for this omission by describing the shroud as 'clean'. Mark's vague reference to 'a tomb' is transformed into 'his own new tomb'. The adjective 'new' is most probably inspired by the previously mentioned sense of what would have been fitting for the body of Jesus. As the linen shroud in which Jesus' body was wrapped was clean, so the tomb of Jesus the Messiah was new and worthy of him.

The indication that the tomb was owned by Joseph may have been inspired by Isa 22:16, 'What have you to do here and whom have you here, that you have hewn here a tomb for yourself, you who hew a tomb on the height, and carve a habitation for yourself in the rock?' The clause may also have been influenced by Isa 53:9.

Verse 61:   Mary Magdalene and the other Mary were there, sitting opposite the sepulchre.

The problem posed by Mk 15:47 and 16:1 is solved in different ways. Mt 27:61 and 28:1 both read 'Mary Magdalene and the other Mary'. In our present verse we are told that they 'were there, sitting opposite the sepulchre'. This seems to refer to the clause '(they) went to see the sepulchre' in Mt 28:1. The repetition of the names in Mt 28:1 is readily understandable and useful because of the insertion of the account of the guards at the tomb, Mt 27:62–66. While in Mk 15:47 the apologetic character of the reference to the women's presence is still clear, this is no longer so in Matthew.

Summing up, we may say that Matthew's redaction shows the following tendencies:

(1)   The motive of the day of rest ('the day before the sabbath') is omitted.

(2)   The personal motivation of Joseph of Arimathea, which Mark already added to the tradition ('who was also looking for the kingdom of God'), is stressed ('who also was a disciple of Jesus').

(3)   Matthew shows a greater interest in the tomb ('his own new tomb'; Joseph is 'a rich man').

(4)   The importance of the burial is stressed (related to the previous element; 'a new tomb'; 'a great stone'; the women witnessed the entire burial).

III. Luke 23:50–56

Verses 50–51:   Now there was a man named Joseph from the Jewish town of Arimathea. He was a member of the council, a good and righteous man, (51) who had not consented to their purpose and deed, and he was looking for the kingdom of God.

Luke, always interested in a person's moral qualities, describes Joseph as 'a good and righteous man' who, although a member of the Sanhedrin, is explicitly dissociated from complicity in Jesus' condemnation. Luke does not describe Joseph as a 'disciple of Jesus' but, following Mark literally, as 'looking for the kingdom of God'.

Verse 52:   This man went to Pilate and asked for the body of Jesus.

At first Luke follows Mark almost literally. Then he omits Mk 15:44–45. Previously Luke omitted the time indications found in Mk 15:25, 'And it was the third hour', and Mk 15:34, 'And at the ninth hour', to which Mk 15:44–45 is probably related. Luke's omission of these verses is thus consistent with his previous handling of Mark.

Verse 53:   Then he took it down and wrapped it in a linen shroud, and laid him in a rock-hewn tomb, where no one had ever yet been laid.

The final clause of this verse has practically the same meaning as Matthew's reference to Joseph's own *new* tomb, and is inspired by the feeling of what would have been most suitable for the body of the Lord.

It reminds us also of Mk 11:2 and Lk 19:30, 'on which no one has ever (yet) sat'.

Verse 54: It was the day of Preparation, and the sabbath was beginning.

The time indication, omitted at the beginning of the pericope, is now given, but without motivating in any way the action of Joseph of Arimathea, as was the case in the pre-Marcan tradition and still to some extent in Mk 15:42.

Verse 55: The women who had come with him from Galilee followed, and saw the tomb, and how his body was laid;

Luke drastically revises the lists of names found in Mark. He has already mentioned Mary Magdalene and two others, Joanna and Susanna, at Lk 8:2f., a passage which deals with the Galilean ministry of Jesus. Lk 23:49, 55 and 24:1, which parallel, respectively, Mk 15:40f., 47, and 16:1, contain elements of all these verses, but mention no names at all. However, in Lk 24:10 we are told that the women involved were 'Mary Magdalene and Joanna and Mary the mother of James and the other women with them'.

The clause 'and saw the tomb, and how his body was laid' draws our attention to the body of Jesus and seems to be related to a similar interest expressed in Lk 24:3 where the failure to find the body is explicitly recorded. These and other texts are said to belong to the 'assumption' scheme found in Luke (cf. Lk 9:51; 24:51).

Verse 56: then they returned, and prepared spices and ointments. On the sabbath they rested according to the commandment.

Luke adds this verse to connect the burial account to its Easter sequel. Luke's transfer of the women's preparations to the burial account, before the intervening sabbath (compare Mk 16:1), is part of a deliberate involvement of the women in the action of burial, and hence a skilful fusion of the two Marcan pericopes into one. Luke indeed pares the two pericopes down to a single episode, with the women becoming central figures throughout. The new, single episode, fashioned within the limits of the Marcan master-copy, may then be considered the threshold for the main Easter narratives which follow it. On Friday the women 'prepared spices and ointments', and then 'they rested according to the commandment'. Luke apparently wants to explain why the women waited until Sunday morning to anoint the corpse. The apparently smooth transition he obtains thereby is weakened by the fact that anointing a corpse was one activity explicitly allowed on the sabbath.

In summary, we may say that the tendencies found in Luke's redaction are very similar to and run parallel with Matthew's:

(1)   The motive of the day of rest is omitted in connection with Joseph's activity. It appears briefly to explain the attitude of the women.

(2)   The personal motivation of Joseph of Arimathea is emphasized. Luke adds to Mark's description that Joseph was 'a good and righteous man'.

(3)   Luke too shows a greater interest than Mark in the tomb ('where no one had ever yet been laid').

(4)   The importance of the burial is emphasized (related to the previous element; 'saw the tomb, and how his body was laid; then they returned and prepared spices and ointments').

(5)   Luke makes the women function actively in Jesus' burial. As a result of this and other editorial interventions the burial and the women's discovery of the tomb are as it were condensed into a single progressive sequence at Jesus' tomb, so that the combined narratives can function together as a prelude to the birth of Easter faith.

7 Theological and Pastoral Perspectives

Speaking of the evangelists and their predecessors, Gerard S. Sloyan says:

> They were greatly concerned that God had acted in history, and they told of his action in terms of human, historical activity. In fact, however, they were reporting on what they were convinced was the outworking of a providential plan foreshadowed in the scriptures, fulfilled in terms of the conflict of good and evil. They made their report in a highly sophisticated way in the context of the theology of the times, but unsophisticatedly as regards the historiography of our day.[8]

After our rather lengthy study of the passion narrative in the three synoptic gospels, throughout which we attempted to summarize the more interesting results of our research at the end of each section, we should come to the point now and try to state the main characteristics of each of these passion narratives. At the same time we would like to show that these characteristics are in keeping with the overall theological tendencies of each of the evangelists. We are, therefore, no longer interested now in the various materials they incorporated and edited, but in the final results and the theological implications of their activity.

I. Mark

(1)   The most important theological characteristic of Mark's gospel is *the* so-called *messianic secret*, according to which Jesus' messianic identity (*that* he is the Messiah) is not revealed before Mk 8:27–33, the turning point of the gospel. After this pivotal text, the nature of his Messiahship (*how* he is the Messiah) is gradually revealed. He is not only the celestial Son of man who will come at the end in the clouds of heaven to establish the glorious reign of God. What is seen at present is the Son of man in his role of the suffering servant of God. The suffering of the Son of man is announced three times (Mk 8:31; 9:31; 10:32–34), and is as many times completely misunderstood by the

disciples. These predictions are followed by instructions on the conditions of discipleship – defined as service, self-denial, taking up one's cross, and giving one's life to gain life.

The mystery of the suffering Son of man is ultimately expressed in the Christological title 'Son of God', which controls the whole gospel, but which for Mark expresses first of all a divine sonship characterized by obedience and death. We find it in the title of the gospel, which is certainly from Mark's hand and expresses his thesis: 'the beginning of the gospel of Jesus Christ, the Son of God'. Gradually, Mark leads his readers to this confession. In the beginning only demons confess Jesus to be the Son of God, but they are rebuked because they accept only the glorious aspect of the divine sonship and thus represent a Christology which Mark opposes throughout the gospel.

In Mark's account of the trial before the Sanhedrin the titles 'Christ' (=Messiah), 'Son of God' (or 'Son of the Blessed'), and 'Son of man' are brought together and we approach the solution of the messianic secret. But March reaches the real acme of his gospel when, after Jesus has expired with a loud cry, the centurion confesses in words which echo the title verse of the gospel. 'Truly this man was the Son of God' (Mk 15:39). This confession is of the highest significance. That Jesus is the Son of God entirely in his suffering and death is a conclusion which Mark wants to impress on his readers. Only when Jesus is 'seen' as the one who suffered, died and will come again, can he be called Son of God in the proper sense, and the messianic secret be totally lifted.

(2) *The disciples' lack of understanding*, emphasized throughout the gospel, especially in connection with the predictions of the passion, reaches its climax in the passion narrative where 'they all forsook him and fled' (Mk 14:50). The young man who followed him ran away naked (Mk 14:51–52), and Peter, who had followed him at a distance (Mk 14:54), denied him (Mk 14:66–72). They behaved in such a cowardly way that Mark refuses to call them disciples from the Gethsemane incident (Mk 14:32) to the message of the young man in white sitting at the entrance of the empty tomb, '. . . But go, tell his disciples and Peter . . .' (Mk 16:7).

(3)   In the same context, *the true suffering of the Son of man* is caused not by the physical pains, which are not at all emphasized, but by his isolation: at the moment he identifies himself with sinful man the Son of man is left alone. He is betrayed by one of the twelve, forsaken by his disciples, rejected by the Sanhedrin, denied by Peter, condemned to death, mocked by those who pass by the cross, until he finally cries out, 'My God, my God, why have you forsaken me?' (Mk 15:34). In our reflection and homilies on Jesus' passion we should do justice to this particular aspect of the gospel message.

(4) *The disconcerting realization of God's design* is evoked in Mark's composition which makes ample use of contrasts and paradox. This can be seen especially in his treatment of the hearing before the Sanhedrin, where Mark's narrative skill brings about a strongly contrasted composition. A first paradox is that the hearing leads to the opposite of the result expected: instead of establishing Jesus' guilt, it ends with the revelation of his supreme dignity. Then we have the second paradox: the revelation of Jesus' true dignity does not raise any positive response. It arouses only opposition. He is accused of blasphemy; he is said to deserve death; he is ill-treated and Peter denies him. Through the arrangement adopted, Mark emphasizes the paradoxical contrast between Jesus' affirmation of his dignity and the succeeding treatment. Similarly the proceedings before Pilate are presented as a strange trial, since the Jews are the accusers and the King remains silent. He is compared with Barabbas, who is set free, while he is condemned to the cross. In an epilogue, the soldiers illustrate the verdict in an appropriate setting: purple robe, crown and homage become part of a mocking scene. God's designs are pictured in disconcerting images. Throughout all this Mark maintains Jesus' innocence and messianic dignity. The narrative does not leave the slightest doubt that an enormous injustice is being committed. Jesus is not only innocent, a victim sacrificed to the hatred of the Jewish leaders, but it is the Messiah, God's Son, who suffers this injustice. It is the representative of God among men who is at the mercy of their injustice. In complete isolation he stands up for God's cause.

(5) *The anti-Temple theme.* Before the passion narrative, Mark tells us three times that the authorities planned to kill Jesus (Mk 3:6; 11:18; 12:12). The first reference is found at the beginning of the gospel, following the healing of the man with the withered hand: 'The Pharisees went out, and immediately held counsel with the Herodians against him, how to destroy him' (Mk 3:6). The other two references occur in the context of Jesus' opposition to the Temple.

First, the accounts of Jesus' triumphal entry, the cursing of the fig tree, and the cleansing of the Temple show a marked anti-Jerusalem and anti-Temple bias. The acclamation of Jesus takes place outside the city and the Marcan addition to the acclamation, 'Blessed is the kingdom of our father David that is coming' (Mk 11:10) points to a substitution of the coming kingdom for the city. The two passages dealing with the fig tree (Mk 11:12–14 and 20–25) provide an eschatological context for the cleansing of the Temple (Mk 11:15–19), and the prohibition against carrying anything through the Temple abrogates the cultic role of the Temple which will be replaced by an eschatological 'house of prayer for all the nations' (Mk 11:17). In reaction against the whole of Jesus' action (Mk 11:15–18) and especially his words (Mk 11:17), the authorities plan to kill him: '(they) sought a way to destroy him' (Mk 11:18, clearly referring to Mk 3:6, 'how to destroy him'; Mark thus creates a parallel between the beginning of Jesus' ministry in Galilee and the beginning in Jerusalem, placing the whole of Jesus' ministry under the shadow of the cross).

Secondly, the same theme is found in Mark's version of the parable of the wicked tenants (Mk 12:1–12), which ends with the Marcan addition, 'And they tried to arrest him . . .' (Mk 12:12).

But the same theme is again continued in the eschatological discourse pronounced by Jesus after leaving the Temple (Mk 13:1) never to return to it again. Then follows the prediction of the destruction of the Temple and the city (Mk 13:2). The discourse proper is pronounced by Jesus 'as he sat on the Mount of Olives *opposite the temple*' (Mk 13:3), leading up to the reference to the 'desolation' (Mk 13:14), an event which has certainly something to do with the Temple, after which the community is to flee from the Temple. Thus Mark moves the anti-Temple theme from the time of Jesus to the time of his readers. The theme may reflect the growing estrangement of Mark's Church from Judaism and provides Mark's readers with an acceptable explanation for the destruction of the Temple. But Mk 13 looks beyond the destruction of the Temple to the formation of the new community when it speaks of the coming of the Son of man and the gathering of the elect (Mk 13:26–27). Thus along with the anti-Temple motif there is the motif of the *eschatological community* (Mk 12:10–11; 13:27).

This whole anti-Temple section leads to the beginning of the (longer) passion narrative, Mk 14:1, '. . . the chief priests and the scribes were seeking how to arrest him by stealth, and kill him'. In the context of the final redaction of the gospel, this verse has a double focus. On the one hand, it describes the authorities' response to the anti-Temple attitude in Mk 11 – 13, and this indicates that Mark intends to portray the death of Jesus as arising out of his opposition to the Jerusalem Temple. On the other hand, it refers the reader of the gospel to the motif of the end of the Temple and the promise of the new community found in Mk 13:5–37.

The motif of opposition to the Temple culminates in the narrative of the trial before the Sanhedrin, more specifically in the saying concerning the destruction of the Temple: 'I will destroy this temple that is made with hands, and in three days I will build another, not made with hands' (Mk 14:58). Jesus will build another temple not made with hands (the eschatological community) in place of the rejected Jerusalem Temple. In this saying Mark combines two traditions to picture Jesus in opposition to the Jerusalem Temple and as the *founder of the new community*.

II. Matthew

It is widely accepted that the final verses of Matthew constitute the key to a proper understanding of this gospel: 'All authority in heaven and on earth has been given to me. Go therefore and make disciples of all nations, baptizing them in the name of the Father and of the Son and of the Holy Spirit, teaching them to observe all that I have commanded you; and lo, I am with you always, to the close of the age' (Mt 28:18–20). Throughout the writing of the gospel, Matthew had this solemn ending constantly in mind. It intends to express that in the present situation of the Church,

(1)   the rule of God (the kingdom of God) is realized in the rule of the Lord (the kingdom of the Son of man), and
(2)   the reality of God's people is now found (actualized) in the Church, the community of disciples of the Lord, who are initiated through baptism and instructed into the Law of Christ by those commissioned for that task. This text has for some time past been recognized as a *covenant*-formula: 'I am', and therefore, I am God with you, my people.

In fact, the recurrent phrase 'with you' (and the corresponding 'with us') expresses an important aspect of Matthew's theology. It is found from the beginning of the gospel, 'his name shall be called Emmanuel (which means God with us)' (Mt 1:23), until its very end, 'I am with you always, to the close of the age' (Mt 28:20). This *covenant*-idea is emphasized in Matthew's version of the Last Supper, 'I shall not drink again of this fruit of the vine until that day when I drink it new *with you* in my Father's kingdom' (Mt 26:29; compare Mk 14:25, '. . . when I drink it new in the kingdom of God'). Again Matthew writes that 'Jesus went *with them* to a place called Gethsemane' (Mt 26:36; compare Mk 14:32, 'they went').

To Jesus' 'being with them' corresponds, of course, their 'being with Jesus' which is equally emphasized: 'remain here, and watch *with me*' (Mt 26:38; compare Mk 14:34, 'remain here, and watch'). And a little further Jesus' complaint reads: 'So could you not watch *with me* one hour?' (Mt 26:40; compare Mk 14:37, 'could you not watch one hour?'). In both instances the preposition 'with' describes the disciples' participation in Jesus' suffering as a specific form of Jesus' 'being with' his disciples.

However, during the passion, the disciples fail to live up to these standards, since it is 'one of those who were *with Jesus*' who struck the slave of the high priest (Mt 26:51; compare Mk 14:47, 'one of those who stood by'). Because of their 'little faith' (Mt 6:30; 8:26; 14:31; 16:8), 'all the disciples forsook him and fled' (Mt 26:56), and Peter denied repeatedly that he was *with Jesus* (Mt 26:69–71), so that they were not with Jesus in his suffering. It would take the initiative of the risen Christ to restore the covenant and realize it beyond all expectation: 'I am with you always, to the close of the age' (Mt 28:20). This whole perspective gives a strongly *ecclesial* character to the gospel.

Ecclesiology

How the kingdom of God is now actualized in the Church appears clearly from the Matthean conclusion of the parable of the wicked tenants: 'Therefore I tell you, the kingdom of God will be taken away from you and given to a nation producing the fruits of it' (Mt 21:43). The same theme is developed in the parable that follows it, that of the wedding feast (Mt 22:1–14), where those who were initially called are not worthy, and where the people found along the thoroughfares are then invited. Throughout this section of the gospel, two Matthean themes come to the fore:

(a) *The anti-Jewish theme*. Matthew, a Jewish Christian writing for Jewish Christians, faced the tragedy of their own people who, by the time of the composition of the gospel (about A.D. 85), had rejected Christ and Christianity.

Developing this anti-Jewish theme, Matthew emphasizes first of all that Jesus was their Messiah, sent first of all to them (Mt 10:5–6; 15:24). But then he shows how Israel rejected this Messiah. This is already touched upon in the infancy narrative (Mt 2:1–12; 2:22) and again at the beginning of Jesus' ministry (Mt 4:12–17). We have also the parable of the wicked tenants (Mt 21:33–46) and the parable of the wedding feast (Mt 22:1–14) mentioned above.

But this theme is especially prominent in the passion narrative where, e.g., in the pericope about the fate of Judas (Mt 27:3–10), the chief priests accept responsibility for Jesus' death by taking the blood money returned by Judas. Then the Matthean additions in Mt 27:19 and 24 show us Pilate's wife and the governor himself knowing of Jesus' innocence. But the *people* accept full responsibility for Jesus' death: 'His blood be on us and on our children!' (Mt 27:25, another Matthean addition). However, this is not the end, since in the story of the guard at the tomb, we are told that they persecute Jesus even beyond his death (Mt 27:62–66; 28:11–15). At the end of this story they are called 'the Jews' (Mt 28:15) and have definitively lost their status as a people of God. Then the disciples are sent to establish Jesus' Lordship, given to him in the resurrection, by making all nations his disciples in the missionary era between Jesus' resurrection and the 'close of the age', i.e., the consummation of history (Mt 28:16–20).

(b) *The positive ecclesial theme*. The conclusion of the parable of the wicked tenants does not only speak of the kingdom of God being taken away from the Jews, but also of the kingdom being given to a people producing the fruits of it. The theme of 'producing fruit' refers to a moral life resulting from this gift of the kingdom. The same two themes, gift of the kingdom and producing fruit, are also found in the conclusion of the parable of the wedding feast (Mt 22:1–14). At the end of this parable Matthew adds a warning addressed to Gentile Christians (those invited who were found along the thoroughfares) to live up to their baptismal grace (the wedding garment) in the era between the moment of their calling and the consummation of history, when the king will come to inspect the guests (Mt 22:11–14).

Matthew realized that the Church would have to live in the world for quite some time and was therefore more explicitly concerned with the theme of the Church and Christian morality. That is why this gospel contains so much didactic material arranged in five discourses on Christian morality and Church 'structures' (Mt 5 – 7, the Sermon on the Mount; Mt 10, the Missionary Discourse; Mt 13, the Parable Discourse; Mt 18, the Church Community Discourse; Mt 24 – 25, the Eschatological Discourse), to which the risen Christ is made to refer when he orders the eleven disciples to go, 'teaching them to observe all that I have commanded you' (Mt 28:19).

The past Jewish attitudes to law and institution constituted a constant temptation for Matthew's Christians. The warning 'not so among you' (Mt 23:8–12) is implicit in several other Matthean compositions, e.g., in Mt 18, the Church Community Discourse, addressed to Church leaders who might understand their position in Jewish fashion and would not care for the 'little ones' – simple people without power and influence. It is this type of (Jewish) Church leadership we see in action in the passion narrative, e.g., during the hearing before the Sanhedrin (Mt 26:57–75) and in the pericope about the fate of Judas (Mt 27:3–10). This type of Church leadership would not hesitate to crucify Christ again, a Christ who stands not for legalism but for the law of the gospel, which is the expression of the kingdom received, of the love for Christ, the Son of man who identifies himself with the poor (Mt 25:31–46).

Throughout Matthew's gospel the Church appears as a *brotherhood* in which nobody is despised (Mt 18:10), in which one sees to it that nobody perishes and that the 'little ones' do not get lost (Mt 18:12–14), and the brother is forgiven 'seventy times seven' (Mt 18:22). They are all brothers for they have one Father in heaven (Mt 23:8–9). They are a brotherhood of *sons* who call on God as their Father, just as Jesus addresses his Father. In this connection it has been noted that the phrases 'my father' and 'your father' are repeatedly found in the same context. Thus we are led from the Church, a community of brothers and sons, to *the Son*, and therefore, to some considerations concerning Matthew's Christology.

Christology

(a) *The Son of God*. In no other gospel is Christ's sonship and God's fatherhood so frequently emphasized. In the first main part of his gospel (Mt 1:1 – 4:16), Matthew sets forth the truth that, while Jesus Messiah is the Son of David and the Son of Abraham, he is first of all the Son of God. In the second main part (Mt 4:17 – 16:20), he then portrays the public ministry of Jesus Messiah, the Son of God, to Israel. But Israel rejects him, and Matthew devotes the third main part of the gospel (Mt 16:21 – 28:20) to showing how the ministry of Jesus Messiah, the Son of God, leads to death (and resurrection). At the same time he also shows that somehow Jesus' sonship always goes together with the sonship of the disciples: they are sons in the Son.

In the passion narrative, Jesus' sonship is emphasized in the crucifixion account, more specifically in the taunts of those who mock Jesus: '*If you are the Son of God*, come down from the cross' (Mt 27:40, reminding us of Satan's words at the temptation, Mt 4:3, 6; compare Mk 15:30, where 'Son of God' is lacking) and a little further: '. . . for he said, "I am the Son of God" ' (Mt 27:43; the whole verse is lacking in Mark). Finally the title is found in the confession of the centurion and those who were with him, 'Truly this was the Son of God' (Mt 27:54; compare Mk 15:39). So we have three references to the title Son of God as against only one in Mark.

So far as the Church is concerned, it seems that the raising of the saints (Mt 27:51b–53) and the confession of the centurion *and those who were with him* (Mt 27:54; compare Mk 15:39 where only the centurion is mentioned) are important texts. Both are understood to be the result of God's action in response to the death of Jesus. The texts prefigure Matthew's Church of Jewish and Gentile Christians. These Christians are the sons of God because the Son of God has died for their sins and has been raised. All this has been possible because Jesus chose to do the will of God. This mention of the will of God leads us again to another aspect of Matthew's gospel which receives special emphasis in the passion narrative: the fulfilment of God's will as expressed in the scriptures.

(b) *The obedient Son: the fulfilment of scripture*. One of Matthew's chief concerns is to show that Jesus fulfils the will of God as expressed in the Old Testament scriptures and hence is the Messiah. From the very beginning of his gospel, in the infancy narrative, he pursues his aim by means of *fulfilment* or *formula quotations*, introduced by the formula 'to fulfil what was spoken by the prophet' (or similar: Mt 1:22; 2:15, 17, 23) and *contextual quotations* (Mt 2:5–6). Throughout his account of Jesus' public ministry all important stages or aspects of his activity are accompanied by explicit or implicit references to scripture (e.g., Mt 4:14–16; 8:17; 13:14–15, 35; 21:4–5, 16, 42).

The same concern is evident in the passion narrative. In the account of Jesus' arrest, Matthew adds, 'But how then should the scriptures be fulfilled, that it must be so?' (Mt 26:54), and Mark's vague statement 'But let the scriptures be fulfilled' (Mk 14:49b) is changed into 'But all this has taken place, that the scriptures of the prophets might be fulfilled' (Mt 26:56). The account of the fate of Judas fulfils what was said by the prophet Jeremiah (Mt 27:9–10). At the cross the mockery of the chief priests is further developed by means of an almost literal quotation from Ps 22(21):8 and Wis 2:18–20. Matthew also takes over all of Mark's allusions to the scriptures and repeatedly alters his Marcan source to get closer to the text referred to or to include allusions to other Old Testament passages (e.g., Matthew's addition that Joseph of Arimathea was 'a rich man' is probably an allusion to Isa 53:9). All these editiorial interventions emphasize that Jesus dies on the cross as Messiah and obedient Son of God.

III. Luke

Luke is the evangelist of God's plan. He wrote a real salvation history presented in the form of a travel account. Jesus travels along a straight line from Nazareth in Galilee to the centre of salvation history, Jerusalem. All other geographical indications in Mark which would either break that straight line or take Jesus to a place where he had already been before, are either changed or omitted. From Jerusalem then, Christ, present in his apostles through the Holy Spirit, travels to the end of the world (Acts 1:8, an outline of the Book of Acts), or at least to what Luke understood to be the centre of the Roman world, Rome itself.

This salvation history is set forth in three clearly delimited periods: (1) the period of the Old Testament, of which John the Baptist is the last prophet; (2) the period of Jesus, from his baptism to his ascension; (3) the period of the Church, beginning with Pentecost, which is separated from the ascension by forty days of preparation of God's new people for the new Sinai (Acts 2:1–13).

Luke's situation and theological perspective is clearly expressed in Acts 1. The disciples ask: 'Lord, will you *at this time* restore the kingdom to *Israel*?' (Acts 1:6). Jesus replies: neither at this time, nor to Israel alone: 'You shall receive power when the Holy Spirit has come upon you; and you shall be my witness in Jerusalem and in all Judea and Samaria and to the end of the earth' (Acts 1:8). An endless space and time lie ahead of Luke's Church. It is the time of the Church in the world, the time of the Spirit sent forth by the Lord sitting at the right hand of the Father (Lk 22:69, quoting Ps 110[109]:1, but omitting the quotation from Dan 7:13, the Son of man coming on the clouds of heaven, which constitutes the second half of Jesus' words in

Mark and Matthew). With this last remark we are immediately occupied with Luke's passion narrative.

(1)   Luke presents the passion first of all as a *martyrium*, as a *witness*, not for one or another idea or conviction, but because it was God's will: 'The Son of man goes as it has been determined' (Lk 22:22). Jesus' passion happened according to God's plan. The passion narrative too is included in Luke's theocentric vision.

Luke emphasizes the features which will in future define the martyr: silence and patience before accusations and insults (Lk 23:9); innocence admitted by Pilate and Herod (Lk 23:4, 14f., 22); overlooking his own sufferings (Lk 23:28); welcome given to the repentant 'criminal' (Lk 23:43); pardon granted to Peter (Lk 22:61) and to his persecutors and executioners themselves (Lk 22:51; 23:34).

To the disciples this *martyrium* or witness is an appeal: they are called to follow Jesus on his way of the cross in the manner Jesus did it first: he reacts to his passion with prayer and forgiveness (Lk 22:32, 51; 23:34, 40, 43) and the true disciple, exemplified by Stephen, does the same: 'And as they were stoning Stephen, he prayed, "Lord Jesus, receive my spirit." And he knelt down and cried with a loud voice, "Lord, do not hold this sin against them" ' (Acts 7:59–60). Thus Luke pictures the first martyr or witness. The disciples are to be Jesus' martyrs or witnesses (Acts 1:8; Greek: *martures*). No wonder that the theme of witness occurs so often in the Book of Acts (Acts 1:8, 22; 2:32; 3:15; 5:32; 10:39, 41; 13:31; 22:15, 20; 26:16). The disciples are to be witnesses to the resurrection, to Jesus' word, to all that he has done. In Acts 22:15; 26:16 Paul is referred to as a witness.

(2)   The motif of *Jesus' innocence* is closely related to the previous theme. It is also found in the other gospels but, unlike Mark and Matthew, Luke first carefully exposes the three political charges the Jewish authorities accuse Jesus of (Lk 23:2) and then has Pilate three times declare Jesus innocent (Lk 23:4, 14, 22). Herod does the same (Lk 23:15). That the pious women follow Jesus to the cross lamenting him implies that he is not a criminal (Lk 23:27), and the repentant 'criminal' admits that Jesus 'has done nothing wrong' (Lk 23:41). Finally, the centurion's confession is formulated, 'Certainly this man was innocent' (Lk 23:47; not 'Truly this (man) was the Son of God' as in Mk 15:39 and Mt 27:54).

The same motif is continued in the Book of Acts (Acts 3:13–16; 7:52; 10:37–39; 13:27–28). Similarly, the Jewish authorities repeatedly accuse Paul of political crimes, intending to brand him as an insurgent and rebel (Acts 17:7; 24:2–5; 25:7–8). Every time, Luke makes it very clear that the Roman authorities acquit Paul of all charges (e.g., Acts 24:2f.; 25:18, 25f.; 26:31f.). Luke untiringly insists that the Roman authorities had no serious conflict with either Jesus or his followers.

(3)   At the beginning of Jesus' ministry, Luke places a programmatic speech (Lk 4:16–30) in which Jesus is described as the *saviour of the poor*, of all those who are *oppressed* and *downcast*, including the women who were not given their due rights in contemporary society, the tax collectors, the criminals, and finally the Gentiles (cf. the quotation from Isa 61:1–2 and 58:6 in Lk 4:18–19). Thus Luke's picture of Jesus is that of a 'philanthropic' Christ. This appears particularly in Luke's version of the miracle stories: Jesus shows great compassion for all those who suffer, and their plight is described in such a way as to enhance Jesus' kind attention for them. He is concerned with a widow's 'only son' (Lk 7:13), a father's 'only daughter, about twelve years of age' (Lk 8:42), and another father's epileptic 'only child' (Lk 9:38–42). Several features of the passion narrative should be understood in line with this Lucan picture of Jesus.

At his arrest Jesus cures the slave of the high priest whose right ear was cut off (Lk 22:50–51). After Peter's denial, Jesus turns and forgivingly looks at him (Lk 22:61). When Jesus is led to the place of crucifixion he overlooks his own suffering and compassionately turns to the *women* who follow him (Lk 23:27–31).

Luke also seems to provide a place for the *Gentiles* at the crucifixion. Unlike the portrayal in Mark and Matthew, Jesus is not only followed by Simon of Cyrene but also by an unidentified great multitude (Lk 23:27), which presumably includes Gentiles, and after the crucifixion Luke again refers to the multitude who assembled to witness the events, and who go home repenting (Lk 23:48).

Ultimately, Luke's Christ dies for and as the *representative of these poor*. Luke says literally that 'two other criminals were led away together with him to be finished off' (Lk 23:32). Then 'they crucified him, and the criminals, one on the right and one on the left' (Lk 23:33), as if Jesus were their leader. The evangelist no doubt refers back to the passage about 'the two swords' (Lk 22:35–38), where Jesus is quoted as saying: 'For I tell you that this scripture must be fulfilled in me, "And he was reckoned with transgressors" (*anomoi*, literally, 'lawless'); for what is written about me has its fulfilment'. In fact, the first to join Jesus to be with him in paradise is the 'criminal' crucified with him (Lk 23:39–46). Finally, the centurion says literally that 'Certainly this man was the just one (*dikaios*)' (Lk 23:47), the one who according to Isa 53:11 and Wis 2:10–20 ('Let us oppress the righteous poor man . . .') suffers and dies for the poor and the oppressed of this world.

(4)   The gospel of Luke is also the *gospel of prayer*. Jesus himself gives the supreme example of prayer. This fact is also referred to by Mark and Matthew, but Luke speaks of the prayer of Jesus in eight further circumstances (Lk 3:21; 5:16; 6:12; 9:18; 11:1; 22:32; 23:34; 23:46). At the same time Luke's gospel also contains a strong

paraenesis (exhortation and warning) on prayer: Jesus often recommends prayer to his disciples (e.g. Lk 11:1–13; 18:1–8). They must pray to obtain the Holy Spirit (Lk 11:13), their prayer must be true prayer (Lk 18:13), they ought to pray at all times (Lk 21:36), and they should pray that they may not enter into temptation (Lk 22:40). It should also be noted that prayer and praying are referred to twenty-five times in the Acts of the Apostles.

This prayer theme is also emphasized in Luke's passion narrative. The prayer motif is stressed in the Gethsemane account (compare Mk 14:32–42 and Lk 22:40–46), but it is especially the scenes of Jesus' crucifixion and death which are transformed into an act of prayer. During the crucifixion only Luke quotes Jesus as praying for his executioners, 'Father, forgive them; for they know not what they do' (Lk 23:34), and at the moment of death Luke quotes Jesus as reciting Ps 31(30):5, 'Into your hand I commit my spirit', to which he adds the address 'Father' (Lk 23:46). Thus Jesus' death on the cross is framed by two prayers to the Father and is presented, therefore, as the supreme act of prayer and surrender to the Father.

Conclusion: Preaching the passion narratives

At the end of our first chapter we stated that each of the synoptic passion narratives has its own theological perspective. We feel that the detailed study of the texts has borne out our initial statement. In this final chapter we have shown that the perspectives of the synoptic passion narratives are in keeping with the theology of the gospels as a whole.

When we preach on any of these passion narratives or on any part of them we should do justice to the proper theological perspective of the evangelist. Thus we will resist the temptation just to tell the passion 'story'. Homiletics is not story-telling, and a homily on a passion narrative is not a summary report of a passion play. The homilist should take pains to ensure that what he says of Jesus' passion conforms to the actual message of the gospel. For instance, we should do justice to the fact that none of the evangelists emphasizes the physical sufferings of Jesus. However, popular devotion tends to focus on physical suffering and cruel details at the expense of the real gospel message. We should not reject or ridicule this popular approach, but we should not simply go along with it either. As true pastors, we should try to lead our people to the genuine riches of scripture by gradually but effectively reorienting their approach.

The evangelists and the early Christian communities did not intend the passion narratives to be accurate reconstructions of what actually happened, but rather faith-interpretations of the passion, developed after, and in the light of, Easter. The preaching of the passion narratives, therefore, should not be an attempt to retell the story as realistically as possible. This would almost certainly lead to the inclusion of elements which are not found in the gospel and would turn the interest of the listeners away from the genuine message of the text. If the homilist acts as though he were retelling in his own words a precise eyewitness report of what happened, then he is misleading his hearers.

In preaching the message of the passion narratives, we should refrain from all attempts at imaginative reconstruction, and apply ourselves to the proclamation of the living and ever-present Christ. The homilist should first of all serve the interests of the Word of God and not the ill-considered expectations of his audience. In fact, he will serve his listeners today best by faithfully adhering to the authentic message of the gospels.

Notes

1. D. Senior, *The Passion Narrative According to Matthew. A Redactional Study* (Bibliotheca Ephemeridum Theologicarum Lovaniensium 39; Louvain: Leuven University Press, 1975), pp. 141–2.
2. The historical problems concerning the trial or hearing of Jesus are very complicated and difficult to solve. For an easily accessible treatment of this question, see D. E. Nineham, *The Gospel of St Mark* (The Pelican Gospel Commentaries; Harmondsworth, Middx/Baltimore: Penguin Books, 1964) pp. 400–5; also E. Schweizer, *The Good News According to Mark* (trans. D. H. Madvig; Richmond, Va.: John Knox Press, 1970/London: SPCK, 1971), pp. 321–8. For more detailed studies, see the Bibliography.
3. J. R. Donahue, *Are You the Christ? The Trial Narrative in the Gospel of Mark* (Society of Biblical Literature Dissertation Series 10; Missoula, Mont.: University of Montana, 1973), p. 69.
4. We find a similar piling up of Christological titles in Mk 8:27 – 9:1, a scene closely related to the trial narrative, but here the titles are spread over thirteen verses.
5. Q (from the first letter of German *Quelle*, 'source'): the hypothetical non-Marcan source common to Matthew and Luke.
6. Cf. H. Hendrickx, *The Infancy Narratives* (revised ed.; London: Geoffrey Chapman, 1984), pp. 4–7.
7. D. Senior, 'Book review on Maria Riebl, *Auferstehung Jesu in der Stunde seines Todes? Zur Botschaft von Mt 27, 51b–53* (Stuttgart: KBW Verlag, 1978)', *The Catholic Biblical Quarterly* 42 (1980), 583.
8. G. S. Sloyan, *Jesus on Trial. The Development of the Passion Narratives and Their Historical and Ecumenical Implications* (Philadelphia: Fortress Press, 1973), p. 127.

The synoptic passion narratives

I. The arrest of Jesus

Matthew 26:47–56

(47)While he was still speaking Judas came, one of the twelve, and with him a great crowd with swords and clubs, from the chief priests and the elders of the people. (48)Now the betrayer had given them a sign, saying, 'The one I shall kiss is the man; seize him.' (49)And he came up to Jesus at once and said, 'Hail, Master!' And he kissed him. (50)Jesus said to him, 'Friend, why are you here?' Then they came up and laid hands on Jesus and seized him.

Mark 14:43–52

(43)And immediately, while he was still speaking, Judas came, one of the twelve, and with him a crowd with swords and clubs, from the chief priests and the scribes and the elders. (44)Now the betrayer had given them a sign, saying, 'The one I shall kiss is the man; seize him and lead him away safely.' (45)And when he came, he went up to him at once, and said, 'Master!' And he kissed him. (46)And they laid hands on him and seized him.

Luke 22:47–53

(47)While he was still speaking, there came a crowd, and the man called Judas, one of the twelve, was leading them. He drew near to Jesus to kiss him; (48)but Jesus said to him, 'Judas, would you betray the Son of man with a kiss?' (49)And when those who were about him saw what would follow, they said, 'Lord, shall we strike with the sword?'

(51)And behold, one of those who were with Jesus stretched out his hand and drew his sword, and struck the slave of the high priest, and cut off his ear. (52)Then Jesus said to him, 'Put your sword back into its place; for all who take the sword will perish by the sword. (53)Do you think that I cannot appeal to my Father, and he will at once send me more than twelve legions of angels? (54)But how then should the scriptures be fulfilled, that it must be so?'	(47)But one of those who stood by drew his sword, and struck the slave of the high priest and cut off his ear.	(50)And one of them struck the slave of the high priest and cut off his right ear. (51)But Jesus said, 'No more of this!'
		And he touched his ear and healed him.
(55)At that hour Jesus said to the crowds,	(48)And Jesus said to them,	(52)Then Jesus said to the chief priests and captains of the temple and elders, who had come out against him,
'Have you come out as against a robber, with swords and clubs to capture me? Day after day I sat in the temple teaching,	'Have you come out as against a robber, with swords and clubs to capture me? (49)Day after day I was with you in the temple teaching,	'Have you come out as against a robber, with swords and clubs? (53)When I was with you day after day in the temple, you

and you did not seize me. (56)But all this has taken place, that the scriptures of the prophets might be fulfilled.' Then all the disciples forsook him and fled.

and you did not seize me. But let the scriptures be fulfilled.' (50)And they all forsook him and fled. (51)And a young man followed him, with nothing but a linen cloth about his body; and they seized him, (52)but he left the linen cloth and ran away naked.

did not lay hands on me. But this is your hour, and the power of darkness.'

II. Jesus before the Sanhedrin and Peter's denial

1. Introduction

Matthew 26:57–60a

(57)Then those who had seized Jesus led him to Caiaphas the high priest, where the scribes and the elders had gathered. (58)But Peter followed him at a distance, as far as the court-

Mark 14:53–55

(53)And they led Jesus to the high priest; and all the chief priests and the elders and the scribes were assembled. (54)And Peter had followed him at a distance, right into the court-

Luke 22:54

(54)Then they seized him and led him away, bringing him into the high priest's house. Peter followed at a distance; (55)and when they

yard of the high priest, and going inside he sat with the guards to see the end.

(59)Now the chief priests and the whole council sought false testimony against Jesus that they might put him to death, (60a)but they found none,

had kindled a fire in the middle of the courtyard and sat down together, Peter sat among them.

yard of the high priest; and he was sitting with the guards, and warming himself at the fire. (55)Now the chief priests and the whole council sought testimony against Jesus to put him to death; but they found none.

Luke 22:55–62

(55)and when they had kindled a fire in the middle of the courtyard and sat down together, Peter sat among them. (56)Then a maid, seeing him as he sat in the light and gazing at him, said, 'This man also was with him.' (57)But he denied it, saying, 'Woman, I do not know him.' (58)And a little later some one else saw him and said, 'You also are one of them.' But Peter said, 'Man, I am not.' (59)And after an interval of about an hour still another insisted, saying, 'Certainly this man also was with him; for he is a Galilean.' (60)But Peter said, 'Man, I do not know what you are saying.' And immediately, while he was still speaking, the cock crowed. (61)And the Lord turned and looked at Peter. And Peter remembered the word of the Lord, how he had said to him, 'Before the cock crows today, you will deny me three times.' (62)And he went out and wept bitterly.

Luke 22:63–65

(63)Now the men who were holding Jesus mocked him and beat him; (64)they also blindfolded him and asked him, 'Prophesy! Who is it that struck you?' (65)And they spoke many other words against him, reviling him.

Luke 22:66

(66)When day came, the assembly of the elders of the people gathered together, both chief priests and scribes; and they led him away to their council,

2. The Accusation by False Witnesses

Mark 14:56–59

(56)For many bore false witness against him, and their witness did not agree. (57)And some stood up and bore false witness against him, saying, (58)"We heard him say, "I will destroy this temple that is made with hands, and in three days I will build another, not made with hands."" (59)Yet not even so did their testimony agree.

Matthew 26:60b–61

(60b)though many false witnesses came forward.

At last two came forward (61)and said, 'This fellow said, "I am able to destroy the temple of God, and to build it in three days."'

3. Interrogation, Answer, Reaction

Matthew 26:62-66	Mark 14:60-64	Luke 22:66-71
(62)And the high priest stood up and said 'Have you no answer to make? What is it that these men testify against you?' (63)But Jesus was silent.	(60)And the high priest stood up in the midst, and asked Jesus, 'Have you no answer to make? What is it that these men testify against you?' (61)But he was silent and made no answer.	(66)*When day came, the assembly of the elders of the people gathered together, both chief priests and scribes; and they led him away to their council,* and they said,
And the high priest said to him, 'I adjure you by the living God, tell us if you are the Christ, the Son of God.'	Again the high priest asked him, 'Are you the Christ, the Son of the Blessed?'	(67)'If you are the Christ, tell us.' But he said to them, 'If I tell you, you will not believe; (68)and if I ask you, you will not answer.
(64)Jesus said to him, 'You have said so. But I tell you, hereafter you will see the Son of man seated at the	(62)And Jesus said, 'I am; and you will see the Son of man sitting at the	(69)But from now on the Son of man shall be seated at

right hand of Power, and coming on the clouds of heaven.'

(65)Then the high priest tore his robes, and said, 'He has uttered blasphemy. Why do we still need witnesses? You have now heard his blasphemy. (66)What is your judgment?' They answered, 'He deserves death.'

right hand of Power, and coming with the clouds of heaven.'

(63)And the high priest tore his mantle, and said, 'Why do we still need witnesses? (64)You have heard his blasphemy. What is your decision?' And they all condemned him as deserving death.

the right hand of the power of God.'

(70)And they all said, 'Are you the Son of God, then?' And he said to them, 'You say that I am.'

(71)And they said, 'What further testimony do we need? We have heard it ourselves from his own lips.'

4. The Mocking Scene

Matthew 26:67–68

(67)Then they spat in his face, and struck him, and some slapped him,

Mark 14:65

(65)And some began to spit on him, and to cover him, and to strike him, saying

(Lk 22:63–65)

(63)*Now the men who were holding Jesus mocked him and beat him;* (64)*they also blindfolded him*

Matthew 26:69-75

(68)saying, 'Prophesy to us, you Christ! Who is it that struck you?'

(69)Now Peter was sitting outside in the courtyard. And a maid came up to him, and said, 'You also were with Jesus the Galilean.' (70)But he denied it before them all, saying, 'I do not know what you mean.' (71)And when he went out to the porch, another maid saw him, and she said to the bystanders, 'This man was with Jesus of Nazareth.' (72)And again he denied it with an oath, 'I do not know the man.' (73)After a little while the

Mark 14:66-72

to him, 'Prophesy!'

And the guards received him with blows.

5. *The Denial of Peter*

(66)And as Peter was below in the courtyard, one of the maids of the high priest came; (67)and seeing Peter warming himself, she looked at him, and said, 'You also were with the Nazarene, Jesus.' (68)But he denied it, saying, 'I neither know nor understand what you mean.' And he went out into the gateway, (69)And the maid saw him, and began again to say to the bystanders, 'This man is one of them.' (70)But again he denied it.

And after a little while again

(Luke 22:55—62)

and asked him, 'Prophesy! Who is it that struck you?' (65)And they spoke many other words against him, reviling him.

(56)Then a maid, seeing him as he sat in the light and gazing at him, said, 'This man also was with him.' (57)But he saying, 'Woman, I do not know him.' denied it.

(58)And a little later some one else saw him and said, 'You also are one of them.'

But Peter, said, 'Man, I am not.'

(59)And after an interval of

bystanders came up and said to Peter, 'Certainly you are also one of them; for your accent betrays you.' (74)Then he began to invoke a curse on himself and to swear, 'I do not know the man.' And immediately the cock crowed.

(75)And Peter remembered the saying of Jesus,

'Before the cock crows, you will deny me three times.' And he went out and wept bitterly.

the bystanders said to Peter, 'Certainly you are one of them; for you are a Galilean.' (71)But he began to invoke a curse on himself and to swear, 'I do not know this man of whom you speak.' (72)And immediately the cock crowed a second time.

And Peter remembered how Jesus had said to him, 'Before the cock crows twice, you will deny me three times.' And he broke down and wept.

about an hour still another insisted, saying, 'Certainly this man was also with him; for he is a Galilean.' (60)But Peter said,

'Man, I do not know what you are saying.' And immediately, while he was still speaking, the cock crowed.

(61)And the Lord turned and looked at Peter. And Peter remembered the word of the Lord, how he had said to him, 'Before the cock crows today, you will deny me three times.' (62)And he went out and wept bitterly.

6. Conclusion of Jewish trial and Jesus delivered to Pilate

Matthew 27:1–2

(1)When morning came, all the chief priests and the elders of the people took counsel against Jesus to put him to

Mark 15:1

(1)And as soon as it was morning the chief priests, with the elders and scribes, and the whole council held a con-

Luke (22:66); 23:1

(66)When day came, the assembly of the elders of the people gathered together, both chief priests and scribes;

Matthew	Mark	Luke
death; (2)and they bound him and led him away and delivered him to Pilate, the governor.	sultation; and they bound Jesus and led him away and delivered him to Pilate.	*and they led him away to their council.* (1)Then the whole company of them arose, and brought him before Pilate.

7. The Fate of Judas

Matthew 27:3–10

(3)When Judas, his betrayer, saw that he was condemned, he repented and brought back the thirty pieces of silver to the chief priests and the elders, (4)saying, 'I have sinned in betraying innocent blood.' They said, 'What is that to us? See to it yourself.' (5)And throwing down the pieces of silver in the temple, he departed; and he went and hanged himself. (6)But the chief priests, taking the pieces of silver, said, 'It is not lawful to put them into the treasury, since they are blood money.' (7)So they took counsel, and bought with them the potter's field, to bury strangers in. (8)Therefore that field has been called the Field of Blood to this day. (9)Then was fulfilled what had been spoken by the prophet Jeremiah, saying, 'And they took the thirty pieces of silver, the price of him on whom a price had been set by some of the sons of Israel, (10)and they gave them for the potter's field, as the Lord directed me.'

III. The trial before Pilate

1. Initial Interrogation by Pilate

Matthew 27:11–14	Mark 15:2–5	Luke 23:2–5
		(2)And they began to accuse him, saying, 'We found this

man perverting our nation, and forbidding us to give tribute to Caesar, and saying that he himself is Christ a king.'

(3)And Pilate asked him, 'Are you the King of the Jews?' And he answered him, 'You have said so.'

(2)And Pilate asked him, 'Are you the King of the Jews?' And he answered him, 'You have said so.' (3)And the chief priests accused him of many things. (4)And Pilate again asked him, 'Have you no answer to make? See how many charges they bring against you.' (5)But Jesus made no answer, so that Pilate wondered.

(4)And Pilate said to the chief priests and the multitudes, 'I find no crime in this man.' (5)But they were urgent, saying, 'He stirs up the people, teaching throughout all Judea, from Galilee even to this place.'

(11)Now Jesus stood before the governor; and the governor asked him, 'Are you the King of the Jews?' Jesus said to him, 'You have said so.' (12)But when he was accused by the chief priests and elders, he made no answer. (13)Then Pilate said to him, 'Do you not hear how many things they testify against you?' (14)But he gave them no answer, not even to a single charge; so that the governor wondered greatly.

Jesus Before Herod

Luke 23:6–16

(6)When Pilate heard this, he asked whether the man was a Galilean. (7)And when he learned that he belonged to Herod's jurisdiction, he sent him over to Herod, who was himself in Jerusalem at that time. (8)When Herod saw Jesus, he was very glad, for he had long desired to see him, because he had heard about him, and he was hoping to see some sign done by him. (9)So he questioned him at some length; but he made no answer. (10)The chief priests and the scribes stood by, vehemently accusing him. (11)And Herod with his soldiers treated him with contempt and mocked him; then, arraying him in gorgeous apparel, he sent him back to Pilate. (12)And Herod and Pilate became friends with each other that very day, for before this they had been at enmity with each other.

(13)Pilate then called together the chief priests and the rulers and the people, (14)and said to them, 'You brought me this man as one who was perverting the people; and after examining him before you, behold, I do not find this man guilty of any of your charges against him; (15)neither did Herod, for he sent him back to us. Behold, nothing deserving death has been done by him; (16)I will therefore chastise him and release him.'

2. The Barabbas Incident and Death Sentence

Matthew 27:15–26   **Mark 15:6–15**   Luke 23:18–25

Matthew 27:15–26

(15)Now at the feast the governor was accustomed to release for the crowd any one prisoner whom they wanted. (16)And they had then a notorious prisoner called Barabbas.

(17)So when they had gathered,

Mark 15:6–15

(6)Now at the feast he used to release for them one prisoner whom they asked. (7)And among the rebels in prison, who had committed murder in the insurrection, there was a man called Barabbas. (8)And the crowd came up and began to ask Pilate to do as he was

Pilate said to them, 'Whom do you want me to release for you, Barabbas or Jesus who is called Christ?' (18)For he knew that it was out of envy that they had delivered him up. (19)Besides, while he was sitting on the judgment seat, his wife sent word to him, 'Have nothing to do with that righteous man, for I have suffered much over him today in a dream.' (20)Now the chief priests and the elders persuaded the people to ask for Barabbas and destroy Jesus.

(21)The governor again said to them, 'Which of the two do you want me to release for you?' And they said, 'Barabbas.' (22)Pilate said to them, 'Then what shall I do with Jesus who is called Christ?'

They all said, 'Let him be crucified.'

wont to do for them. (9)And he answered them, 'Do you want me to release for you the King of the Jews?' (10)For he perceived that it was out of envy that the chief priests had delivered him up.

(11)But the chief priests stirred up the crowd to have him release for them Barabbas instead.

(12)And Pilate again said to them,

'Then what shall I do with the man whom you call the King of the Jews?'
(13)And they cried out again 'Crucify him.'

(18)But they all cried out together, 'Away with this man, and release to us Barabbas' — (19)a man who had been thrown into prison for an insurrection started in the city, and for murder. (20)Pilate addressed them once more, desiring to release Jesus;

(21)but they shouted out, 'Crucify, crucify him!'

(23)And he said,
'Why, what evil has he done?'

But they shouted all the more,
'Let him be crucified.'

(24)So when Pilate saw that he was gaining nothing, but rather that a riot was beginning, he took water and washed his hands before the crowd, saying, 'I am innocent of this man's blood; see to it yourselves.' (25)And all the people answered, 'His blood be on us and on our children!'

(26)Then he released for them Barabbas,

and having scourged Jesus, delivered him to be crucified.

---

(14)And Pilate said to them 'Why, what evil has he done?'

But they shouted all the more, 'Crucify him.'

(15)So Pilate, wishing to satisfy the crowd, released for them Barabbas;

and having scourged Jesus, he delivered him to be crucified.

---

(22)A third time he said to them, 'Why, what evil has he done? I have found in him no crime deserving death; I will therefore chastise him and release him.' (23)But they were urgent, demanding with loud cries that he should be crucified. And their voices prevailed.

(24)So Pilate gave sentence that their demand should be granted. (25)He released the man who had been thrown into prison for insurrection and murder, whom they asked for; but Jesus he delivered up to their will.

3. The Mocking by the Soldiers

Matthew 27:27-31

(27)Then the soldiers of the governor took Jesus into the praetorium, and they gathered the whole battalion before him. (28)And they stripped him and put a scarlet robe upon him, (29)and plaiting a crown of thorns they put it on his head, and put a reed in his right hand. And kneeling before him they mocked him, saying, 'Hail, King of the Jews!' (30)And they spat upon him, and took the reed and struck him on the head.

(31)And when they had mocked him, they stripped him of the robe, and put his own clothes on him, and led him away to crucify him.

Mark 15:16-20

(16)And the soldiers led him away inside the palace (that is, the praetorium); and they called together the whole battalion.

(17)And they clothed him in a purple cloak, and plaiting a crown of thorns they put it on him.

(18)And they began to salute him, 'Hail, King of the Jews!' (19)And they struck his head with a reed, and spat upon him, and they knelt down in homage to him. (20)And when they had mocked him, they stripped him of the purple cloak, and put his own clothes on him. And they led him out to crucify him.

IV. Crucifixion and Death

1. Requisition of Simon of Cyrene

Matthew 27:32

(32)As they were marching out, they came upon a man of Cyrene, Simon by name; this man they compelled to carry his cross.

Mark 15:21

(21)And they compelled a passer-by, Simon of Cyrene, who was coming in from the country, the father of Alexander and Rufus, to carry his cross

Luke 23:26

(26)And as they led him away, they seized one Simon of Cyrene, who was coming in from the country, and laid on him the cross, to carry it behind Jesus.

Luke 23:27–32

(27)And there followed him a great multitude of the people, and of women who bewailed and lamented him. (28)But Jesus turning to them said, 'Daughters of Jerusalem, do not weep for me, but weep for yourselves and for your children. (29)For behold, the days are coming when they will say, "Blessed are the barren, and the wombs that never bore, and the breasts that never gave suck!" (30)Then they will begin to say to the mountains, "Fall on us"; and to the hills, "Cover us." (31)For if they do this when the wood is green, what will happen when it is dry?' (32)Two others also, who were criminals, were led away to be put to death with him.

2. *The Crucifixion*

Matthew 27:33–38

(33)And when they came to a place called Golgotha, (which means the place of a skull), (34)they offered him wine to drink, mingled with gall; but when he tasted it, he would not drink it.

(35)And when they had crucified him,

Mark 15:22–27

(22)And they brought him to the place called Golgotha (which means the place of a skull). (23)And they offered him wine mingled with myrrh; but he did not take it.

(24)And they crucified him,

Luke 23:33–34

(33)And when they came to the place which is called The Skull,

there they crucified him, and the criminals, one on the right and one on the left. (34)And Jesus said, 'Father, forgive them; for they know not what they do.' And they

they divided his garments among them by casting lots;

(36)then they sat down and kept watch over him there.

(37)And over his head they put the charge against him, which read, 'This is Jesus the King of the Jews.'

(38)Then two robbers were crucified with him, one on the right and one on the left.

Matthew 27:39–44

(39)And those who passed by derided him, wagging their heads (40)and saying, 'You who would destroy the temple and built it in three days, save yourself! If you are the Son of God, come down from the cross.'

and divided his garments among them, casting lots for them, to decide what each should take.

(25)And it was the third hour, when they crucified him.

(26)And the inscription of the charge against him read, 'The King of the Jews.'

(27)And with him they crucified two robbers, one on his right and one on his left.

3. *The Mockery*

Mark 15:29–32

(29)And those who passed by derided him, wagging their heads, and saying, 'Aha! You who would destroy the temple and build it in three days, (30)save yourself, and come down from the cross!'

cast lots to divide his garments.

Luke 23:35–43

(35)And the people stood by, watching;

(41)So also the chief priests, with the scribes and elders, mocked him, saying, (42)'He saved others; he cannot save himself. He is the King of Israel; let him come down now from the cross, and we will believe in him. (43)He trusts in God; let God deliver him now, if he desires him; for he said, "I am the Son of God."'

(44)And the robbers who were crucified with him also reviled him in the same way.

(31)So also the chief priests mocked him to one another with the scribes, saying, 'He saved others; he cannot save himself. (32)Let the Christ, the King of Israel, come down now from the cross, that we may see and believe.'

Those who were crucified with him also reviled him.

but the rulers scoffed at him, saying, 'He saved others; let him save himself, if he is the Christ of God, his Chosen One!'

(36)The soldiers also mocked him, coming up and offering him vinegar, (37)and saying, 'If you are the King of the Jews, save yourself!' (38)There was also an inscription over him, 'This is the King of the Jews.'

(39)One of the criminals who were hanged railed at him, saying, 'Are you not the Christ? Save yourself and us!' (40)But the other rebuked him, saying, 'Do you not fear God, since you are under the same sentence of condemnation? (41)And we indeed justly; for we are receiving the due reward of our deeds; but this man has done nothing wrong.' (42)And he said, 'Jesus, remember me when you come in your kingly power.' (43)And he said to him, 'Truly, I say to you, today you will be with me in Paradise.'

Luke 23:44-45

(44)It was now about the sixth hour, and there was darkness over the whole land until the ninth hour. (45)while the sun's light failed; and the curtain of the temple was torn in two.

4. The Darkness

Matthew 27:45-49

(45)Now from the sixth hour there was darkness over all the land until the ninth hour.

(46)And about the ninth hour Jesus cried with a loud voice, 'Eli, Eli, lama sabachthani?' that is, 'My God, my God, why hast thou forsaken me?'

Mark 15:33-36

(33)And when the sixth hour had come, there was darkness over the whole land until the ninth hour.

(34)And at the ninth hour Jesus cried with a loud voice, 'Eloi, Eloi, lama sabachthani?' which means, 'My God, my God, why hast thou forsaken me?'

(47)And some of the bystanders hearing it said, 'This man is calling Elijah.' (48)And one of them at once ran and took a sponge, filled it with vinegar, and put it on a reed, and gave it to him to drink. (49)But the others said, 'Wait, let us see whether Elijah will come to save him.'

(35)And some of the bystanders hearing it said, 'Behold, he is calling Elijah.' (36)And one ran and, filling a sponge full of vinegar, put it on a reed and gave it to him to drink, saying, 'Wait, let us see whether Elijah will come to take him down.'

5. The Death of Jesus and its Repercussions

Matthew 27:50-54	Mark 15:37-39	Luke 23:46-48
(50)And Jesus cried again with a loud voice and yielded up his spirit. (51)And behold, the curtain of the temple was torn in two, from top to bottom; and the earth shook, and the rocks were split; (52)the tombs also were opened, and many bodies of the saints who had fallen asleep were raised, (53)and	(37)And Jesus uttered a loud cry, and breathed his last. (38)And the curtain of the temple was torn in two, from top to bottom.	(46)Then Jesus, crying with a loud voice, said, 'Father, into your hands I commit my spirit!' And having said this he breathed his last.

coming out of the tombs after his resurrection they went into the holy city and appeared to many. (54)When the centurion and those who were with him, keeping watch over Jesus, saw the earthquake and what took place, they were filled with awe, and said, 'Truly this was the Son of God!'

(39)And when the centurion, who stood facing him, saw that he thus breathed his last,

he said

'Truly this man was the Son of God!'

(47)Now when the centurion saw what had taken place, he praised God,

and said, 'Certainly this man was innocent!' (48)And all the multitudes who assembled to see the sight, when they saw what had taken place, returned home beating their breasts.

6. The Mention of the Women

Matthew 27:55–56

(55)There were also many women looking on from afar, who had followed him from Galilee, ministering to him; (56)among whom were Mary Magdalene, and Mary the mother

Mark 15:40–41

(40)There were also women looking on from afar,

among whom were Mary Magdalene, and Mary the mother

Luke 23:49

(49)And all his acquaintances and the women who had followed him from Galilee stood at a distance and saw these things.

V. The burial of Jesus

Matthew 27:57–61	Mark 15:42–47	Luke 23:50–56
of James and Joseph, and the mother of the sons of Zebedee.	of James the younger and of Joses, and Salome, (41)who when he was in Galilee, followed him, and ministered to him; and also many other women who came up with him to Jerusalem.	
(57)When it was evening,	(42)And when evening had come, since it was the day of Preparation, that is, the day before the sabbath, (43)Joseph of Arimathea,	(50)Now there was a man named Joseph from the Jewish town of Arimathea. He was a member of the council, a good and righteous man, (51)who had not consented to their purpose and deed, and he was looking for the kingdom of God.
there came a rich man from Arimathea, named Joseph,	a respected member of the council,	
who also was a disciple of Jesus.	who was also himself looking for the kingdom of God, took courage	
(58)He went to Pilate and asked for the body of Jesus.	and went to Pilate, and asked for the body of Jesus. (44)And Pilate wondered if	(52)This man went to Pilate and asked for the body of Jesus.

Then Pilate ordered it to be given him.

(59)And Joseph took the body, and wrapped it in a clean linen shroud, (60)and laid it in his own new tomb, which he had hewn in the rock; and he rolled a great stone to the door of the tomb, and departed.

(61)Mary Magdalene and the other Mary were there, sitting opposite the sepulchre.

he were already dead; and summoning the centurion, he asked him whether he was already dead. (45)And when he learned from the centurion that he was dead, he granted the body to Joseph.

(46)And he bought a linen shroud, and taking him down, wrapped him in the linen shroud, and laid him in a tomb which had been hewn out of the rock; and he rolled a stone against the door of the tomb.

(47)Mary Magdalene and Mary the mother of Joses saw where he was laid.

(53)Then he took it down and wrapped it in a linen shroud, and laid him in a rock-hewn tomb, where no one had ever yet been laid.

(54)It was the day of Preparation and the sabbath was beginning.

(55)The women who had come with him from Galilee followed, and saw the tomb, and how his body was laid;

(56)then they returned, and prepared spices and ointments. On the sabbath they rested according to the commandment.

For Further Reading

Benoit, P., *The Passion and Resurrection of Jesus Christ* (New York: Herder and Herder/London: Darton, Longman and Todd, 1969).

Blinzler, J., *The Trial of Jesus* (Westminster, Md.: The Newman Press, 1959).

Donahue, J. R., *Are You the Christ? The Trial Narrative in the Gospel of Mark* (Society of Biblical Literature Dissertation Series 10; Missoula, Mont.: University of Montana, 1973).

Lacomora, A. (ed.), *The Language of the Cross* (Chicago: Franciscan Herald Press, 1977).

O'Collins, G., *The Calvary Christ* (Philadelphia: The Westminster Press/London: SCM Press, 1977).

Sloyan, G. S., *Jesus on Trial. The Development of the Passion Narratives and Their Historical and Ecumenical Implications* (Philadelphia: Fortress Press, 1973).

Vanhoye, A., *Structure and Theology of the Accounts of the Passion in the Synoptic Gospels* (Collegeville, Minn.: The Liturgical Press, 1967).

Weber, H.-R., *The Cross. Tradition and Interpretation* (London: SPCK, 1979).

General Bibliography

Asendorf, U., 'Kreuz und Auferstehung', *Theologische Literaturzeitung* 102 (1977), 785–94.

Aubry, J., 'Valeur salvifique de la mort et de la résurrection de Jésus', *Assemblées du Seigneur* 24 (1969), 66–81.

Bajsic, A., 'Pilatus, Jesus und Barabbas', *Biblica* 48 (1967), 7–28.

Bammel, E. (ed.), *The Trial of Jesus. Cambridge Studies in Honour of C. F. D. Moule* (Studies in Biblical Theology, 2nd series 13; London: SCM Press/Naperville, Ill.: A. R. Allenson, 1970).

Barrick, W. B., 'The Rich Man from Arimathea (Matt 27:57–60) and 1QIsa^a', *Journal of Biblical Literature* 96 (1977), 235–9.

Bartsch, H. W., 'Historische Erwägungen zur Leidensgeschichte', *Evangelische Theologie* 22 (1962), 449–59.

Bartsch, H. W., 'Die Bedeutung des Sterbens Jesu nach den Synoptikern', *Theologische Zeitschrift* 20 (1964), 87–102.

Bartsch, H. W., 'Jesu Schwertwort, Lukas XXII, 35–38', *New Testament Studies* 20 (1973–74), 190–203.

Bartsch, H. W., 'The Sword-Word of Jesus (Luke 22:35–38)', *Brethren of Life and Thought* (1974), 149–56.

Bastin, M., *Jésus devant sa Passion* (Lectio Divina 92; Paris: Éditions du Cerf, 1976).

Bastin, M., 'L'annonce de la passion et les critères de l'historicité', *Revue de Sciences Religieuses* 50 (1976), 289–329.

Beaude, M., 'Mort et mis par écrit', *Christus* 24 (1977), 32–42.

Beckmann, J., 'Die Heilsbedeutung des Kreuzes Jesu' in *Freispruch und Freiheit. Festschrift für W. Kreck* (ed. H. G. Geijer; Munich: Kösel-Verlag, 1973), pp. 19–32.

Benoit, P., 'Jésus devant le Sanhédrin', *Angelicum* 20 (1943), 143–65 (=*Exégèse et Théologie* I, pp. 290–311).

Benoit, P., 'La Mort de Judas' in *Exégèse et Théologie* I (Paris: Éditions du Cerf, 1961), pp. 340–59.

Benoit, P., 'Les outrages à Jésus prophète (Mc 14,65 et par.)' in *Exégèse et Théologie* III (Paris: Éditions du Cerf, 1968), pp. 251–69.

Best, E., *The Temptation and the Passion. The Markan Soteriology* (Society for New Testament Studies Monograph Series 2; Cambridge: University Press, 1965).

Black, M., 'The "Son of Man" Passion Sayings in the Gospel Tradition', *Zeitschrift für die neutestamentliche Wissenschaft* 60 (1969), 1–8.

Blevins, J. L., 'The Passion Narrative: Luke 19:28–24:53', *Review and Expositor* 64 (1967), 513–22.

Bligh, J., 'Christ's Death Cry', *Heythrop Journal* 1 (1960), 142–6.

Bligh, J., 'Scripture Reading: Matching Passages 2: St Matthew's Passion Narrative', *The Way* 9 (1969), 59–73.

Blinzler, J., 'Passionsgeschehen und Passionsbericht des Lukasevangeliums', *Bibel und Kirche* 24 (1969), 1–4.

Blinzler, J., 'The Trial of Jesus in the Light of History', *Judaism* 20 (1971), 49–55.

Borgen, P., 'John and the Synoptics in the Passion Narrative', *New Testament Studies* 5 (1958–59), 246–59.

Borsch, F. H., 'Mark XIV.62 and I Enoch LXII.5', *New Testament Studies* 14 (1967–68), 565–8.

Bouwman, G., 'Lijden en offer', *Tijdschrift voor Geestelijk Leven* 33 (1977), 34–50.

Bovon, F., *Les derniers jours de Jésus. Textes et événements* (Collection 'Flèches'; Neuchâtel/Paris: Delachaux & Niestlé, 1974).

Bowman, J., 'The Significance of Mt 27:25', *Milla wa-Milla* 14 (1974), 26–31.

Brandenburger, E., '*Stauros*. Kreuzigung und Kreuzestheologie', *Wort und Dienst* 10 (1969), 17–43.

Brandon, S. G. F., *The Trial of Jesus of Nazareth* (New York: Stein and Day/London: Batsford, 1968).

Braun, F. M., 'La sépulture de Jésus', *Revue Biblique* 43 (1936), 34–52; 184–200; 346–63.

Broer, I., *Die Urgemeinde und das Grab Jesu: Eine Analyse der Grablegungsgeschichte im Neuen Testament* (Studien zum Alten und Neuen Testament 31; Munich: Kösel-Verlag, 1972).

Brown, S., *Apostasy and Perseverance in the Theology of Luke* (Analecta Biblica 36; Rome: Pontifical Biblical Institute, 1969).

Büchele, A., *Der Tod Jesu im Lukasevangelium. Eine redaktionsgeschichtliche Untersuchung zu Lk 23* (Frankfurt: J. Knecht, 1978).

Buijtenen, C. van, ' "En hij vluchtte naakt weg . . ." (Mc 14,52)', *Emmaüs* 10 (1979), 57–60.

Bultmann, R., *The History of the Synoptic Tradition* (trans. J. Marsh; revised ed.; Oxford: Basil Blackwell/New York: Harper and Row, 1968).

Burkill, T. A., 'St Mark's Philosophy of the Passion', *Novum Testamentum* 2 (1958), 245–71.

Burkill, T. A., *Mysterious Revelation. An Examination of the Philosophy of St Mark's Gospel* (Ithaca, N.Y.: Cornell University Press, 1963).

Buse, I., 'St John and the Marcan Passion Narrative', *New Testament Studies* 4 (1957–58), 215–19.

Buse, I., 'St John and the Passion Narratives of St Matthew and St Luke', *New Testament Studies* 7 (1960–61), 65–76.

Bussmann, C., 'Christus starb für unsere Sunden. Eine Anfrage an die Exegese angesichts des Unverständnisses, das dieser Satz heute trifft' in *Biblische Randbemerkungen* (ed. H. Merklein *et al.*; Würzburg: Echter Verlag, 1974), pp. 337–45.

Callan, T., 'Psalm 110:1 and the Origin of the Expectation that Jesus Will Come Again', *The Catholic Biblical Quarterly* 44 (1982), 606–21.

Catchpole, D. R., 'The Answer of Jesus to Caiaphas (Matt. XXVI.64)', *New Testament Studies* 17 (1970–71), 213–26.

Catchpole, D. R., *The Trial of Jesus* (Leiden: J. Brill, 1971).

Chabrol, C., 'Analyse des "Textes" der Passion' in *Erzählende Semiotik nach Berichten der Bibel* (Munich: Kösel-Verlag, 1973), pp. 123–55.

Chenderlin, F. P., 'Old Testament Sacrificial Memorial and Calvary', *The Bible Today* no. 59 (March 1972), 684–90.

Chordat, J. L., *Jésus devant sa mort* (Lire la Bible; Paris: Éditions du Cerf, 1970).

Chronis, H. L., 'The Torn Veil: Cultus and Christology in Mark 15:37–39', *Journal of Biblical Literature* 101 (1982), 97–114.

Cohn, H. H., *The Trial and Death of Jesus* (New York: Harper and Row, 1971/London: Weidenfeld and Nicolson, 1972; repr. New York: Ktav, 1977).

Cohn-Sherbok, D., 'Jesus' Cry on the Cross: An Alternative View', *Expository Times* 93 (7; 1982), 215–17.

Conzelmann, H., 'History and Theology in the Passion Narratives of the Synoptic Gospels', *Interpretation* 24 (1970), 178–97.

Corbin, M., 'Jésus devant Hérode. Lecture de Luc 23,6–12', *Christus* 25 (98; 1978), 190–7.

Cousin, H., *Le prophète assassiné. Histoire des textes évangéliques de la Passion* (Paris: J. Delarge, 1976).

Crossan, J. D., 'Mark and the Relatives of Jesus', *Novum Testamentum* 15 (1973), 81–113.

Culpepper, R. A., 'The Passion and Resurrection in Mark', *Review and Expositor* 75 (1978), 583–600.

Czerski, J., 'Die Passion Christi in den synoptischen Evangelien im Lichte der historisch-literarischen Kritik', *Collectanea Theologica* 46 (Sonderheft 1976), 81–96.

Dahl, N. A., 'Die Passionsgeschichte bei Matthäus', *New Testament Studies* 2 (1955–56), 17–32.

Dahl, N. A., *The Crucified Messiah and Other Essays* (Minneapolis: Augsburg, 1974).

Dahl, N. A., 'The Passion Narrative in Matthew' in *Jesus in the Memory of the Early Church* (Minneapolis: Augsburg, 1976), pp. 37–51.

Danker, F. W., 'The Demonic Secret in Mark. A Reexamination of the Cry of Dereliction (15,34)', *Zeitschrift für die neutestamentliche Wissenschaft* 61 (1970), 48–69.

Davies, A. T., 'The Jews and the Death of Jesus: Theological Reflections', *Interpretation* 23 (1969), 207–17.

Davies, P. E., 'Did Jesus die as a Martyr-Prophet?', *Biblical Research* 19 (1974), 37–47.

Davies, S. L., 'Who is called Bar Abbas?', *New Testament Studies* 27 (1980–81), 260–2.

Delling, G., *Der Kreuzestod Jesu in der urchristlichen Verkündigung* (Göttingen: Vandenhoeck & Ruprecht, 1972).

Delorme, J., 'Le Procès de Jésus ou la parole risquée (Lc 22,54–23,25)' in *La Parole de Grâce. Études lucaniennes à la mémoire d'Augustin George* (ed. J. Delorme and J. Duplacy; Paris: Recherches de Science Religieuse, 1981), pp. 123–46.

Derrett, J. D. M., 'Midrash in the New Testament: The Origin of Luke XXII, 67–68', *Studia Theologica* 29 (1975), 147–56.

Derrett, J. D. M., ' "Have nothing to do with that just man!" (Matt. 27, 19). Haggadah and the Account of the Passion', *Downside Review* 97 (329; 1979), 308–15.

Derrett, J. D. M., 'The Two Malefactors (Lk XXIII,33,39–43)' in *Studies in the New Testament* III: *Midrash, Haggadah, and the Character of the Community* (Leiden: Brill, 1982), pp. 200–14.

Derrett, J. D. M., 'Daniel and Salvation-History', *Downside Review* 100 (338; 1982), 62–8.

Derrett, J. D. M., 'The Reason for the Cock-Crowings', *New Testament Studies* 29 (1983), 142–4.

Descamps, A., 'Rédaction et christologie dans le récit matthéen de la Passion' in *L'Évangile selon Matthieu* (ed. M. Didier; Bibliotheca Ephemeridum Theologicarum Lovaniensium 29; Gembloux: Éditions J. Duculot, 1972), pp. 359–415.

Dibelius, M., *From Tradition to Gospel* (trans. B. L. Woolf; London: Ivor Nicholson & Watson, 1934/New York: Charles Scribner's Sons, 1935; repr. Cambridge: James Clarke & Co., 1971).

Dodd, C. H., 'The Historical Problem of the Death of Jesus' in *More New Testament Studies* (Manchester: University Press/Grand Rapids: Eerdmans, 1968).

Dormeyer, D., *Die Passion Jesu als Verhaltensmodel. Literarische und theologische Analyse der Traditions- und Redaktionsgeschichte der Markuspassion* (Neutestamentliche Abhandlungen, N.F. 11; Münster: Aschendorff, 1974).

Dormeyer, D., *Der Sinn des Leidens Jesu. Historisch-kritische und textpragmatische Analysen zur Markuspassion* (Stuttgarter Bibelstudien 96; Stuttgart: KBW Verlag, 1979).

Dunkerley, R., 'Was Barabbas also Called Jesus?', *Expository Times* 74 (1962–63), 126–7.

Dupont, J., 'Die individuelle Eschatologie im Lukas-Evangelium und in der Apostelgeschichte' in *Orientierung an Jesus. Zur Theologie der Synoptiker* (ed. P. Hoffmann, N. Brox and W. Pesch; Freiburg/Basel/Vienna: Herder, 1973), pp. 37–47.

Eltester, W., ' "Freund, wozu du gekommen bist" (Mt XXVI,50)' in *Neotestamentica et Patristica. Freundesgabe für Oscar Cullmann* (Leiden: Brill, 1962), pp. 70–91.

Ernst, J., 'Noch einmal: Die Verleugnung Jesu durch Petrus (Mk 14,54. 66–72)', *Catholica* 30 (1976), 207–26.

Ernst, J., 'Die Passionserzählung des Markus und die Aporien der Forschung', *Theologie und Glaube* 70 (1980), 160–80.

Escande, J., 'Judas et Pilate prisonniers d'une même structure (Mt 27,1–26)', *Foi et Vie* 78 (1979), 92–100.

Evans, C. A., ' "Peter Warming Himself": The Problem of an Editorial "Seam" ', *Journal of Biblical Literature* 101 (1982), 245–9.

Evans, C. F., 'The Passion of Christ', *Explorations in Theology* 2 (1977), 1–66, 185–8.

Feuillet, A., 'Le Triomphe du Fils de l'Homme d'après la déclaration du Christ aux Sanhédrites (Mc 14,62; Mt 26,64; Lc 22,69)' in *La Venue du Messie.*

Messianisme et Eschatologie (Recherches Bibliques VI; Bruges: Desclée, 1962), pp. 149–71.

Fitzmyer, J., 'Anti-semitism and the Cry of "All the People" (Mt 27:25)', *Theological Studies* 26 (1965), 667–71.

Fleddermann, H., 'The Flight of a Naked Young Man (Mark 14:51–52)', *The Catholic Biblical Quarterly* 41 (1979), 412–18.

Flusser, D., 'The Crucified One and the Jews', *Immanuel* 7 (1977), 25–37.

Flusser, D.,' "Sie wissen nicht was sie tun". Geschichte eines Herrenwortes' in *Kontinuität und Einheit. Festschrift für Franz Mussner* (ed. P. G. Müller and W. Stenger; Freiburg/Basel/Vienna: Herder, 1981), pp. 393–410.

Flusser, D., *Die letzten Tage Jesu in Jerusalem. Das Passionsgeschehen aus judischer Sicht. Bericht über neueste Forschungsergebnisse* (Stuttgart: Calwer Verlag, 1982).

Foulon-Piganiol, C. L., 'Le rôle du peuple dans le procès de Jésus. Une hypothèse juridique et théologique', *Nouvelle Revue Théologique* 98 (1976), 627–37.

Ford, J. M.,' "Crucify him, crucify him" and the Temple Scroll', *Expository Times* 87 (1975–76), 275–8.

France, R. T., 'Jésus devant Caïphe', *Hokhma* 15 (1980), 20–35.

Frankemölle, H., *Jahwebund und Kirche Christi. Studien zur Form- und Traditionsgeschichte des 'Evangeliums' nach Matthäus* (Neutestamentliche Abhandlungen, N.F. 10; Münster: Aschendorff, 1974).

Friedrich, G., *Die Verkündigung des Todes Jesu im Neuen Testament* (Biblisch-theologische Studien 6; Neukirchen-Vluyn: Neukirchener Verlag, 1982).

Frost, F., 'Jesus and Death', *The Clergy Review* 64 (1979), 117–22.

Genest, O., *Le Christ de la Passion. Perspective structurale. Analyse de Marc 14,53 – 15,47, des parallèles bibliques et extra-bibliques* (Tournai: Desclée, 1978).

George, A., 'Le sens de la mort de Jésus pour Luc', *Revue Biblique* 80 (1973), 186–217.

Gerhardsson, B., 'Jésus livré et abandonné d'après la Passion selon saint Matthieu', *Revue Biblique* 76 (1969), 206–27.

Gerhardsson, B., 'Confession and Denial before Men: Observations on Matt 26:57 – 27:2', *Journal for the Study of the New Testament* 13 (1981), 46–66.

Gewalt, D., 'Die Verleugnung des Petrus', *Linguistica Biblica* 43 (1978), 113–44.

Giblin, C. H., 'Structural and Thematic Correlations in the Matthean Burial-Resurrection Narrative (Matt. XXVII,57 – XXVIII,20)', *New Testament Studies* 21 (1974–75), 406–20.

Glasson, T. F., 'The Reply to Caiaphas (Mark XIV.62)', *New Testament Studies* 7 (1960–61), 88–93.

Glasson, T. F., 'Davidic Links with the Betrayal of Jesus', *Expository Times* 85 (1973–74), 118–19.

Grassi, J., 'Ezekiel XXXIV, 1–14 and the New Testament', *New Testament Studies* 11 (1964–65), 162–4.

Grelot, P.,' "Aujourd'hui tu seras avec moi dans le Paradis" (Luc XXIII,43)', *Revue Biblique* 74 (1967), 194–214.

Gubler, M.-L., *Die frühesten Deutungen des Todes Jesu. Eine motiv-*

geschichtliche Darstellung aufgrund der neueren exegetischen Forschung
(Orbis Biblicus et Orientalis 15; Göttingen: Vandenhoek & Ruprecht,
1977).

Hare, D., *The Theme of Jewish Persecution of Christians in the Gospel according to St Matthew* (Society for New Testament Studies Monograph Series
6; Cambridge: University Press, 1967).

Harner, P. B., 'Qualitative Anarthrous Predicate Nouns: Mark 15:39 and
John 1:1', *Journal of Biblical Literature* 92 (1973), 75–87.

Hemelsoet, B., 'Het lijdensverhaal volgens Matteüs', *Getuigenis* 25 (1981),
112–17.

Hengel, M., *Crucifixion in the Ancient World and the Folly of the Message of the
Cross* (London: SCM Press/Philadelphia: Fortress Press, 1977).

Hengel, M., 'The Expiatory Sacrifice of Christ', *Bulletin of the John Rylands
Library, Manchester* 62 (1979–80), 454–75.

Hengel, M., 'Der stellvertretende Sühnetod Jesu. Ein Beitrag zur Entstehung
des urchristlichen Kerygmas', *Internationale katholische Zeitschrift/
Communio* 9 (1980), 1–25, 135–47.

Hoehner, H. W., 'Chronological Aspects of the Life of Christ, Part IV: The
Day of Christ's Crucifixion', *Bibliotheca Sacra* 131 (1974), 332–48.

Horbury, W., 'The Passion Narratives and Historical Criticism', *Theology* 75
(620; 1972), 58–71.

Horvath, T., 'Why was Jesus Brought to Pilate?', *Novum Testamentum* 11
(1969), 174–84.

Janssen, F., 'Die synoptischen Passionsberichte. Ihre theologische Konzeption
und literarische Komposition', *Bibel und Leben* 14 (1973), 40–57.

Jeremias, J., 'Jesu Wörte über sein Leiden und Sterben', *Die Innere Mission* 58
(1968), 119–28.

Johnson, S. L., 'The Death of Christ', *Bibliotheca Sacra* 125 (1968), 10–19.

Jonge, M. de, 'De berichten over het scheuren van het voorhangsel bij Jezus'
dood in de synoptische evangelien', *Nederlands Theologisch Tijdschrift*
21 (1966–67), 90–114.

Jonge, M. de, 'The Use of *ho christos* in the Passion Narratives' in *Jésus aux
origines de la Christologie* (ed. J. Dupont; Bibliotheca Ephemeridum
Theologicarum Lovaniensium 25; Louvain: Leuven University Press,
1975), pp. 169–92.

Josuttis, M., 'Die permanente Passion. Predigt über Markus 15,33–39',
Evangelische Theologie 38 (1978), 160–3.

Juel, D., *Messiah and Temple. The Trial of Jesus in the Gospel of Mark* (Society
of Biblical Literature Dissertation Series 31; Missoula, Mont.: Scholars
Press, 1977).

Käsemann, E., 'Die Gegenwart des Gekreuzigten', *Zeichen der Zeit* 22
(1968), 7–15.

Käsemann, E., 'Proclaiming the Cross of Christ in an Age of Self-Deception',
The Month 236 (1975), 4–8.

Käser, W., 'Exegetische und theologische Erwägungen zur Seligpreisung der
Kinderlosen. Lc 23:29b', *Zeitschrift für die neutestamentliche Wissenschaft* 54 (1963), 240–54.

Keck, L. E., 'Mark and the Passion', *Interpretation* 31 (1977), 432–4.

Kelber, W. H., *The Kingdom in Mark. A New Place and a New Time* (Philadelphia: Fortress Press, 1974).

Kelber, W. H., *The Passion in Mark. Studies on Mark 14–16* (Philadelphia: Fortress Press, 1976).

Kempthorne, R., 'The Marcan Text of Jesus' Answer to the High Priest (Mark XIV,62)', *Novum Testamentum* 19 (1977), 197–208.

Kempthorne, R., 'Anti-Christian Tendency in pre-Markan Traditions of the Sanhedrin Trial' in *Studia Evangelica* VII (Texte und Untersuchungen 126; Berlin: Akademie Verlag, 1982), pp. 283–5.

Kertelge, K., 'Der allgemeine Tod und der Tod Jesu', *Trierer Theologische Zeitschrift* 83 (1974), 146–56.

Kertelge, K. (ed.), *Der Tod Jesu. Deutungen im Neuen Testament* (Quaestiones Disputatae 74; Freiburg: Herder, 1976).

Kingsbury, J. D., *Matthew: Structure, Christology, Kingdom* (Philadelphia: Fortress Press, 1975/London: SPCK, 1976).

Kistemaker, S. J., 'The Seven Words from the Cross', *Westminster Theological Journal* 38 (1975–76), 182–91.

Klein, G., 'Die Verleugnung des Petrus. Eine traditionsgeschichtliche Untersuchung', *Zeitschrift für Theologie und Kirche* 58 (1961), 286–328.

Klein, H., 'Die lukanisch-johanneische Passionstradition', *Zeitschrift für die neutestamentliche Wissenschaft* 67 (1976), 155–86.

Klijn, A. F. J., 'Scribes, Pharisees, High Priests and Elders in the New Testament', *Novum Testamentum* 3 (1959), 259–67.

Knoch, O., 'Zur Diskussion über die Heilsbedeutung des Todes Jesu', *Theologisch-praktische Quartalschrift* 124 (1976), 3–14.

Knoch, O., 'Die Heilsbedeutung des Todes Jesu', *Theologisch-praktische Quartalschrift* 126 (1976), 221–37.

Kodell, J., 'Luke's Use of *Laos*, "People," Especially in the Jerusalem Narrative (Lk 19,28–24,53)', *The Catholic Biblical Quarterly* 31 (1969), 327–43.

Kosmala, H., 'Matthew XXVI.52 – A Quotation from the Targum', *Novum Testamentum* 4 (1960), 3–5.

Kosmala, H., 'The Time of Cock-Crow', *Annual of the Swedish Theological Institute* 2 (1963), 118–20; 6 (1968), 132–4.

Kosmala, H., ' "His Blood on Us and Our Children" (The Background of Mat. 27,24–25)', *Annual of the Swedish Theological Institute* 7 (1968–69), 94–126.

Kreck, W., 'Zum Verständnis des Todes Jesu', *Evangelische Theologie* 28 (1968), 277–93.

Kremer, J., 'Verurteilt als "König der Juden" – verkündigt als "Herr und Christus" ', *Bibel und Liturgie* 45 (1972), 23–32.

Kwaak, H. van der, *Het Proces van Jezus. Een vergelijkend onderzoek van de beschrijvingen der evangelisten* (Assen: Van Gorcum & Comp., 1969).

Lamarche, P., 'Le "blasphème" de Jésus devant le Sanhédrin', *Recherches de Science Religieuse* 50 (1962), 74–85.

Lamarche, P., 'La mort du Christ et le voile du temple selon Marc', *Nouvelle Revue Théologique* 106 (1974), 583–99.

Lamarche, P., 'L'humiliation du Christ', *Christus* 26 (104; 1979), 461–70.

Lampe, G. W. H., 'St Peter's Denial', *Bulletin of the John Rylands Library, Manchester* 55 (1973), 348–68.

Lange, H. D., 'The Relationship between Ps 22 and the Passion Narrative', *Concordia Theological Monthly* 43 (1972), 610–21.

186 *The Passion Narratives of the Synoptic Gospels*

Lange, J., 'Zur Ausgestaltung der Szene vom Sterben Jesu in den synoptischen Evangelien' in *Biblische Randbemerkungen* (ed. H. Merklein and J. Lange; Würzburg: Echter Verlag, 1974), pp. 40–55.

Lee, G. M., 'Matthew XXVI.50: *Hetaire, eph' ho parei*', *Expository Times* 81 (1969–70), 50.

Lee, G. M., 'Mark 14:72: *epibalōn eklaien*', *Biblica* 53 (1972), 411–12.

Lee, G. M., 'Mark XV,21, The Father of Alexander and Rufus', *Novum Testamentum* 17 (1975), 303.

Lee, G. M., 'Mark VIII 24. Mark XV 8', *Novum Testamentum* 20 (1978), 74.

Légasse, S., 'Jésus devant le Sanhédrin. Recherche sur les traditions évangéliques', *Revue Théologique de Louvain* 5 (1974), 170–97.

Légasse, S., 'Les voiles du Temple de Jérusalem. Essai de parcours historique', *Revue Biblique* 87 (1980), 560–89.

Léon-Dufour, X., 'Mt et Mc dans le récit de la Passion', *Biblica* 40 (1959), 684–96.

Léon-Dufour, X., 'Autour des récits de la Passion', *Recherches de Science Religieuse* 48 (1960), 489–507.

Léon-Dufour, X., 'La mort rédemptrice du Christ selon le Nouveau Testament' in *Mort pour nos péchés* (Brussels: Facultés Universitaires Saint-Louis, 1976), pp. 11–44.

Léon-Dufour, X., 'Le dernier cri de Jésus', *Études* 348 (1978), 666–82.

Léon-Dufour, X., 'Der Todesschrei Jesu', *Theologie der Gegenwart* 21 (1978), 172–8.

Léon-Dufour, X., *Face à la Mort. Jésus et Paul* (Parole de Dieu; Paris: Éditions du Seuil, 1979).

Linnemann, E., *Studien zur Passionsgeschichte* (Forschungen zur Religion und Literatur des Alten und Neuen Testaments 102; Göttingen: Vandenhoeck & Ruprecht, 1970).

Linton, O., 'The Trial of Jesus and the Interpretation of Psalm CX', *New Testament Studies* 7 (1960–61), 258–63.

Loader, W. R. G., 'Christ at the Right Hand. Ps CX.1 in the New Testament', *New Testament Studies* 24 (1977–78), 199–217.

Lohfink, G., *Der Letzte Tag Jesu: Die Ereignisse der Passion* (Freiburg/Basel/Vienna: Herder, 1981).

Lohse, E., *History of the Suffering and Death of Jesus Christ* (trans. M. O. Dietrich; Philadelphia: Fortress Press, 1967).

Lührmann, D., 'Markus 14.55–64: Christologie und Zerstörung des Tempels im Markusevangelium', *New Testament Studies* 27 (1980–81), 457–74.

Luke, K., 'The Thirty Pieces of Silver (Zch 11:12f.)', *Indian Theological Studies* 19 (1982), 15–22.

McArthur, H. K., 'Mark XIV.62', *New Testament Studies* 4 (1957–58), 156–8.

Maccoby, H. Z., 'Jesus and Barabbas', *New Testament Studies* 16 (1969–70), 55–60.

Mahoney, R., 'A New Look at "The Third Hour" of Mk 15,25', *The Catholic Biblical Quarterly* 21 (1966), 292–9.

Mahoney, R., *Two Disciples at the Tomb: The Background and Message of John 20:1–10* (Theologie und Wirklichkeit 6; Berne/Frankfurt: Lang, 1974).

Maier, P. L., 'Who was responsible for the Trial of Jesus?', *Christ Today* 18 (1974), 806–9.

Mann, D., *Mein Gott, mein Gott, warum hast du mich verlassen? Eine Auslegung der Passionsgeschichte nach Markus* (Neukirchen-Vluyn: Neukirchener Verlag, 1980).

Manns, F., 'Un midrash chrétien: le récit de la mort de Judas', *Revue de Sciences Religieuses* 54 (1980), 197–203.

Marin, L., *The Semiotics of the Passion Narrative. Topics and Figures* (Pittsburgh: Pickwick Press, 1981).

Matera, F., *The Kingship of Jesus: Composition and Theology in Mark 15* (Chico, Cal.: Scholars Press, 1981).

Maurer, C., 'Knecht Gottes und Sohn Gottes im Passionsbericht des Markus', *Zeitschrift für Theologie und Kirche* 50 (1953), 1–51.

Michaels, J. R., 'The Centurion's Confession and the Spear Thrust', *The Catholic Biblical Quarterly* 29 (1967), 102–9.

Michiels, R., 'Het oudste passieverhaal (Marcus)', *Tijdschrift voor Liturgie* 63 (1979), 272–89.

Miller, D. L., '*Empaizein*: Playing the Mock Game (Luke 22:63–64)', *Journal of Biblical Literature* 90 (1971), 309–13.

Mitscherlich, P., *Unter dem Kreuz. Begegnungen mit dem Leiden Jesu* (Topos-Taschenbücher 82; Mainz: Matthias-Grünewald, 1979).

Moore, S., *The Crucified is no Stranger* (London: Darton, Longman and Todd, 1977).

Müller, K., 'Jesus vor Herodes. Eine redaktionsgeschichtliche Untersuchung zu Lk 23,6–12' in *Zur Geschichte des Urchristentums* (ed. G. Dautzenberg *et al.*; Quaestiones Disputatae 87; Freiburg/Basel/Vienna: Herder, 1979), pp. 111–41.

Neirynck, F., 'La rédaction matthéenne et la structure du premier évangile', *Ephemerides Theologicae Lovanienses* 43 (1967), 41–73.

Neirynck, F., 'Duality in Mark', *Ephemerides Theologicae Lovanienses* 47 (1971), 394–463.

Neirynck, F., 'La fuite du jeune homme en Mc 14,51–52', *Ephemerides Theologicae Lovanienses* 55 (1979), 43–66.

Nevius, R., 'A Reply to Dr Dunkerly', *Expository Times* 74 (1962–63), 255.

Neyrey, J. H., 'Jesus' Address to the Women of Jerusalem (Lk 23.27–31) – A Prophetic Judgment Oracle', *New Testament Studies* 29 (1983), 74–86.

Nickelsburg, W. E., 'The Genre and Function of the Markan Passion Narrative', *Harvard Theological Review* 73 (1980), 153–84.

O'Collins, G., 'The Crucifixion', *Doctrine and Life* 26 (1976), 247–63.

O'Neill, J. C., 'The Silence of Jesus', *New Testament Studies* 15 (1968–69), 153–67.

O'Neill, J. C., 'The Charge of Blasphemy at Jesus' Trial before the Sanhedrin' in *The Trial of Jesus. Cambridge Studies in Honour of C. F. D. Moule* (ed. E. Bammel; London: SCM Press/Naperville, Ill.: A. R. Allenson, 1970), pp. 72–7.

Osborne, G. R., 'Redactional Trajectories in the Crucifixion Narrative', *Evangelical Quarterly* 51 (1979), 80–96.

Oswald, J., 'Die Beziehung zwischen Psalm 22 und dem vormarkinischen Passionsbericht', *Zeitschrift für Katholische Theologie* 101 (1979), 53–66.

Overstreet, R. L., 'Roman Law and the Trial of Jesus', *Bibliotheca Sacra* 135 (1978), 323–32.

Packer, J. I., 'What Did the Cross Achieve? The Logic of Penal Substitution', *Tyndale Bulletin* 25 (1974), 3–45.

Patte, D., and Patte, A., *Structural Exegesis: From Theory to Practice. Exegesis of Mark 15 and 16. Hermeneutical Implications* (Philadelphia: Fortress Press, 1978).

Pelletier, A., 'La tradition synoptique du "voile déchiré" à la lumière des réalités archéologiques', *Recherches de Science Religieuse* 46 (1958), 162–80.

Perrin, N., *A Modern Pilgrimage in New Testament Christology* (Philadelphia: Fortress Press, 1974).

Pesch, R., 'Die Verleuchnung des Petrus. Eine Studie zu Mk 14,55.66–72 (und Mk 14,26–31)' in *Neues Testament und Kirche* (ed. J. Gnilka; Freiburg/Basel/Vienna: Herder, 1974), pp. 42–62.

Pesch, R., 'Die Überlieferung der Passion Jesu' in *Rückfrage nach Jesus* (ed. K. Kertelge; Quaestiones Disputatae 63; Freiburg/Basel/Vienna: Herder, 1974), pp. 148–73.

Pesch, R., 'Der Schluss der markinischen Passionsgeschichte und des Markusevangeliums: Mk 15,42 – 16,8' in *L'Évangile de Marc. Tradition et rédaction* (ed. M. Sabbe; Bibliotheca Ephemeridum Theologicarum Lovaniensium 24; Louvain: Leuven University Press, 1974), pp. 365–409.

Pesch, R., 'Die Passion des Menschensohnes' in *Jesus und der Menschensohn. Festschrift für Anton Vögtle* (ed. R. Pesch and R. Schnackenburg; Freiburg/Basel/Vienna: Herder, 1975), pp. 166–95.

Pobee, J., 'The Cry of the Centurion – A Cry of Defeat' in *The Trial of Jesus. Cambridge Studies in Honour of C. F. D. Moule* (ed. E. Bammel; London: SCM Press/Naperville, Ill.: A. R. Allenson, 1970), pp. 91–102.

Punnakottil, G., 'The Passion Narrative According to Matthew. A Redaction Critical Study', *BibleBhashyam* 3 (1977), 20–47.

Quinn, J. F., 'The Pilate Sequence in the Gospel of Matthew', *Dunwoodie Review* 10 (1970), 154–77.

Rau, G., 'Das Volk in der lukanischen Passionsgeschichte, eine Konjektur zu Lk 23,13', *Zeitschrift für die neutestamentliche Wissenschaft* 56 (1965), 41–51.

Reid, W. S., 'The Death of Christ, Historical and Contemporaneous', *Evangelical Quarterly* 45 (1973), 69–80.

Reumann, J. H., 'Psalm 22 at the Cross. Lament and Thanksgiving for Jesus Christ', *Interpretation* 28 (1974), 39–45.

Rice, G. E., 'The Role of the Populace in the Passion Narrative of Luke in Codex Bezae', *Andrews University Seminary Studies* 19 (1981), 147–53.

Riches, J., 'The Dense and Driven Passion – The Story according to Mark', *The Furrow* 33 (1982), 195–202.

Riebl, M., *Auferstehung Jesu in der Stunde seines Todes? Zur Botschaft von Mt 27:51b–53* (Stuttgarter biblische Beiträge; Stuttgart: KBW Verlag, 1978).

Riedl, J., 'Die evangelische Leidensgeschichte und ihre theologische Aussage', *Bibel und Liturgie* 61 (1968), 70–111.

Roloff, J., 'Anfänge der soteriologischen Deutung des Todes Jesu (Mk X.45 und Lk XXII.27)', *New Testament Studies* 19 (1972–73), 38–64.

Ruppert, L., 'Das Skandalon eines gekreuzigten Messias und seine Überwindung mit Hilfe der geprägten Vorstellung vom leidenden Gerechte' in *Kirche und Bibel. Festgabe für Bischof E. Schick* (ed. A. Winter *et al.*; Paderborn/Munich/Vienna/Zurich: Schöningh, 1979), pp. 319–41.

Sanders, W., 'Das Blut Jesu und die Juden. Gedanken zu Matth. 27,25', *Una Sancta* 27 (1972), 168–71.

Sawyer, J. F. A., 'Why is a Solar Eclipse Mentioned in the Passion Narrative (Luke XXIII.44–45)', *Journal of Theological Studies* 23 (1972), 124–8.

Schelkle, K. H., *Die Passion Jesu in der Verkündigung des Neuen Testaments: Ein Beitrag zur Formgeschichte und zur Theologie des Neuen Testaments* (Heidelberg: Kerle Verlag, 1949).

Schenk, W., *Der Passionsbericht nach Markus: Untersuchungen zur Überlieferungsgeschichte der Passionstraditionen* (Gütersloh: Mohn, 1974).

Schenke, L., *Studien zur Passionsgeschichte des Markus. Tradition und Redaktion in Markus 14:1–42* (Forschung zur Bibel 4: Würzburg: Echter Verlag, 1971).

Schenke, L., *Der gekreuzigte Christus: Versuch einer literarischen und traditionsgeschichtlichen Bestimmung der vormarkinischen Passionsberichte* (Stuttgarter Bibelstudien 69; Stuttgart: KBW Verlag, 1974).

Schille, G., 'Das Leiden des Herrn. Die evangelische Passionstradition und ihr "Sitz im Leben" ', *Zeitschrift für Theologie und Kirche* 52 (1955), 161–205.

Schlier, H., *Die Markuspassion* (Kriterien 32; Einsiedeln: Johannes Verlag, 1974).

Schneider, G., *Verleugnung, Verspöttung und Verhor Jesu nach Lukas 22,54–71. Studien zur lukanischen Darstellung der Passion* (Studien zum Alten und Neuen Testament 22; Munich: Kösel-Verlag, 1969).

Schneider, G., 'Jesus vor dem Synedrium', *Bibel und Leben* 11 (1970), 1–15.

Schneider, G., 'Gab es eine vorsynoptische Szene "Jesus vor dem Synedrium"? ', *Novum Testamentum* 12 (1970), 22–39.

Schneider, G., 'Das Problem einer vorkanonische Passionserzählung', *Biblische Zeitschrift* 16 (1972), 222–44.

Schneider, G., 'Die Verhaftung Jesu. Traditionsgeschichte von Mk 14,43–52', *Zeitschrift für neutestamentliche Wissenschaft* 63 (1972), 188–209.

Schneider, G., *Die Passion Jesu nach den drei älteren Evangelien* (Biblische Handbibliothek 11; Munich: Kösel-Verlag, 1973).

Schneider, G., 'A Precanonical Passion Narrative?', *Theology Digest* 24 (1976), 188–9.

Schneider, G., 'Die theologische Sicht des Todes Jesu in den Kreuzigungsberichten der Evangelien', *Theologisch-praktische Quartalschrift* 126 (1978), 14–22.

Schnellbächer, E. L., 'Das Rätsel des *neaniskos* bei Markus', *Zeitschrift für die neutestamentliche Wissenschaft* 73 (1982), 127–35.

Schottroff, L., 'Maria Magdalena und die Frauen am Grabe Jesu', *Evangelische Theologie* 42 (1982), 3–25.

Schottroff, L., 'Die Nachfolge Jesu and das Kreuz' in *Die Bibel als politisches Buch* (ed. D. Schirmer; Urban-Taschenbücher; Stuttgart: Kohlhammer, 1982), pp. 35–46.

Schreiber, J., *Die Markuspassion. Wege zur Erforschung der Leidensgeschichte Jesu* (Hamburg: Furche-Verlag, 1969).

Schreiber, J., 'Die Bestattung Jesu. Redaktionsgeschichtliche Beobachtungen zu Mk 15:42–47 par.', *Zeitschrift für die neutestamentliche Wissenschaft* 72 (1981), 141–77.

Schürmann, H., *Jesu Tod – unser Leben. Ein Versuch zu Verstehen* (Antwort des Glaubens 18; Freiburg: Informationszentrum Berufe der Kirche, 1980).

Schütz, F., *Der leidende Christus. Die angefochtene Gemeinde und das Christuskerygma der lukanischen Schriften* (Beiträge zur Wissenschaft vom Alten und Neuen Testament 89; Stuttgart: Kohlhammer, 1969).

Schützeichel, H., 'Der Todesschrei. Bemerkungen zu einer Theologie des Kreuzes', *Trierer Theologische Zeitschrift* 83 (1974), 1–16.

Scroggs, R., and Groff, K. I., 'Baptism in Mark: Dying and Rising with Christ', *Journal of Biblical Literature* 92 (1973), 531–48.

Senior, D., 'The Fate of the Betrayer. A Redactional Study of Matthew XXVII, 3–10', *Ephemerides Theologicae Lovanienses* 48 (1972), 372–426.

Senior, D., 'The Passion Narrative in the Gospel of Matthew' in *L'Évangile selon Matthieu* (ed. M. Didier; Bibliotheca Ephemeridum Theologicarum Lovaniensium 29; Gembloux: Éditions J. Duculot, 1972), pp. 343–57.

Senior, D., 'A Death Song', *The Bible Today* no. 69 (February 1974), 1457–63.

Senior, D., 'A Case Study in Matthean Creativity. Matthew 27:3–10', *Biblical Research* 19 (1974), 23–46.

Senior, D., *The Passion Narrative According to Matthew. A Redactional Study* (Bibliotheca Ephemeridum Theologicarum Lovaniensium 39; Louvain: Leuven University Press, 1975).

Senior, D., 'The Death of Jesus and the Resurrection of the Holy Ones (Mt 27:51–53)', *The Catholic Biblical Quarterly* 38 (1976), 312–29.

Sloyan, G. S., 'Recent Literature on the Trial Narratives of the Four Gospels' in *Critical History and Biblical Faith* (ed. T. J. Ryan; Villanova, Pa.: CTS Annual Publications, 1979), pp. 136–76.

Smalley, A., 'Translating Luke's Passion Story from the TEV', *The Bible Translator* 28 (1977), 231–5.

Smith, R. H., 'Darkness at Noon: Mark's Passion Narrative', *Concordia Theological Monthly* 44 (1973), 325–38.

Smith, R. H., 'Paradise Today: Luke's Passion Narrative', *Currents in Theology and Mission* 3 (1976), 323–36.

Sobosan, J. G., 'The Trial of Jesus', *Journal of Ecumenical Studies* 10 (1973), 72–91.

Stock, K., 'Das Bekenntnis des Centurio. Mk 15, 39 im Rahmen des Markusevangeliums', *Zeitschrift für Katholische Theologie* 100 (1978), 289–301.

Stöger, A., 'Eigenart und Botschaft der lukanischen Passionsgeschichte', *Bibel und Kirche* 24 (1969), 4–8.

Strecker, G., 'The Passion- and Resurrection Predictions in Mark's Gospel', *Interpretation* 22 (1968), 421–42.

Taylor, V., 'The Narrative of the Crucifixion', *New Testament Studies* 8 (1961–62), 333–4.

Taylor, V., *The Passion Narrative of St Luke. A Critical and Historical Investigation* (Society for New Testament Studies Monograph Series 19; Cambridge: University Press, 1972).

Theissen, G., 'Die Tempelweissagung Jesu. Prophetie im Spannungsfeld von Stadt und Land', *Theologische Zeitschrift* 32 (1976), 144–58.

Tilborg, S. van, 'Als mens temidden van het geweld. Een uitleg van Mattheüs 26,36–56', *Ons Geestelijk Leven* 55 (1978), 132–9.

Trilling, W., 'Der Tod Jesu, Ende der alten Weltzeit (Mk 15,33–41)' in *Christusverkündigung in den synoptischen Evangelien* (Biblische Handbibliothek 4; Munich: Kösel-Verlag, 1969), pp. 191–211.

Trilling, W., 'Le Christ, roi crucifié, Lc 23,35–43', *Assemblées du Seigneur* 65 (1973), 56–65.

Trocmé, É., *The Formation of the Gospel According to Mark* (trans. P. Gaughan; Philadelphia: Westminster Press/London: SPCK, 1975).

Trocmé, É., *The Passion as Liturgy. A Study in the Origin of the Passion Narrative in the Four Gospels* (London: SCM Press, 1983).

Trudinger, L. P., ' "Eli, Eli, Lama Sabachthani": A Cry of Dereliction? or Victory?', *Journal of the Evangelical Theological Society* 17 (1974), 235–8.

Trudinger, L. P., 'Davidic Links with the Betrayal of Jesus. Some Further Observations', *Expository Times* 86 (1974–75), 278–9.

Tyson, J. B., 'The Lucan Version of the Trial of Jesus', *Novum Testamentum* 3 (1959), 249–58.

Tyson, J. B., 'Jesus and Herod Antipas', *Journal of Biblical Literature* 79 (1960), 239–246.

Unnik, W. C. van, 'The Death of Judas in Saint Matthew's Gospel', *Anglican Theological Review*, Supplementary Series no. 3 (March 1974), 44–57.

Untergassmair, F. G., *Kreuzweg und Kreuzigung Jesu. Ein Beitrag zur lukanischen 'Kreuzestheologie'* (Paderborner theologische Studien 10; Paderborn: Schöningh, 1980).

Untergassmair, F. G., 'Thesen zur Sinndeutung des Todes Jesu in den lukanischen Passionsgeschichte', *Theologie und Glaube* 70 (1980), 180–93.

Upton, J. A., 'The Potter's Field and the Death of Judas', *Concordia Journal* 8 (1982), 213–19.

Vanhoye, A., 'La fuite de l'homme nu (Mc 14,51–52)', *Biblica* 52 (1971), 401–6.

Veerkamp, T., 'Vom ersten Tag nach jenen Sabbat. Der Epilog des Markusevangeliums: 15,33 – 16,8', *Texte und Kontexte* no. 13 (1982), 5–34.

Walaskay, P. W., 'The Trial and Death of Jesus in the Gospel of Luke', *Journal of Biblical Literature* 94 (1975), 81–93.

Walker, N., 'Pauses in the Passion Story and Their Significance for Chronology', *Novum Testamentum* 6 (1963), 16–19.

Walker, N., 'Yet Another Look at the Passion Chronology', *ibid.*, 286–9.

Walker, R., *Die Heilsgeschichte im ersten Evangelium* (Göttingen: Vandenhoeck & Ruprecht 1967).

Walter, N., 'Die Verleugnung des Petrus' in *Theologische Versuche* VII (ed. J. Rogge and G. Schille; Berlin: Evangelische Verlagsanstalt, 1977), pp. 45–62.

Wansbrough, H., 'The Crucifixion of Jesus', *Clergy Review* 56 (1971), 251–61.

Wead, D. W., 'We Have a Law', *Novum Testamentum* 11 (1969), 185–9.

Weber, H.-R., *Kreuz. Überlieferung und Deutung der Kreuzigung Jesu im neutestamentlichen Kulturraum* (Bibliothek Themen der Theologie,

Ergänzungsband; Stuttgart: Kreuz Verlag, 1975 (for English trans., see *For Further Reading* above).

Weeden, T. J., *Mark – Traditions in Conflict* (Philadelphia: Fortress Press, 1971).

Wenham, J. W., 'How Many Cock-Crowings? The Problem of Harmonistic Text-Variants', *New Testament Studies* 25 (1978–79), 523–5.

Wilcox, M., 'The Denial-Sequence in Mark XIV.26–31, 66–72', *New Testament Studies* 17 (1970–71), 426–36.

Winter, P., 'Markus 14:53b.55–64. Eine Gebilde des Evangelisten', *Zeitschrift für die neutestamentliche Wissenschaft* 53 (1962), 260–3.

Winter, P., 'The Marcan Account of Jesus' Trial by the Sanhedrin', *Journal of Theological Studies* N.S. 14 (1963), 94–102.

Winter, P., 'The Trial of Jesus and the Competence of the Sanhedrin', *New Testament Studies* 10 (1963–64), 494–9.

Winter, P., *On the Trial of Jesus* (Studia Judaica I; revised and ed. T. A. Burkill and G. Vermes; Berlin/New York: de Gruyter, 1974).

Zehrer, F., 'Jesus, der leidende Gerechte in der Passion', *Bibel und Liturgie* 47 (1974), 104–11.

Zeller, D., 'Die Handlungsstruktur der Markuspassion. Ein Ertrag strukturalistischer Literaturwissenschaft für die Exegese', *Theologische Quartalschrift* 159 (1979), 213–27.